Lecture Notes in Computer Science   10214

Commenced Publication in 1973
Founding and Former Series Editors:
Gerhard Goos, Juris Hartmanis, and Jan van Leeuwen

More information about this series at http://www.springer.com/series/7412

Bertrand Kerautret · Miguel Colom
Pascal Monasse (Eds.)

Reproducible Research in Pattern Recognition

First International Workshop, RRPR 2016
Cancún, Mexico, December 4, 2016
Revised Selected Papers

Springer

Editors
Bertrand Kerautret
University of Lorraine
Nancy
France

Miguel Colom
CMLA
Ecole Normale Supérieure
Cachan
France

Pascal Monasse
LIGM Ecole des Ponts, UPE
Marne-la-Vallée
France

ISSN 0302-9743   ISSN 1611-3349   (electronic)
Lecture Notes in Computer Science
ISBN 978-3-319-56413-5   ISBN 978-3-319-56414-2   (eBook)
DOI 10.1007/978-3-319-56414-2

Library of Congress Control Number: 2017936468

LNCS Sublibrary: SL6 – Image Processing, Computer Vision, Pattern Recognition, and Graphics

Printed on acid-free paper

This Springer imprint is published by Springer Nature
The registered company is Springer International Publishing AG
The registered company address is: Gewerbestrasse 11, 6330 Cham, Switzerland

Preface

This volume contains the papers presented at the First Workshop on Reproducible Research in Pattern Recognition (RRPR 2016) held on December 4, 2016, in Cancún. This workshop aims to give an overview of reproducible research (RR) for authors, with a special focus on pattern recognition algorithms. The call for papers was organized into two main tracks: RR Frameworks and RR Results. The first track was dedicated to the general topic of reproducible research in computer science with papers describing experiences, frameworks, and platforms. The second track focus on the description of previous works in terms of RR. The latter track contained ICPR companion papers describing their quality of RR. A total of 16 submissions were received with eight papers submitted to track 1 of RR Frameworks, six papers to track 2 of RR Results, and two papers associated with the invited talks. After a reviewing process including mostly three reviewers per paper, six papers were accepted as oral presentations and four as posters.

The different topics of the workshop were equitably represented with six presentations for the RR Framework track and five presentations for the RR Result track. Two invited presentations were given during the workshop. The first one was a presentation of the *Image Processing On Line* journal (IPOL) presented by Pascal Monasse in a common work with Miguel Colom. The second invited talk was given by Daniel Lopresti and Bart Lamiroy with a presentation of the DAE platform in the context of RR. There were around 30 attendees.

For its first edition, the RRPR committee introduced the "Reproducible Label in Pattern Recognition" in order to highlight the reproducible aspects of the RRPR and ICPR works. The work of the authors who obtained the this label is archived and publicly available in the GitHub account of the Organizing Committee, https://github.com/RLPR. Finally a selection of papers will be invited to an RRPR IPOL special issue (www.ipol.im).

We are pleased that RRPR received, for its first edition, the endorsement of the International Association of Pattern Recognition (IAPR). We would like to thank this association, all contributors, invited speakers, and the scientific committee for the high-quality works including papers, algorithms, and source code reviews. We also express our gratitude to the ICPR 2016 committees and in particular to the ICPR Workshop chairs: Prof. Humberto Sossa Azuela, Prof. Markus Vincze, and Prof. Hugues Talbot. We also thank the Springer Computer Sciences team, and in particular Alfred Hofmann and Anna Kramer, for allowing us to publish the proceedings as an LNCS volume. Finally we also thank Jean-Michel Morel for supporting our initiative and Audrey Bichet of the MMI department of Saint Dié-des-Vosges for designing the logo and the poster of this workshop.

February 2017

Bertrand Kerautret
Miguel Colom
Pascal Monasse

Organization

Chairs

Miguel Colom   CMLA, ENS Cachan, France
Bertrand Kerautret   LORIA, University of Lorraine, France
Pascal Monasse   LIGM, École des Ponts, France
Jean-Michel Morel   CMLA, ENS Cachan, France

Co-organizers

Pablo Arias   CMLA, ENS Cachan, France
Nicolas Aubry   LORIA, University of Lorraine, France
Adrien Krähenbühl   LaBRI, France
Enric Meinhardt-Llopis   CMLA, ENS Cachan, France
Nelson Monzón López   CTIM, University of Las Palmas de Gran Canaria, Spain

Program Committee

Pablo Arias   CMLA, ENS Cachan, France
Fabien Baldacci   LaBRI, University of Bordeaux, France
Joost Batenburg   University of Antwerp, Belgium
Jenny Benois-Pineau   LaBRI, University of Bordeaux, France
Partha Bhowmick   Indian Institute of Technology, Kharagpur, India
Arindam Biswas   Indian Institute of Engineering Science and Technology, Shibpur, India
Alexandre Boulch   ONERA, France
Luc Brun   GREYC, Caen Normandy University, France
Leszek Chmielewski   Warsaw University of Life Sciences, Poland
David Coeurjolly   LIRIS, CNRS, France
Miguel Colom   CMLA, ENS Cachan, France
Isabelle Debled-Rennesson   LORIA, University of Lorraine, France
Pascal Desbarats   LaBRI, University of Bordeaux, France
Philippe Even   LORIA, University of Lorraine, France
Yukiko Kenmochi   LIGM, CNRS, France
Bertrand Kerautret   LORIA, University of Lorraine, France
Adrien Krähenbühl   LaBRI, France
Jacques-Olivier Lachaud   LAMA, University Savoie Mont Blanc, France
Enric Meinhardt-Llopis   CMLA, ENS Cachan, France
Nicolas Mellado   UPS, IRIT, CNRS, Université de Toulouse, France
Pascal Monasse   LIGM, École des Ponts, France

Nelson Monzón López	CTIM, University of Las Palmas de Gran Canaria, Spain
Jean-Michel Morel	CMLA, ENS Cachan, France
Khadija Musayeva	LORIA, University of Lorraine, France
Benoît Naegel	ICube, Université de Strasbourg, France
Phuc Ngo	LORIA, University of Lorraine, France
Thanh Phuong Nguyen	University of Toulon, France
Nicolas Normand	IRCCyN Université de Nantes, France
Nicolas Passat	Université de Reims Champagne-Ardenne, France
Francois Rousseau	Télécom Bretagne, France
Loïc Simon	GREYC, Caen Normandy University, France
Isabelle Sivignon	GIPSA-lab, CNRS, France
Robin Strand	Centre for Image Analysis, Uppsala, Sweden
Jonathan Weber	MIPS, Université de Haute-Alsace, France
Laurent Wendling	LIPADE, Université Paris Descartes, France

Additional Reviewers

Hoel Le Capitaine	LS2N, Université de Nantes, France
Sánchez, Javier	CTIM, University of Las Palmas de Gran Canaria, Spain

Contents

Invited Talks

The IPOL Demo System: A Scalable Architecture of Microservices for Reproducible Research

Martín Arévalo[1], Carlos Escobar[2], Pascal Monasse[3], Nelson Monzón[4], and Miguel Colom[2(✉)]

[1] Department of Biological Engineering, Universidad de la República, Montevideo, Uruguay
marevalo@cup.edu.uy
[2] CMLA, ENS Cachan, CNRS, Université Paris-Saclay, 94235 Cachan, France
carlos.escobar101@alu.ulpgc.es, colom@cmla.ens-cachan.fr
[3] LIGM, UMR 8049, École des Ponts, UPE, Champs-sur-Marne, France
pascal.monasse@enpc.fr
[4] CTIM, University of Las Palmas de Gran Canaria, Las Palmas, Spain
monzon@ctim.es

Abstract. We identified design problems related to the architecture, ergonomy, and performance in the previous version of the Image Processing on Line (IPOL) demonstration system. In order to correct them we moved to an architecture of microservices and performed many refactorings. This article first describes the state of the art in Reproducible Research platforms and explains IPOL in that context. The specific problems which were found are discussed, along with the solutions implemented in the new demo system, and the changes in its architecture with respect to the previous system. Finally, we expose the challenges of the system in the short term.

Keywords: IPOL · Reproducible research · Research · Journal · SOA · Microservices · Service-oriented · Platform · Continuous integration

1 Introduction

Image Processing on Line (IPOL) is a research journal started in 2010 on Reproducible Research in the field of Signal Processing (mainly Image Processing, but also video, sounds, and 3D data), giving a special emphasis on the role of mathematics in the design of the algorithms [1]. This article discusses the current system after the changes that were anticipated in [2], and towards which direction it plans to move in the future.

As pointed by Donoho et al. [3], there is a crisis of scientific credibility since in many published papers it is not possible for the readers to reproduce exactly

---

All authors contributed equally.

© Springer International Publishing AG 2017
B. Kerautret et al. (Eds.): RRPR 2016, LNCS 10214, pp. 3–16, 2017.
DOI: 10.1007/978-3-319-56414-2_1

the same results given by the authors. The causes are many, including incomplete descriptions in the manuscripts, not releasing the source code, or that the published algorithm does not correspond to what actually is implemented. Each IPOL article has an online demo associated which allows users to run the algorithms with their own data; the reviewers of the IPOL articles must carefully check that both the description and the implementation match.

Since it started in 2010, the IPOL demo system has been continuously improved and according to usage statistics collected along these years, it has about 250 unique visitors per day. However, several problems of design and potential improvement actions were identified and, on February 2015, it was decided to build a second version of the system based on microservices [4]. Among these problems can be listed: the lack of modularity, tightly-coupled interfaces, difficulties to share the computational load along different machines, or complicated debugging of the system in case of malfunction.

The plan of the article follows. Section 2 discusses the state of the art in Reproducible Research and microservices platforms. Section 3 discusses the particularities of IPOL as a journal, and Sect. 4 presents the architecture of microservices of the new IPOL demo system. Section 5 reveals the software development methodologies in the software engineering process the IPOL team is applying internally. Section 6 refers to a particular tool we designed for the IPOL editors which allows them to manage the editorial process. Section 7 presents a very important novelty of the new system, which is the capability of quickly creating new demos from a textual description. Finally, Sect. 8 presents the conclusions.

2   State of the Art in Reproducible Research Platforms

Some very well-known platforms whose use is closely related to Reproducible Research exist nowadays. Some of them are domain-specific while others are more general.

In the case of Biology, the Galaxy project [5] is a platform for genomic research which makes available tools which can be used by non-expert users too. Galaxy defines a *workflow* as a reusable template which contains different algorithms applied to the input data. In order to achieve reproducibility the system stores: the input dataset, the tools and algorithms which were applied to the data within the chain, the parameters, and the output dataset. Thus, performing the same workflow with the same data ensures that the same results are obtained given that the version of all the elements is kept the same.

In the field of Document Image Analysis, the Document Analysis and Exploitation platform (DAE) was designed to share and distribute document image with algorithms. Created from 2012, the DAE platform also adds tools to exploit annotation and perform benchmarking [6].

Generic tools for Reproducible Research include the IPython tool and its notebooks. This mature tool created in 2001 allows to create reproducible articles by not only editing text in the notebook, but allowing code execution and creating figures *in situ*. This approach follows closely the definition of a "reproducible scientific publication" given by Claerbout and followed also by Buckheit and Donoho: *An article about computational science in a scientific publication is not the scholarship itself, it is merely advertising of the scholarship. The actual scholarship is the complete software development environment and the complete set of instructions which generated the figures* [7].

In 2014 the Jupyter project was started as a spin-off of IPython in order to separate the Python language part of IPython to all the other functionalities needed to run the notebooks, such as the notebook format, the web framework, or the message protocols. IPython turns then into just another computation kernel for Jupyter, which nowadays supports more than 40 languages that can be used as kernels[1].

There are also other generic tools which can be seen as *dissemination* platforms since their main objective is to make source code and data widely available to the public. In this category we find for example Research Compendia[2] focused on reaching reproducible research by storing data, code, in a form that is *accessible, traceable, and persistent*, MLOSS[3] for machine learning, datahub[4] to create, register, and share generic datasets, and RunMyCode[5] to associate code and data to scientific publications. Compared to these platforms, IPOL differs from them in the sense that it is a peer reviewed journal, and not only a dissemination platform.

Regarding the system architecture of IPOL, it is built as a Service-Oriented Architecture (SOA) made of microservices. This type of architecture allows IPOL to have simple units (called *modules* in its own terminology) which encapsulate isolated high-level functions (see in Sect. 4.1). Specifically, we use the CherryPy framework to provide the REST HTTP [8] services. Microservices in distributed system are specially useful for those system which need to serve millions of simultaneous requests. A good example of SOAs made of microservices is the Amazon AWS API Gateway[6] used by millions of users. Also, multimedia streaming services such as Netflix[7] which receives about two-billion daily requests or Spotify[8] are usually based on SOAs of microservices.

3   IPOL as a Peer-Reviewed Scientific Journal

IPOL is a scientific journal on mathematical signal processing algorithms (image, video, audio, 3D) which focuses on the importance of reproducibility. It differs from other classic journals in its editorial policy: each IPOL article must present a complete description of its mathematical details together with a precise explanation of its methods with pseudo-codes. These ones must describe exactly the

---

[1] https://github.com/ipython/ipython/wiki/IPython-kernels-for-other-languages.
[2] http://104.130.4.253/.
[3] http://mloss.org.
[4] https://datahub.io/.
[5] http://www.runmycode.org/.
[6] https://aws.amazon.com/api-gateway.
[7] https://media.netflix.com/en/company-blog/completing-the-netflix-cloud-migration.
[8] http://es.slideshare.net/kevingoldsmith/microservices-at-spotify.

implementation that achieves the results depicted in the paper. The idea is that readers with sufficient skills could implement their own version (in any programming language or environment) from the IPOL article. Furthermore, submitting an IPOL paper means to upload the manuscript coupled with the original source codes. Both are reviewed in depth by the referees to ensure the quality of the publication and that the pseudo-codes match exactly with the attached program, before the editor's decision. The publication process is divided in two stages: first, the reviewers evaluate the scientific interest, the experiments and the reproducibility of the work; secondly, if this evaluation is positive, the authors submit the original code and the online demo is published.

Each IPOL article contains [1]:

1. A description of *one algorithm* and its *source code*;
2. a PDF article associated with an *online demonstration*;
3. *archived experiments* run by users.

All these data, accessible through different tabs of the article webpage, make IPOL an open science journal in favor of reproducible research. The philosophy of the journal follows the guidelines on reproducible research topics, by obeying the standards of reproducible research [9,10]. This is meant as an answer to the credibility crisis in scientific computation pointed out by Donoho et al. [3].

IPOL publishes algorithms along with their implementation, but not compiled/binary software. Neither is it a software library, since each code must have minimal dependencies. The objective of IPOL is not simply to be a software or code diffusion platform. In this sense, the code must be as transparent to the reader as possible, not using implementation tricks unless they are described in the article. It should be seen as a reference implementation, always preferring clarity over run time optimization.

The current form of an IPOL article is illustrated in Fig. 1. The first tab (a) presents the links to the low- and high-resolution PDF manuscripts, and also to the reference source code. An embedded PDF viewer presents a preview of the manuscript. The second tab (b) is the interface of the demonstration system, proposing some illustrative input data. The user can also upload its own data from this page. Clicking on one proposed input dataset or uploading a new one brings to a page presenting a list of adjustable parameters of the algorithm, and possibly an image selection tool, used for example for cropping an image too big for real-time processing by the system (almost all demonstrations are expected to achieve their processing in at most 30 s). A click on the "Run" button brings to a waiting page, while the server runs the author's code, which finally updates into a webpage showing the results. At this stage, the user has the option to re-run on the same input data but modifying the parameters, or to change the input data. Running the algorithm on newly uploaded input data proposes to archive them and their results. The archived data of tab (c) in Fig. 1 have permanent URL. This facilitates online communication between distant collaborators working on an algorithm. The archived data allow to understand what usages are aimed at by visitors, can reveal failure cases not anticipated by the authors, etc. The amount of archived data can also serve as a crude measure of the interest an algorithm raises in the community, as a kind of substitute or complement to the number of citations in a standard journal. The most cited IPOL articles have also tens of thousands of archived online experiments.

Each IPOL demo downloads and compiles by itself the source code. This ensures that the users can reproduce exactly the results claimed by the authors. However, the authors of the demo can additionally add scripts or data, which is not peer-reviewed, but is needed to show the results in the website. This allows to avoid mixing the peer-reviewed source code of the submitted method with support extra codes needed only by the demo. This approach differs from classic publishing, where the method and some details about the implementation are usually described but it is not possible to reproduce and thus confirm the published results.

(a)　　　　　　　　　(b)　　　　　　　　　(c)

Fig. 1. The current form of an IPOL article with its three tabs: (a) article with manuscript, online viewer, and link to source code, (b) demonstration system, and (c) archived experiments.

Apart from this specific form of the articles, IPOL presents the same aspects as a classic scientific journal, with an editorial committee, contributors in the form of authors and editors, a reviewing process, an ISSN, a DOI, etc. Some special issues are proposed, for example some selected papers from the 16th IAPR International Conference on Discrete Geometry for Computer Imagery (DGCI) in 2011. There is also an agreement for publishing companion papers in SIAM Journal of Imaging Sciences (SIIMS) and IPOL, the first submission concentrating on the theory and general algorithm and the second one on practical implementation and algorithmic details. Note that originality of the algorithm is *not* a prerequisite for IPOL publication: the usefulness and efficiency of an algorithm are the decisive criteria. IPOL articles are indexed by all major indexers, such as Scirus, Google Scholar, DBLP, SHERPA/RoMEO, CVonline, etc.

The role of the reviewer is not restricted to the evaluation of the manuscript. The reviewers are also expected to test the online demonstration, check the algorithmic description in the article, and the source code. Most importantly, they must verify that the description of the algorithm and its implementation code match. An important requirement is that the code be readable and well documented.

4   The IPOL System Architecture

The architecture of the new IPOL demo system is an SOA based on microservices. This change was motivated by the problems found in the previous version of the demo system. First, it was designed as a monolithic program[9] which made it quite easy to deploy in the servers and to run it locally, but at the cost of many disadvantages. Given that it was a monolithic system, it was difficult to split it into different machines to share the computational load of the algorithms being executed. A simple solution would be to create specialized units to run the algorithms and to call them from the monolithic code, but this clearly evokes the first step to move to a microservices architecture. Indeed, this first step of *breaking the monolith* [4] can be iterated until all the functions of the system have been delegated in different modules. In the case of IPOL, we created specialized modules and removed the code from the monolith until the very monolith became a module itself: the Core. This Core module is in charge of all the system and delegates the operations to other modules. Figure 2 summarizes the IPOL modules and other components of the system.

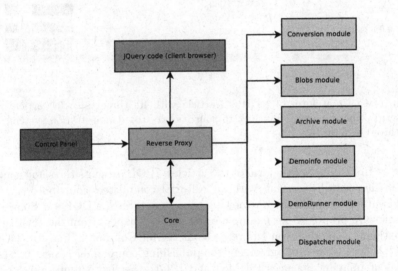

Fig. 2. IPOL as a modular system.

Other problems we had in the previous version of the demo system got solved when we moved to the microservices architecture. Since there is a loose coupling between the Core and the other modules, different members of the development team can work at the same time without worrying about the implementation details or data structures used in other parts of the system. Also, tracking down malfunctions is easier: since the Core centralizes all the operations, when a bug

---

[9] Of course, with a good separation of functionality among different classes.

shows it can only be generated either at the Core or at the involved module, but not at any other part of the system. In the old system a bug could be caused by complex conditions which depend on the global state of the program, making debugging a complex task. And as noted before, the fact that the architecture of the system is distributed and modular by design makes it very natural and simple to have mechanisms to share the computational load among several machines.

Hiding the internal implementation details behind the interfaces of the modules is an essential part of the system, and it is needed to provide loose coupling between its components. The internal architecture of the system is of course hidden from the users when they interact with the system, but it is also hidden *from the inside*. This means that any module (the Core included) does not need to know the location of the modules. Instead, all of them use a published API.

Once the API is defined, the routing to the modules is implemented by a reverse proxy[10]. It receives the requests from the clients according to this pattern: `/api/<module>/<service>` and redirects them to the corresponding module. Figure 3 shows how the API messages received by the proxy are routed to the corresponding modules, thus hiding the internal architecture of the system.

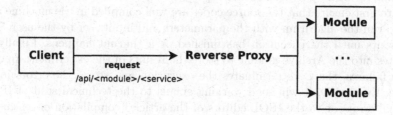

Fig. 3. The reverse proxy routes the API messages to the corresponding modules.

4.1   The IPOL Demo System Modules

The IPOL demo system is made of several standalone units used by the Core module to delegate specialized and well isolated functions. This section describes briefly these microservices modules.

Archive. The archive module stores all the experiments performed by the IPOL with their original data. The database stores the experiments and blobs, which are related with a junction table with a many-to-many relationship. It is worth noting that the system does not save file duplicates of the same blob, but detects them from their SHA1 hash.

This module offers several services, such as adding (or deleting) an experiment or deleting all the set of experiments related to a particular demo. The archive also has services to show particular experiments or several pages with all the experiments stored since the first use of the archive.

---

[10] We use Nginx as the reverse proxy.

Blobs. Each demo of IPOL offers the user a set of default blobs which can be tagged and linked to different demos. Thus, the users are not forced to supply their own files for the execution of the algorithms. This module introduces the concept of *templates*, which are sets of blobs which can be associated to a particular demo. For example, this allows all the demos of an specific type (e.g., denoising) to share the same images as default input data. Instead of editing each demo one by one, the editors can simply edit their template to make changes in all the demos, and then particular changes to each specific demo.

Core. This module is the centralized controller of the whole IPOL system. It delegates most of the tasks to the other modules, such as the execution of the demos, archiving experiments, or retrieving metadata, among others.

When an execution is requested, it obtains first the textual description of the corresponding demo by using the Demo Description Lines (DDL) from the DemoInfo module and it copies the blobs chosen by the users as the algorithm's input. Then, it asks for the workload of the different DemoRunners and gives this information to the Dispatcher module in order to pick the best DemoRunner according to the Dispatcher's selection policy. The Core asks the chosen DemoRunner to first ensure that the source codes are well compiled in the machine and then to run the algorithm with the parameters and inputs set by the user. The Core waits until the execution has finished or a timeout happens. Finally, it delegates into the Archive module to store the results of the experiment. In case of any failures, the Core terminates the execution and stores the errors in its log file. Eventually, it will send warning emails to the technical staff of IPOL (internal error) or to the IPOL editors of the article (compilation or execution failure).

Dispatcher. In order to distribute the computational load along different machines, this module is responsible of assigning a concrete DemoRunner according to a configurable policy. The policy takes into account the requirements of a demo and the workload of all the DemoRunners and returns the DemoRunner which best fits. The DemoRunners and their workloads are provided by the Core. Figure 4 shows the communication between the Core, Dispatcher, and the DemoRunner modules.

Currently the Dispatcher implements three policies:

- **random:** it assigns a random DemoRunner
- **sequential:** it iterates sequentially the list of DemoRunners;
- **lowest workload:** it chooses the DemoRunner with the lowest workload.

Any policy selects only the DemoRunners satisfying the requirements (for example, having MATLAB installed, or a particular version of openCV).

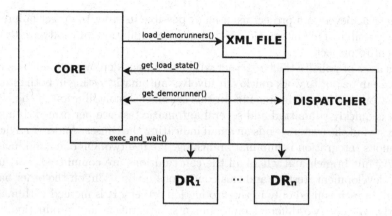

Fig. 4. Communication between the Core, Dispatcher, and the DemoRunner modules.

DemoInfo. The DemoInfo module stores the metadata of the demos. For example, the title, abstract, ID, or its authors, among others. It also stores the abstract textual description of the demo (DDL). All this information can be required by the Core when executing a demo or by the Control Panel when the demo is edited with its website interface.

It is possible that the demo requires non-reviewed support code to show results. In this case, the demo can use custom scripts to create result plots. Note that this only refers to scripts and data which is not peer-reviewed. In case they are important to reproduce the results or figures in the article, they need to be in the peer-reviewed source code package.

DemoRunner. This module controls the execution of the IPOL demos. The DemoRunner module is responsible of informing the Core about the load of the machine where it is running, of ensuring that the demo execution is done with the last source codes provided by the authors (it downloads and compiles these codes to maintain them updated), and of executing the algorithm with the parameters set by the users. It takes care of stopping the demo execution if a timeout is reached, and to inform the Core about the causes of a demo execution failure so the Core can take the best action in response.

5   Software Engineering in the IPOL Demo System

The current IPOL project tries to follow the best practices in software engineering. Specifically, for this kind of project we found that Continuous Integration was a good choice in order to achieve fast delivery of results and ensuring quality. Continuous Integration is a methodology for software development proposed by Martin Fowler, which consists of making automatic integrations of each increment achieved in a project as often as possible in order to detect failures as soon as possible. This integration includes the compilation and software testing of the entire project.

It is a set of policies that, together with continuous deployment, ensures that the code can be put to work quickly. It involves automatic testing in both integration and production environments. In this sense, each contribution in the IPOL system is quickly submitted and several automatic test are performed. If any of these tests fail the system sends an email indicating the causes. Another advice of Continuous Integration is minimal branching. We use two. On one hand, master is the default branch and where all the contributions are committed. It is used for the development, testing and this continuous integration; on the other hand, the prod branch is used only in the production servers. It is merged with master regularly. We use two different environments: integration and production. The integration server is where the master branch is pulled after each commit. The prod branch is used for the production servers and the code in this branch is assumed to be stable. However, the code in the integration server is also assumed to be stable and theoretically the code in the master branch could be promoted to production at any time once it has been deployed to the integration server and checked that is fully functional and without errors.

Quality is perhaps the most important requirement in the software guidelines of the IPOL development team. The code of the modules must be readable and the use of reusable solution is advised [11]. The modules must be simple, well tested and documented, with loose interface coupling, and with proper error logging. Note that it is not possible to ensure that any part of the IPOL will not fail, but in case of a failure we need to limit the propagation of the problem through the system and to end up with diagnostic information which allows to determine the causes afterwards. Refactoring [12] is performed regularly and documentation is as important as the source code. In fact, any discrepancy between the source code and the documentation is considered as a bug.

5.1   Tools

The IPOL development team has created so far three main tools for the system administrators, developers, and editors to interact with the IPOL system. Some of their capabilities might be duplicated or overlapping with the Control Panel (for example, reading and modifying the DDL of the demos is a function implemented in the DDL tool and in the Control Panel, but they are still useful to perform massive changes or to automatize tasks).

Terminal. The Terminal is a small Python standalone application intended for system administrators which allows to start, stop, and query the status of each module. The current list of commands is: **start:** launches the specified module; **ping:** checks if the module is up; **shutdown:** stops the specified module;

info: prints the list of available commands of the module; **modules:** displays the list of the modules of the system.

Control Panel. The Control Panel web application offers a unified interface to configure and manage the platform. It provides a navigation menu option for each module, which allows the editors to edit the demos or the modules directly (say, the add or remove images of a demo, or to delete experiments from the Archive upon request). Look at Sect. 6 for more information on the Control Panel.

DDL Tool. This tool is a standalone Python script which allows to read and write the DDLs of each demo. The main justification for this tool is to perform massive changes in the DDLs and automatize some needed tasks. It admits the following list of commands. **Read:** downloads the DDLs of the specified demos; **Read all:** downloads the DDLs of all the demos known by the system; **Write:** uploads the content of the file with the DDLs of the specified demos.

6   Editorial Management: The Control Panel

The Control Panel is a Django web application which offers a unified interface to configure and manage the platform. Its graphical interface gives to the editors a menu with options to access the different modules available on the system. It provides many editing options to the users. The first option is the Status, that shows a list of the modules with summarized information about them, allowing the user to monitor if they are currently running. In second place there is an Archive Module option to provide a list of the demos with stored experiments, as a result of an execution with original data. It allows the editor to remove specific experiments upon request (e.g., inappropriate images). There is also a Blobs Module option, which allows to add and remove blobs for a particular demo.

Additionally, the DemoInfo Module option permits the user to access information about the demos, authors and editors stored on the IPOL demo system, organized in three sections. The Demos section is the option selected by default, and makes it possible to edit the demo metadata, such as its ID, title, or the source code URL, the assigned editors, or its support scripts, among others. Figure 5 shows a screen capture of the Control Panel application as shown in the browser.

7   Automatic Demo Generation

In the previous version of the IPOL demo system the demo editors had to write Python code to create a new demo. Specifically, to override some methods in a base demo class in order to configure its input parameters, to call the program

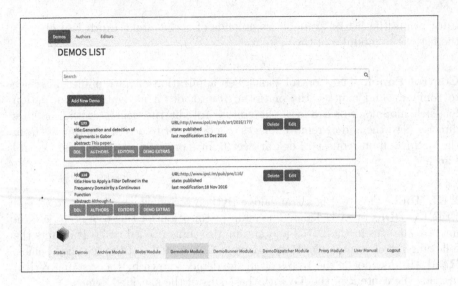

Fig. 5. List of demos in DemoInfo Module option of the Control Panel.

implementing the algorithm, and also to design Mako HTML templates for the results page.

This approach does not really solve anything, since it simply moves the inability to generate demos from a simple description from the system to the demo editors. Since the Python code is written by the demo editors, it is prone to bugs which are specific to each demo. Moreover, fixing a bug in a demo does not prevent the others the have similar problems, with different implementations.

In fact, it is evident that this is a bad design, since to completely define a demo all that is needed is: (1) The title of the demo; (2) the URL where the system should download the source code of the demo; (3) the compilation instructions; (4) a description of the input parameters; (5) a description of what needs to be shown as results.

This information is not tied to any particular language or visualization technique, but it can be a simple abstract textual description. In IPOL we called this abstract textual description the Demo Description Lines (DDL). The IPOL editors only need to write such a description and the system takes care of making available the demo according to it. This not only avoids any coding problems (since there is nothing to code, but writing the short DDL), but also allows IPOL to have non-expert demo editors, and makes it possible to edit and publish demos quickly.

As an example, the following DDL listing is from a published IPOL demo:

```
1  { "archive": {
2        "files": {
3            "derivative1.png":" Derivative 1",
4            "sinc3.png":"Sinc 3"
5        },
6        "params": [
7            "a1","a2","variable","orientation","sigma"
8        ]
9    },
10    "build": {
11        "build1": {
12            "url":"http://www.ipol.im/pub/art/2016/116/filtering_1.00.zip",
13            "construct":"cmake filtering_1.00 && make -C filtering_1.00",
14            "move":"main_comparison"
15        }
16    },
17    "general": {
18        "demo_title":"How to Apply a Filter Defined in the Frequency Domain by a Continuous Function",
19        "xlink_article":"http://www.ipol.im/pub/art/2016/116/"
20    },
21    "inputs": [
22        {
23            "description":"input",
24            "dtype":"3x8i","ext":".png",
25            "max_pixels":"700*700","max_weight":"10*1024*1024",
26            "type":"image"
27        }
28    ],
29    "params": [
30        {
31            "id":"a1",
32            "label":"x-component shifting",
33            "type":"range",
34            "values": {
35                "default": 0.25,"max": 1,"min": 0,"step": 0.05
36            }
37        },
38        (...)
39    ],
40    "results": [
41        {
42            "contents": {
43                "Derivative 1":"derivative1.png",
44                "Sinc 3":"sinc3.png"
45            },
46            "label":"Filtered and difference images",
47            "type":"gallery"
48        },
49    ],
50    "run":"main_comparison input_0.png -a $a1 -b $a2 -V $variable -g $sigma -Q $orientation -e png"
51 }
```

8   Conclusions

The first version of the IPOL demo system has been working since the first article was published in 2010, with a total of 1434 citations and h- and i10-indexes of 20 and 36 respectively; its demo system is receiving about 250 unique visitors per day. While it is clear that the system is functional, some problems were detected: the system was difficult to debug to track down malfunctions, it suffered from tightly coupled interfaces, it was complicated to distribute the computational load among different machines, and the editors needed to write Python code to create and edit demos. These problems compromised the durability of the system at the same time they started to create a bottleneck that prevented to create and edit demos quickly.

The new system moved to a distributed architecture of microservices which solved many of these problems. It introduced however the typical problems of moving the complexity from the monolithic code to the boundaries of the microservices, but in general the balance has been quite positive. The system is made now of simple parts and the development team has gained flexibility due to the isolation of the microservices. Also, the editors are able now to quickly create and edit demos thanks to the abstract syntax of the DDL.

The next challenges for the very short term are to integrate new data types such as video, audio, and 3D, and the development team is quite optimistic about that, since the system is able to manage generic types (even if we refer to *images*, for the system they are simply *blobs*) and it comes down to a visualization problem in the website interface.

In conclusion, we managed to fix many of the problems found in the previous system by redesign and refactoring and now the system is ready to be expanded again, with a solid architecture and codebase.

Acknowledgments. This work was partly funded by the European Research Council (advanced grant Twelve Labours), the Office of Naval Research (ONR grand N00014-14-1-0023), and the ANR-DGA project ANR-12-ASTR-0035.

References

1. Limare, N.: Reproducible research, software quality, online interfaces and publishing for image processing. Ph.D. thesis, École normale supérieure de Cachan-ENS Cachan (2012)
2. Colom, M., Kerautret, B., Limare, N., Monasse, P., Morel, J.-M.: IPOL: a new journal for fully reproducible research; analysis of four years development. In: 2015 7th International Conference on New Technologies, Mobility and Security (NTMS), pp. 1–5. IEEE (2015)
3. Donoho, D.L., Maleki, A., Rahman, I.U., Shahram, M., Stodden, V.: Reproducible research in computational harmonic analysis. Comput. Sci. Eng. **11**(1), 8–18 (2009)
4. Neuman, S.: Building Microservices: Designing Fine-Grained Systems. O'Reilly Media (2015)
5. Goecks, J., Nekrutenko, A., Taylor, J.: Galaxy: a comprehensive approach for supporting accessible, reproducible, and transparent computational research in the life sciences. Genome Biol. **11**(8), 1 (2010)
6. Lamiroy, B., Lopresti, D.: The DAE platform: a framework for reproducible research in document image analysis. In: Kerautret, B., Colom, M., Monasse, P. (eds.) RRPR 2016. LNCS, vol. 10214, pp. 17–29. Springer, Cham (2017)
7. Buckheit, J.B., Donoho, D.L.: Wavelab and reproducible research. In: Antoniadis, A., Oppenheim, G. (eds.) Wavelets and Statistics. Springer, New York (1995)
8. Berners-Lee, T., Fielding, R., Frystyk, H.: Hypertext transfer protocol-HTTP/1.0, RFC 1945, RFC Editor (1996)
9. Stodden, V.: The legal framework for reproducible scientific research: licensing and copyright. Comput. Sci. Eng. **11**(1), 35–40 (2009)
10. Stodden, V.: Enabling reproducible research: open licensing for scientific innovation. Int. J. Commun. Law Policy **13**, 1–25 (2009)
11. Gamma, E., Helm, R., Johnson, R., Vlissides, J.: Design Patterns: Elements of Reusable Object-Oriented Software. Addison-Wesley, Reading (2008)
12. Fowler, M., Beck, K., Brant, J., Opdyke, W., Roberts, D.: Refactoring: Improving the Design of Existing Programs. Addison-Wesley, Reading (1999)

The DAE Platform: A Framework for Reproducible Research in Document Image Analysis

Bart Lamiroy[1](✉) and Daniel P. Lopresti[2](✉)

[1] Université de Lorraine – Loria (UMR 7503), Campus Scientifique – BP 239,
54506 Vandœuvre-lès-Nancy Cedex, France
bart.lamiroy@loria.fr
[2] Packard Laboratory, P.C. Rossin College of Engineering and Applied Science
Computer Science and Engineering, Lehigh University,
19 Memorial Drive West, Bethlehem, PA 18015, USA
lopresti@cse.lehigh.edu

Abstract. We present the DAE Platform in the specific context of reproducible research. DAE was developed at Lehigh University targeted at the Document Image Analysis research community for distributing document images and associated document analysis algorithms, as well as an unlimited range of annotations and "ground truth" for benchmarking and evaluation of new contributions to the state-of-the-art.

DAE was conceived from the beginning with the idea of reproducibility and data provenance in mind. In this paper we more specifically analyze how this approach answers a number of challenges raised by the need of providing fully reproducible experimental research. Furthermore, since DAE has been up and running without interruption since 2010, we are in a position of providing a qualitative analysis of the technological choices made at the time, and suggest some new perspectives in light of more recent technologies and practices.

1 Introduction

The issue of reproducibility is a fundamental tenant of scientific research. It forms the basis by which a field advances, and fosters a research community that is both competitive and yet collaborative. Advances are made only when it is possible to build on trustworthy work that has come before. Despite the overall high quality of the research being conducted within the international pattern recognition community, and a general awareness of the importance of good scientific practice, our field has recently come to realize there is room for improvement. This observation was one of the motivating factors behind the First Workshop on Reproducible Research in Pattern Recognition, held in conjunction with ICPR 2016 in Cancun, Mexico [1].

Concerns about reproducibility are not limited to our research community; they have also arisen in other fields over the past several years, most famously in US biomedical research [4,6]. In their influential policy statement as leaders of the National Institutes of Health, Collins and Tabak write that a *"growing chorus*

© Springer International Publishing AG 2017
B. Kerautret et al. (Eds.): RRPR 2016, LNCS 10214, pp. 17–29, 2017.
DOI: 10.1007/978-3-319-56414-2_2

of concern, from scientists and laypeople, contends that the complex system for ensuring the reproducibility of biomedical research is failing and is in need of restructuring" [6]. While they note that lack of reproducibility is rarely due to scientific misconduct, the system has evolved to push (or entice) researchers away from good practices. The list of failings they quote, while drawn from a completely different domain, could easily be adapted to apply to the field of pattern recognition. In particular, they call out [6]:

1. The need to make strong (perhaps unjustifiable) claims to get published in the top venues.
2. Missing technical details when papers are published.
3. Bad practices in experimental design, including improper "blinding, randomization, replication, sample-size calculation ..."
4. The use by some scientists of a "secret sauce" (their words) in getting their experiments to work which they fail to reveal in publications to preserve a competitive advantage.
5. Inaccessible and/or proprietary data used in published works.

Collins and Tabak also point out the difficulty in publishing negative results that identify flaws in previously accepted theories. Without the benefit of a publication at the end of the tunnel, few scientists will engage in the hard work of trying to confirm or disprove the outcomes of others. They also assert that datasets are a valuable intellectual contribution in their own right that should be citable.

Their list of simple reasons that work may fail to be reproducible, while drawn from another domain, should also sound familiar to those working in pattern recognition: "*different animal strains, different lab environments or subtle changes in protocol*" [6]. All of these forms of bad behavior have analogs in our field as well. We may think of using different test collections, different implementations of a standard machine learning technique, or different approaches to computing and reporting performance measures.

The DAE platform, to be discussed in this paper, is our attempt to address some of these issues [10, 13]. In particular, DAE provides an open environment for researchers to "publish" their algorithms and their data, and to document and to serve the data used in past experiments so that new techniques can be compared relative to old ones.

Collins and Tabak propose a number of clear steps for addressing the shortcomings they see in biomedical research, including the adoption and enforcement of better experimental practices. We can take such steps in the pattern recognition community, too, many of which involve changes in the social processes we use (*e.g.* the standards by which papers are reviewed and accepted for publication). The DAE server provides some of the functionality they envision for a Data Discovery Index (DDI) [3].

The remainder of this paper is organized as follows: first we will redefine the notion of *Reproducible Research* in the context of Document Image Analysis and the relations it establishes with a broader concept of Open Research (Sect. 2). Section 3 develops the functional architecture of the DAE platform, and explains how it addresses reproducible research, and offers solutions to several of the points raised in the previous sections. Finally, Sect. 4 considers the handling of more complex notions like "Truth" and reference interpretations.

2   Our Definition of Reproducible Research

Reproducible research is not only about documenting processes, availability of experimental data and software, benchmarking and performance evaluation. Is also (and essentially) a comprehensive process of interaction with information that is certified to be reliable, of traceability and provenance, accountable re-use, recycling and re-sampling of pre-existing sources, leading to better practices overall. We already developed these issues in [16].

Research goals for work in pattern recognition and machine perception generally consist of:

– developing algorithms that are robust and approach human levels of performance for specific tasks of interest;
– inventing new methods that are better than known techniques;
– generating experimental results that are well-documented, understandable in context, and reproducible by others;
– building on past knowledge to yield new insights moving us toward solutions for problems of vital importance.

For each if these goals the sections below contain a number of observations regarding general practices and their impact of the global quality of research outcomes.

2.1   Robustness and Human Levels of Performance

In *developing algorithms that are robust and approach human levels of performance*, we want algorithms to be general. This goal expresses the need for perception algorithms to perform well on tasks containing operational conditions or expected results that are difficult to formally define [9] and for which one expects the resulting algorithm to perform equally well on new, previously unseen data.

Measuring this robustness, or reproduce published results in controlled conditions is a challenging task, and often relies on benchmarking using reference data sets. One can observe, however, that too often methods are either tested on small, overused datasets, or – especially in the context of recent deep learning developments – in extremely large datasets that make it difficult to assess the breadth of scope they capture. As a result, many experimental results reported in the literature suffer form the intimate knowledge of the data the algorithm developers have acquired over time and therefore introduce a quite strong bias towards the specifics of the benchmarks. The result is that large segments of current practices lack convincing evidence of generality.

Furthermore, the notion of "human levels of performance" is not quite well defined. In many a situation human experts can disagree on all but the most trivial of cases [9]. This, combined with the natural bias towards the benchmark data described above, means that performance metrics and conclusions from reference data should systematically undergo scrutiny and analysis with respect to the limitations of generality they induce.

While in itself this is not a restriction to reproducibility, it does raise the question of how well it influences (positively or negatively) the emergence of new, robust and assessable approaches and ideas, or on the other hand, may tend to push research towards niche problems.

2.2   Improve upon Known Techniques

The previous section relates to the aim of *inventing new methods that are better than known techniques*, and especially to the question of knowing whether we have succeeded [17]. We already mentioned the fact that the need to compare against previously published results creates over-reliance on standard datasets (which is counter-productive). Notwithstanding, comparing new approaches with previously published ones, under the same conditions and with the same data, is still important for the assessment of progress and ongoing improvement. However, attempts to re-implement a published algorithm are often problematic due to incomplete descriptions or even the inherent conflict of interest that arises when attempting to show that one's own methods improve upon existing techniques [19]. As we already pointed out in [13,16], there are many opportunities for improvement:

1. Access to source code and data used in reported results are part of the basic requirements, but do not solve everything. Code tends to be dependent on technological environments and context, and frequently becomes obsolete (due to API changes of dependency libraries; evolution of the standard version of compilers, interpreters, and frameworks; *etc.*). Notwithstanding, code repositories and initiatives like IPOL [2] are important contributions to reproducibility. There are however situations when source code cannot be made available, or where the execution environment and resources are as important as the code itself. In that case, having access to executable binaries or complete packaged virtualized environments [12,21] can supply supplementary or complementary tools for reproducibility.
2. Even though access to source code or executables is helpful in many cases, a complete description of experimental protocols is essential to guarantee that one measures comparable results when evaluating whether new approaches improve upon the state-of-the-art. This includes, besides the data, the selection criteria, pre-filtering *etc.*
3. Another way of measuring improvement over known techniques is the use of recurring, open competitions. In order for these competitions to fully accomplish their goals, they should be frequent, have consistent and well documented evaluations protocols and metrics, and maintain records over time and subsequent editions. This implies a significant investment of resources by community in question.

2.3 Well-Documented Reproducible Results and Knowledge to Build New Advances

Generating experimental results that are well-documented, understandable in context, and reproducible by others is a real challenge and requires carefully thought out and sufficiently explicit protocols. Some of the difficulties raised here have already be mentioned in the previous sections. It is important that published results clearly establish, describe and provide all relevant data (parameters, description of data selection and filtering process, post-processing, *etc.*) making it possible for others to reproduce experiments under the same conditions.

In many cases, the explicit and/or implicit bias in selecting and using data (*e.g.*, discarding hard cases) makes the full experimental context difficult to recover. Furthermore, "Publish or Perish" mindsets lead to overstated claims and a poor understanding of the generalizability of the published results.

One of the essential by-products of reproducible open research is that it simplifies *building on past knowledge to yield new advances* toward solving problems of importance. This is generally what drives experimental research. However, if all previously enumerated conditions for open reproducible research are not met, it often becomes quite difficult to know if the efforts dedicated to developing methods actually improve upon existing techniques, or if they are well suited for the task at hand. In other cases, much time is risked to be spent "reinventing the wheel." Again, "Publish or Perish" pressure often leads to precipitation that leaves insufficient time to think and construct upon previously existing achievements, very much like trying to build a pyramid out of shifting sand without first forming it into blocks. Fixing this will require a radical paradigm shift within the community, and like the NIH position paper by Collins and Tabak discussed earlier [6], here we propose some steps in that same direction.

2.4 Reference Data and Truth

One of the corollaries of aiming for human performance levels and clearly describing experimental conditions is that there can be no such thing as "ground truth" [9]. Rather, there is the intent of the author (which is hard to determine, although sometimes we have it) or the interpretation arrived at by a reader of the document [8] (which could be a human or an algorithm) within her personal reference frame or context. Subsequently, there may be no single right answer – interpretations may naturally differ – although for some applications, we expect that users who are fluent will agree nearly all of the time.

While this may seem to contradict commonly accepted approaches to the annotation of data and the verification of algorithms, our conviction is that maintaining a *status quo* on unique reference annotations is hindering broad and open extensible or reusable research.

On the other hand, it raises a number of practical questions. With multiple interpretations, how should we proceed in developing new methods that mimic a fluent human expert? Some may be more careful, fluent or expert than others; worse, this can depend entirely on context! How can this be handled in the context of attempting to describe a reproducible experiment? We have suggested elsewhere that on-line reputation, as originally derived in social networking, can determine whose interpretations to trust and in what context [16]. Use of reputation is one key feature of the new paradigm we would like to promote. This is beyond the scope of this paper, however. Section 4 does address some of the more structural issues of handling multiple interpretations and lack of absolute ground truth.

3   The DAE Platform, a Technical Overview

The DAE platform was the outcome of a 2009–2011 DARPA funded project. The acronym DAE refers to Document Analysis and Exploitation: see http:// dae.cse.lehigh.edu. We first reported it in [10]. Complete operational details can be found in [12].

The platform has been running without major interruption since 2010, and hosts a variety of Document Image Analysis data sets, as well as document analysis reference algorithm implementations. Its general architecture is represented in Fig. 1.

DAE was conceived from the beginning with the idea of reproducibility and data provenance in mind. In the following sections, we more specifically analyze

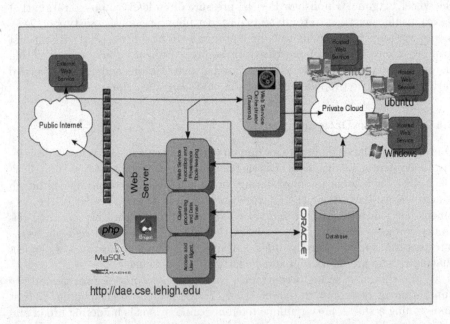

Fig. 1. General Architecture of the DAE Platform: browsing and authentication through a traditional web interface (blue – lower middle), WSDL interaction for querying and executing hosted applications (orange – upper middle); virtualized applications (green – upper right) and back-office database (yellow – lower right) (Color figure online)

how this approach answers a number of challenges raised by the needs of reproducible experimental research. Furthermore, because of the experience gathered by running the platform, we can provide a qualitative analysis of its technological impact and offer new perspectives in light of more recent technologies and practices.

3.1 General Features

From a general point of view, the DAE platform hosts a variety of data sets and algorithm implementations for document image analysis. However, the core feature of the platform is that all data is referenced in a central database on a fine-grained level. The full data model is described here [13]. We are not going to further detail the data structure, here.

This allows the platform to offer the following services:

1. It stores large data collections containing both "raw" document images, as well as an unlimited range of annotations. These annotations vary from high level content interpretations (like, for instance, text transcriptions, author identification or document structure) or pixel level segmentation information (binarization, shape outlines, ...).
2. All data can be hierarchically structured, and allows for convenient browsing through the collections.
3. It can host a wide variety of programs that interact with the data. They are intended to be reference snapshots of the state-of-the-art at some point in time. Thanks to virtualization they run in an isolated and well controlled environment. These programs are published as web services using a standard WSDL[1] interface. The WSDL API also offers SQL querying and interaction with the stored data.

These features contribute in a significant way to handling some of the more fundamental requirements for reproducible research, as shall be made clear in the next section.

3.2 Contributions to Reproducible Research

Data Is a Query: while the DAE data model is fully compatible with the more traditional approach to fixed datasets and reference annotations (or *ground truth*, for that matter) it actually has a much versatile approach to data.

As outlined in Sects. 2.3 and 2.4 data needs to conform to the following properties for efficient reproducible and open research:

1. For the sake of reproducibility, data used for published experiments should be freely and fully accessible in their exact same state as described in the referenced work; this will allow to replay and compare the results by third parties or with other approaches;

---

[1] https://en.wikipedia.org/wiki/Web_Services_Description_Language consulted January, 2017.

2. Since data (and more specifically their associated annotations) are open to various interpretations, contexts and possible disagreements, their annotations should be able to capture this multiplicity, while guaranteeing that every interpretation context can be accessed in a non-ambiguous and repeatable manner;
3. Data collections should be open to recomposition, extension, combination and selection in order to create new collections for other contexts and experimental setups while maintaining legacy and references to previous versions; this will enhance reuse and improvement in new contexts as the state-of-the-art evolves.

This is handled by the DAE platform by having a fine-grained data model [13]. It essentially consists of using a flat data model of *stuff*, and let users organize it in various ways. Most data stored in the platform (raw experimental data, annotations, *etc.*) is a `data_item`, and data items can be freely associated to one another or grouped (in a non-exclusive way) in collections.

As a consequence, all data, annotations, interpretations and collections are stored in such a way that they can be retrieved through well defined queries (SQL, essentially) and that, through the use of appropriate labeling, reference configurations can be frozen and their corresponding query made available as an archival reference. The platform provides a transparent mapping between URLs and queries. More detailed information is available in [13].

Software as a Service in a Controlled Environment: Since availability of experimental data is only one of the requirements for open reproducible research, algorithms and software need to be made available as well. We have made the choice that, where software is concerned, reproducibility through availability of source code is not necessarily the best guarantee for replication of results. Initiatives like IPOL [2], github and others make it possible to thoroughly describe source code such that previously published methods can be reused and reimplemented. DAE pursues another goal: benchmarking and comparison. It therefore offers the possibility to run published reference applications in a controlled environment, as close as possible to the one used at the time of publication.

These implementations are made available in a *Software as a Service* mode through WSDL interfaces (*cf.* [12] for further details). Interested parties can therefore freely launch remote executions of the software, either with their own data or with data provided by the platform itself. This approach has a number of advantages as well as some drawbacks.

– The main advantage is to offer the possibility for any type of software (regardless of complexity, programming language, or execution environment) to be run by the platform. It uses completely isolated virtualized environments, and is therefore immune to dependencies or technological obsolescence, as long as the virtualization remains available.
– It significantly lowers the barrier for contributors to provide their applications: no need for releasing source code, or to conform to specific restrictions related to supporting programming languages *etc.*

- The SAAS/WSDL approach offers the possibility to linearly scale the platform and to distribute it over multiple locations. Individual contributors may choose to host their own software, rather than upload it to the centralized DAE platform.
- The downside, on the other hand, is that the hosting facility supports the costs for all executions, rather than having them supported by the experimenter; popular applications may become a burden for the hosting facility, since execution resources are expended on the server side.

Experimental Protocols Made Explicit: As a by-product of the two previous features (data as a query/url and software as a service) it becomes easy to make experimental protocols explicit, sharable and reusable. We have explored [11] the use of web service orchestrating scripts like Taverna [20] and myexperiment.org.

3.3   Lessons Learned and Possible Upgrades

The DAE server has been up and running without interruption for more than five years. It is currently hosting 113,605 document images (totaling 287 gigabytes of data), 9 algorithms and a total of 357,925 data_items. We are currently in the process of uploading approximately 800 scanned technical drawings from the Lehigh Engineering Collection [5] (representing anther 400 gigabytes of raw image data). Our experience running the environment has suggested a set of possible improvements and extensions, as outlined below.

The general motivations behind these extensions consist of facilitating interactions with other, comparable or complementary initiatives, making access easier and making it possible to distribute the platform over multiple cooperating sites.

Evolution from a WSDL Interface to a REST Interface: The current architecture is based on web services with a Web Service Description Language (WSDL) interface. WSDL has the advantage of having well typed and formalized interfaces, but has the disadvantage of being synchronous. Representational State Transfer (REST) interfaces are much more flexible and have the advantage of allowing asynchronous interactions.

Services in the REST model are better-suited to the different uses of the platform than WSDL services, and will improve interactions with other services and other modern applications. This is what has been implemented by the DIVAServices platform [21], for instance.

Support for Standard Formats: There are a large number of initiatives for the annotation and structuring of data extracted from digital documents, each adapted (or adopted) according to the field of application. TEI[2], for example, is

---

[2] http://www.tei-c.org.

a standard used in various digital humanities projects; PAGE is a format advocated by the European project Impact and the associated European Competence Center [18]; GEDI is a format developed by the University of Maryland [7] and widely used in research circles in document analysis.

It is important for reproducibility and open research that users are not restricted to closed, proprietary formats; open, well documented exchange formats should be used.

Transition to a Distributed Data Model and Infrastructure: The platform currently relies on a back office consisting of an Oracle database and a centralized ZFS file system. In order to allow more flexible interactions with instances hosted at different sites, and thus allow easy extension and sharing of resources it would be appropriate to move to a more scalable structure of the NoSQL type.

Virtualization: One of the obstacles to the adoption of the platform is the need to use web services and encapsulate them in virtualized and safe environments. Virtualization, as deployed on the current version, is not optimal in terms of resource allocation, and will not scale well. It is therefore necessary to switch to more flexible and modernized virtualization technologies. In collaboration with the initiative at the University of Fribourg [21], we plan to employ their solution using Docker.

4   Handling Multiple Interpretations

As already mentioned before, data annotation for the verification and benchmarking of algorithms cannot be assumed to be unique [9]. The traditional approach to using *Ground Truth* for assessing the validity and performance of research generally consists of 3 phases:

- assemble a *representative* collection of reference documents;
- use human annotators to identify, select and provide the expected interpretations (we do not consider cases where test data can be synthetically generated);
- create the set of reference interpretations for the document collection (*Ground Truth*).

Performance evaluation then consists of

- providing part of the annotated data as indication and benchmark for the expected outcome (this allows researchers to define the scope of their algorithms, possibly train them, or otherwise configure them);
- running the resulting algorithms on the remaining part of reference documents (without providing associated *Ground Truth*);
- measuring discrepancy between algorithm outputs and expected *Ground Truth*;

- rank algorithms according to their measured performance.

This general paradigm is well understood, and largely adopted by the community to assess and measure the quality of the state-of-the-art. Notwithstanding, it has a number of limitations and drawbacks, some of which have already been studied [14].

1. Getting the annotations for constructing the ground truth is costly. It requires human intervention, takes time, is subject to human error. Furthermore, recent trends and techniques (essentially those based on supervised Machine Learning) tend to rely on (and require) larger and larger amounts of data. This creates a bottleneck situation.

    Crowd-sourcing has been advanced as a potential solution to this problem, but introduces issues itself. It requires a large commitment and involvement of a community, incentives and motivation are an issue and may largely affect annotation quality and reliability, extra quality control and/or processes for handling ambiguity or disagreement are needed (and may become as costly as the annotation itself) and sometimes ethical issues may arise.

2. Constituted reference annotations progressively get tainted over time: partially because they represent a snapshot of the data that was relevant at a given point in time; partially because once more and more people start to use them, it becomes more and more difficult to maintain the separation between known training data and unknown testing data. The latter eventually loses its neutral status, since it pervasively becomes known and may be used for training.

3. The way the traditional evaluation paradigm is used (very often through the organization of recurring annual or bi-annual contests) is sub-optimal in some situations, in a sense that it is unusual to see explicit loop-back mechanisms that help improving algorithms; that it is difficult to get a detailed account on how the performance of competing algorithms increases over time and sometimes *regression testing* from one contest edition to another would be useful.

4. *Ground Truth* is excessively context bound and it has been formally established [9] that it necessarily contains data that can either be considered as being mislabeled, or as being open to multiple legitimate (yet incompatible) interpretations. This induces the fact that performance evaluation and subsequent ranking may be statistically insignificant if the level of disagreement on the reference annotations is too high.

Our proposed solution consists in directly incorporating, measuring and thus leveraging the level of disagreement/uncertainty of the *Ground Truth* and actually stop calling it *Ground Truth* altogether – call it CRI: *Consensus Reference Interpretation*, for instance.

The DAE platform handles multiple concurrent annotations on the same data, and provides means to filtering, selecting and organizing these annotations. What we currently lack are the appropriate metrics and methods to efficiently handle the associated notions of fuzzy or context related "truth" and the reputation or confidence that can be associated with them [14,15].

5 Conclusion

As we pointed out in our introduction, the stakes and need for awareness regarding reproducible and open research are pervasive to all sciences. Large influential communities like the Health Sciences and Particle Physics are raising concerns and offering standards, in attempts to improve overall practices.

In this paper, we have represented the DAE Platform and highlighted its features in the context of reproducible research in a smaller and specifically targeted community. It was developed with Document Image Analysis research in mind and allows for distributing document images, associated document analysis algorithms as well as an unlimited range of annotations for benchmarking and evaluation of new contributions to the state-of-the-art.

Although DAE was conceived from the beginning with the idea of reproducibility and data provenance in mind, there are still quite a number of challenging technical developments that need to be incorporated on the one hand. On the other hand, the principal and most important challenge is to persuade large research communities that reproducible research is above all an attitude and a collection of practices that do not necessarily depend on technology, but more on collective adoption and enforcement on good practices.

Acknowledgment. The authors acknowledge support from the CNRS PICS-06758 Dia-Tribe. Early stages of this work were supported by a DARPA IPTO grant administered by Raytheon BBN Technologies.

References

1. Workshop on reproducible research in pattern recognition, Cancun, Mexico, December 2016. https://wrrpr2016.sciencesconf.org/
2. IPOL Journal - Image Processing On Line (2009)
3. Resource indexing, data science at NIH, January 2017. https://datascience.nih.gov/bd2k/funded-programs/resource-indexing
4. Alberts, B., Kirschner, M.W., Tilghman, S., Varmus, H.: Rescuing US biomedical research from its systemic flaws. Proc. Natl. Acad. Sci. 111(16), 5773–5777 (2014)
5. Bruno, B., Lopresti, D.P.: The lehigh steel collection: a new open dataset for document recognition research. In: Document Recognition and Retrieval XXI, San Francisco, California, USA, 5–6 February 2014
6. Collins, F.S., Tabak, L.A.: Policy: NIH plans to enhance reproducibility. Nature 505(7485), 612–613 (2014)
7. Doermann, D., Zotkina, E., Li, H.: GEDI - AGroundtruthing environment for document images. In: Ninth IAPR International Workshop on Document Analysis Systems (DAS 2010) (2010)
8. Eco, U.: The Limits of Interpretation. Indiana University Press, Bloomington (1990)
9. Lamiroy, B.: Interpretation, evaluation and the semantic gap... What if we were on a side-track? In: Lamiroy, B., Ogier, J.-M. (eds.) GREC 2013. LNCS, vol. 8746, pp. 221–233. Springer, Heidelberg (2014). doi:10.1007/978-3-662-44854-0_17

10. Lamiroy, B., Lopresti, D.: A platform for storing, visualizing, and interpreting collections of noisy documents. In: Fourth Workshop on Analytics for Noisy Unstructured Text Data - AND 2010. ACM International Conference Proceeding Series, Toronto, Canada. IAPR, ACM, October 2010

11. Lamiroy, B., Lopresti, D.: An open architecture for end-to-end document analysis benchmarking. In: 11th International Conference on Document Analysis and Recognition - ICDAR 2011, Beijing, China, pp. 42–47. International Association for Pattern Recognition, IEEE Computer Society, September 2011. ISBN: 978-1-4577-1350-7

12. Lamiroy, B., Lopresti, D.: The Non-Geek's guide to the DAE platform. In: DAS - 10th IAPR International Workshop on Document Analysis Systems, Gold Coast, Queensland, Australia, pp. 27–32. International Association for Pattern Recognition, IEEE, March 2012

13. Lamiroy, B., Lopresti, D., Korth, H., Heflin, J.: How carefully designed open resource sharing can help and expand document analysis research. In: Gady Agam, C.V.-G. (ed.) Document Recognition and Retrieval XVIII - DRR 2011, Part of the IST/SPIE 23rd Annual Symposium on Electronic Imaging. Document Recognition and Retrieval XVIII, vol. 7874. SPIE, San Francisco, January 2011. ISBN: 9780819484116

14. Lamiroy, B., Pierrot, P.: Statistical performance metrics for use with imprecise ground-truth. In: Lamiroy, B., Dueire Lins, R. (eds.) GREC 2015. LNCS, vol. 9657, pp. 31–44. Springer, Cham (2017). doi:10.1007/978-3-319-52159-6_3

15. Lamiroy, B., Sun, T.: Computing precision and recall with missing or uncertain ground truth. In: Kwon, Y.-B., Ogier, J.-M. (eds.) GREC 2011. LNCS, vol. 7423, pp. 149–162. Springer, Heidelberg (2013). doi:10.1007/978-3-642-36824-0_15

16. Lopresti, D., Lamiroy, B.: Document analysis research in the year 2021. In: Mehrotra, K.G., Mohan, C.K., Oh, J.C., Varshney, P.K., Ali, M. (eds.) IEA/AIE 2011. LNCS (LNAI), vol. 6703, pp. 264–274. Springer, Heidelberg (2011). doi:10.1007/978-3-642-21822-4_27

17. Lopresti, D., Nagy, G.: When is a problem solved? In: Proceedings of the 2011 International Conference on Document Analysis and Recognition, ICDAR 2011, Washington, DC, USA, pp. 32–36. IEEE Computer Society (2011)

18. Pletschacher, S., Antonacopoulos, A.: The page (page analysis and ground-truth elements) format framework. In: Proceedings of the 2010 20th International Conference on Pattern Recognition, ICPR 2010, Washington, DC, USA, pp. 257–260. IEEE Computer Society (2010)

19. Salman, I.: Cognitive biases in software quality and testing. In: Proceedings of the 38th International Conference on Software Engineering Companion, ICSE 2016, New York, NY, USA, pp. 823–826. ACM (2016)

20. Wolstencroft, K., Haines, R., Fellows, D., Williams, A., Withers, D., Owen, S., Soiland-Reyes, S., Dunlop, I., Nenadic, A., Fisher, P., Bhagat, J., Belhajjame, K., Bacall, F., Hardisty, A., de la Hidalga, A.N., Balcazar Vargas, M.P., Sufi, S., Goble, C.: The Taverna workflow suite: designing and executing workflows of web services on the desktop, web or in the cloud. Nucleic Acids Res. **41**(W1), W557 (2013)

21. Würsch, M., Ingold, R., Liwicki, M.: SDK reinvented: document image analysis methods as RESTful web services. In: Document Analysis Systems (DAS), April 2016

Reproducible Research Framework

An Evaluation Framework and Database for MoCap-Based Gait Recognition Methods

Michal Balazia$^{(\boxtimes)}$ (iD) and Petr Sojka (iD)

Faculty of Informatics, Masaryk University, Botanická 68a,
602 00 Brno, Czech Republic
xbalazia@mail.muni.cz, sojka@fi.muni.cz

Abstract. As a contribution to reproducible research, this paper presents a framework and a database to improve the development, evaluation and comparison of methods for gait recognition from motion capture (MoCap) data. The evaluation framework comprises source codes of state-of-the-art human-interpretable geometric features as well as our own approaches where gait features are learned by a modification of Fisher's Linear Discriminant Analysis with the Maximum Margin Criterion, and by a combination of Principal Component Analysis and Linear Discriminant Analysis. It includes a description and source codes of a mechanism for evaluating class separability coefficients of feature space and four classifier performance metrics. This framework also contains a tool for learning a custom classifier and for classifying a custom probe on a custom gallery. We provide an experimental database along with source codes for its extraction from the general CMU MoCap database.

1 Introduction

Gait (walk) pattern has several attractive properties as a soft biometric trait. From a surveillance perspective, gait pattern biometrics is appealing in that it can be performed at a distance without requiring body-invasive equipment or subject cooperation.

Many research groups investigate the discrimination power of gait pattern and develop models that are applied to the automatic recognition of walking people from MoCap data. A number of MoCap-based gait recognition methods have been introduced in the past few years and new ones continue to emerge. In order to move forward with this competitive research, it is necessary to compare their innovative approaches with the state-of-the-art and evaluate them against established evaluation metrics on a benchmark database. New frameworks and databases have been developed recently [10,15].

As a contribution to reproducible research, this paper focuses on our framework for evaluating MoCap-based gait recognition methods and our benchmark MoCap gait database. We provide a large experimental database together with its extraction-and-normalization drive from the general CMU MoCap database,

This is a companion paper to our papers [7,8].

© Springer International Publishing AG 2017
B. Kerautret et al. (Eds.): RRPR 2016, LNCS 10214, pp. 33–47, 2017.
DOI: 10.1007/978-3-319-56414-2_3

as specified in Sect. 2. Implementation details of thirteen relevant methods are summarized in Sect. 3. In Sect. 4 we describe the evaluation mechanism and define four class separability coefficients and four rank-based classifier performance metrics. Finally, Sect. 5 consists of a manual and comments on reproducing the experiments.

2 Data

MoCap technology provides video clips of individuals walking which contain structural motion data. The format keeps an overall structure of the human body and holds estimated 3D positions of major anatomical landmarks as the person moves. These MoCap data can be collected online by a system of multiple cameras (Vicon) or a depth camera (Microsoft Kinect). To visualize MoCap data (see Fig. 1), a simplified stick figure representing the human skeleton (graph of joints connected by bones) can be recovered from body point spatial coordinates in time. Recent rapid improvement in MoCap sensor accuracy has brought affordable MoCap technology to assist human identification in such applications as access control and video surveillance.

For evaluation purposes we have extracted a large number of gait samples from the MoCap database obtained from the CMU Graphics Lab [11], which is available under the Creative Commons license. It is a well-known and recognized database of structural human motion data and contains a considerable number of gait sequences. Motions are recorded with an optical marker-based Vicon system. People wear a black jumpsuit with 41 markers taped on. The tracking space of $30\,m^2$ is surrounded by 12 cameras with a sampling rate of $120\,Hz$ at heights ranging from 2 to 4 m above ground thereby creating a video surveillance

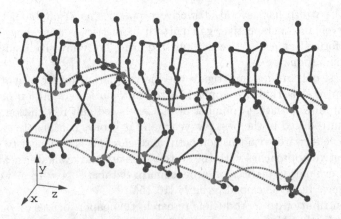

Fig. 1. Motion capture data. A skeleton is represented by a stick figure of 31 joints (only 17 are shown here). Seven selected video frames of a walk sequence contain 3D coordinates of each joint in time. The red and blue lines track trajectories of hands and feet [24]. (Color figure online)

environment. Motion videos are triangulated to get highly accurate 3D data in the form of relative body point coordinates (with respect to the root joint) in each video frame and are stored in the standard ASF/AMC data format. Each registered participant is assigned with their respective skeleton described in an ASF file. Motions in the AMC files store bone rotational data, which is interpreted as instructions about how the associated skeleton deforms over time.

These MoCap data, however, contain skeleton parameters pre-calibrated by the CMU staff. Skeletons are unique to each walker and even a trivial skeleton check could result in 100 % recognition. In order to fairly use the collected data, a prototypical skeleton is constructed and used to represent bodies of all subjects, shrouding the skeleton parameters. Assuming that all walking individuals are physically identical disables the skeleton check from being a potentially unfair classifier. Moreover, this is a skeleton-robust solution as all bone rotational data are linked to one specific skeleton. To obtain realistic parameters, it is calculated as mean of all skeletons in the provided ASF files.

The raw data are in the form of bone rotations or, if combined with the prototypical skeleton, 3D joint coordinates. The bone rotational data are taken from the AMC files without any pre-processing. We calculate the joint coordinates using the bone rotational data and the prototypical skeleton. One cannot directly use raw values of joint coordinates, as they refer to absolute positions in the tracking space, and not all potential methods are invariant to person's position or walk direction. To ensure such invariance, the center of the coordinate system is moved to the position of root joint $\gamma_{\text{root}}(t) = [0,0,0]^\top$ for each time t and the axes are adjusted to the walker's perspective: the X axis is from right (negative) to left (positive), the Y axis is from down (negative) to up (positive), and the Z axis is from back (negative) to front (positive). In the AMC file structure notation it is achieved by setting the root translation and rotation to zero (root 0 0 0 0 0 0) in all frames of all motion sequences.

Since the general motion database contains all motion types, we extracted a number of sub-motions that represent gait cycles. First, an exemplary gait cycle was identified, and clean gait cycles were then filtered out using a threshold for their Dynamic Time Warping (DTW) distance on bone rotations in time. The distance threshold was explicitly set low enough so that even the least similar sub-motions still semantically represent gait cycles. Setting this threshold higher might also qualify sub-motions that do not resemble gait cycles anymore. Finally, subjects that contributed with less than 10 samples were excluded. The final database [2] has 54 walking subjects that performed 3,843 samples in total, which results in an average of about 71 samples per subject.

3 Implementation Details of Algorithms

Recognizing a person from their gait involves capturing and normalizing their walk sample $\mathbf{g}_n$, extracting gait features to compose a template $\hat{\mathbf{g}}_n$, and finally querying the gallery for a set of similar templates $\hat{\mathbf{g}}_{n'}$ – based on a distance function $\hat{\delta}(\hat{\mathbf{g}}_n, \hat{\mathbf{g}}_{n'})$ – to report the most likely identity. This work focuses on extracting robust and discriminative gait features from raw MoCap data.

Many geometric gait features have been introduced over the past few years. They are typically combinations of static body parameters (bone lengths, person's height) [18] with dynamic gait features such as step length, walking speed, joint angles and inter-joint distances [3,6,18,20], along with various statistics (mean, standard deviation or maximum) of their signals [5]. Clearly, these features are schematic and human-interpretable, which is convenient for visualizations and for intuitive understanding, but unnecessary for automatic gait recognition. Instead, our approach [7,8] prefers learning features in a supervised manner that maximally separate the identity classes and are not limited by such dispensable factors.

What follows is a detailed specification of the thirteen gait features extraction methods that we have reviewed in our work to date. Since the idea behind each method has some potential, we have implemented each of them for direct comparison.

- **Ahmed** by Ahmed *et al.* [4] extracts the mean, standard deviation and skew during one gait cycle of horizontal distances (projected on the Z axis) between feet, knees, wrists and shoulders, and mean and standard deviation during one gait cycle of vertical distances (Y coordinates) of head, wrists, shoulders, knees and feet, and finally the mean area during one gait cycle of the triangle of root and two feet.
- **Ali** by Ali *et al.* [5] measures the mean areas during one gait cycle of lower limb triangles.
- **Andersson** by Andersson and Araujo [6] calculates gait attributes as mean and standard deviation during one gait cycle of local extremes of the signals of lower body angles, step length as a maximum of feet distance, stride length as a length of two steps, cycle time and velocity as a ratio of stride length and cycle time. In addition, they extract the mean and standard deviation during one gait cycle of each bone length, and height as the sum of the bone lengths between head and root plus the averages of the bone lengths between root and both feet.
- **Ball** by Ball *et al.* [9] measures mean, standard deviation and maximum during one gait cycle of lower limb angle pairs: upper leg relative to the Y axis, lower leg relative to the upper leg, and the foot relative to the Z axis.
- **Dikovski** by Dikovski *et al.* [12] selects the mean during one gait cycle of step length, height, all bone lengths, then mean, standard deviation, minimum, maximum and mean difference of subsequent frames during one gait cycle of all major joint angles, and the angle between the lines of the shoulder joints and the hip joints.
- **Gavrilova** by Gavrilova *et al.* [3] chooses 20 joint relative distance signals and 16 joint relative angle signals across the whole body, compared using the DTW.
- **Jiang** by Jiang *et al.* [14] measures angle signals between the Y axis and four major lower body (thigh and calf) bones. The signals are compared using the DTW.
- **Krzeszowski** by Krzeszowski *et al.* [16] observes the signals of rotations of eight major bones (humerus, ulna, thigh and calf) around all three axes, the

person's height and step length. These signals are compared using the DTW distance function.

- **Kumar** by Kumar and Babu [17] extracts all joint trajectories around all three axes. Gait samples are compared by a distance function of their covariance matrices.
- **Kwolek** by Kwolek *et al.* [18] processes signals of bone angles around all axes, the person's height and step length. The gait cycles are normalized to 30 frames.
- **Preis** by Preis *et al.* [19] takes height, length of legs, torso, both lower legs, both thighs, both upper arms, both forearms, step length and speed.
- **Sedmidubsky** by Sedmidubsky *et al.* [21] concludes that only the two shoulder-hand signals are discriminatory enough to be used for recognition. These temporal data are compared using the DTW distance function.
- **Sinha** by Sinha *et al.* [22] combines all features of Ball and Preis with mean areas during one gait cycle of upper body and lower body, then mean, standard deviation and maximum distances during one gait cycle between the centroid of the upper body polygon and the centroids of four limb polygons.

We are interested in finding an optimal feature space by maximizing its class separability, which is when gait templates are close to those of the same walker and far from those of other walkers. The method proposed in [7,8] learns gait features directly from joint coordinates by a modification of Fisher's Linear Discriminant Analysis [13] with Maximum Margin Criterion. The framework allows learning from bone rotations as well.

Let the model of a human body have J joints and all samples be linearly normalized to their average length T. Labeled learning data in the sample (measurement) space $\mathcal{G}_L$ are given in the form $\{(\mathbf{g}_n, \ell_n)\}_{n=1}^{N_L}$ where $\mathbf{g}_n = [[\gamma_1(1) \cdots \gamma_J(1)] \cdots [\gamma_1(T) \cdots \gamma_J(T)]]^\top$ is a sample (gait cycle) in which $\gamma_j(t) \in \mathbb{R}^3$ are 3D spatial coordinates of a joint $j \in \{1, \ldots, J\}$ at time $t \in \{1, \ldots, T\}$ normalized with respect to the person's position and direction. See that $\mathcal{G}_L$ has dimensionality $D = 3JT$. Learning on bone rotations is analogical. Each learning sample falls strictly into one of the learning identity classes $\{\mathcal{I}_c\}_{c=1}^C$ determined by ℓ_n. A class $\mathcal{I}_c \subseteq \mathcal{G}_L$ has N_c samples and a priori probability p_c. The classes are complete and mutually exclusive. We say that learning samples $(\mathbf{g}_n, \ell_n)$ and $(\mathbf{g}_{n'}, \ell_{n'})$ share a common walker if and only if they belong to the same class, i.e., $(\mathbf{g}_n, \ell_n), (\mathbf{g}_{n'}, \ell_{n'}) \in \mathcal{I}_c \Leftrightarrow \ell_n = \ell_{n'}$.

Apart from Maximum Margin Criterion (MMC) we also investigated the fusion of Principal Component Analysis (PCA) with Linear Discriminant Analysis (LDA) that has been used for silhouette-based (2D) gait recognition by Su *et al.* [23]. Feature extraction is given by a linear transformation (feature) matrix $\Phi \in \mathbb{R}^{D \times \widehat{D}}$ from a D-dimensional sample space $\mathcal{G} = \{\mathbf{g}_n\}_{n=1}^N$ of not necessarily labeled gait samples to a $\widehat{D}$-dimensional feature space $\widehat{\mathcal{G}} = \{\widehat{\mathbf{g}}_n\}_{n=1}^N$ of gait templates where $\widehat{D} < D$ and gait samples $\mathbf{g}_n$ are transformed into gait templates $\widehat{\mathbf{g}}_n$ by $\widehat{\mathbf{g}}_n = \Phi^\top \mathbf{g}_n$.

On given labeled learning data $\mathcal{G}_L$, Algorithms 1 and 2 are efficient ways of learning the transforms Φ for MMC and PCA+LDA, respectively. Both algorithms [7,8] are of quadratic complexity with respect to the number of learning identity classes due to the singular value decomposition and eigenvalue decomposition.

Algorithm 1. LearnTransformationMatrixMMC $(\mathcal{G}_L)$

1: split $\mathcal{G}_L = \{(\mathbf{g}_n, \ell_n)\}_{n=1}^{N_L}$ into classes $\{\mathcal{I}_c\}_{c=1}^{C_L}$ of $N_c = |\mathcal{I}_c|$ samples and set p_c (we set $p_c = N_c/N_L$)
2: compute overall mean $\mu = \frac{1}{N_L} \sum_{n=1}^{N_L} \mathbf{g}_n$ and individual class means $\mu_c = \frac{1}{N_c} \sum_{n=1}^{N_c} \mathbf{g}_n^{(c)}$
3: compute $\Sigma_B = \sum_{c=1}^{C_L} p_c (\mu_c - \mu)(\mu_c - \mu)^\top$
4: compute $\mathbf{X} = \frac{1}{\sqrt{N_L}}[(\mathbf{g}_1 - \mu) \cdots (\mathbf{g}_{N_L} - \mu)]$
5: compute $\Upsilon = \left[\sqrt{p_1}(\mu_1 - \mu) \cdots \sqrt{p_{C_L}}(\mu_{C_L} - \mu)\right]$
6: compute eigenvectors Ω and corresponding eigenvalues Θ of $\Sigma_T = \mathbf{X}\mathbf{X}^\top$ through SVD of $\mathbf{X}$
7: compute eigenvectors Ξ of $\Theta^{-1/2}\Omega^\top \Sigma_B \Omega \Theta^{-1/2}$ through SVD of $\Theta^{-1/2}\Omega^\top \Upsilon$
8: compute eigenvectors $\Psi = \Omega \Theta^{-1/2} \Xi$
9: compute eigenvalues $\Delta = \Psi^\top \Sigma_B \Psi$
10: return transform Φ as eigenvectors in Ψ that correspond to the eigenvalues of at least $\frac{1}{2}$ in Δ

Algorithm 2. LearnTransformationMatrixPCALDA $(\mathcal{G}_L)$

1: split $\mathcal{G}_L = \{(\mathbf{g}_n, \ell_n)\}_{n=1}^{N_L}$ into classes $\{\mathcal{I}_c\}_{c=1}^{C_L}$ of $N_c = |\mathcal{I}_c|$ samples and set p_c (we set $p_c = N_c/N_L$)
2: compute overall mean $\mu = \frac{1}{N_L} \sum_{n=1}^{N_L} \mathbf{g}_n$ and individual class means $\mu_c = \frac{1}{N_c} \sum_{n=1}^{N_c} \mathbf{g}_n^{(c)}$
3: compute $\Sigma_B = \sum_{c=1}^{C_L} p_c (\mu_c - \mu)(\mu_c - \mu)^\top$
4: compute $\Sigma_W = \sum_{c=1}^{C_L} p_c \sum_{n=1}^{N_c} \left(\mathbf{g}_n^{(c)} - \mu_c\right)\left(\mathbf{g}_n^{(c)} - \mu_c\right)^\top$
5: compute eigenvectors Φ_{PCA} of Σ_T that correspond to the $\overline{D}$ largest eigenvalues (we set $\overline{D} = C_L$)
6: compute eigenvectors Φ_{LDA} of $\left(\Phi_{PCA}^\top \Sigma_W \Phi_{PCA}\right)^{-1}\left(\Phi_{PCA}^\top \Sigma_B \Phi_{PCA}\right)$ by eigendecomposition
7: return transform $\Phi = \Phi_{PCA}\Phi_{LDA}$

In addition to the gait features extraction methods of our fellow researchers, we implemented our own methods as described below. Depending on whether the raw data are in the form of bone rotations or joint coordinates, the methods are referred to with BR or JC subscripts, respectively.

- _MMC learns gait features by MMC (Algorithm 1) and the gait templates are compared by the Mahalanobis distance [7,8].
- _PCALDA learns gait features by PCA+LDA (Algorithm 2) and the gait templates are also compared by the Mahalanobis distance [7,8].
- _Random has no features and classification is performed by picking a random identity that is present in the gallery.

- **_Raw** takes all raw data. The template vector, normalized to the average of $T = 150$ frames, results in a large feature space dimensionality $\widehat{D} = D = 3JT = 13{,}950$, which is why the raw data cannot be directly used for recognition on large databases.

4   Evaluation

Learning data $\mathcal{G}_L = \{(\mathbf{g}_n, \ell_n)\}_{n=1}^{N_L}$ of C_L identities and evaluation data $\mathcal{G}_E = \{(\mathbf{g}_n, \ell_n)\}_{n=1}^{N_E}$ of C_E identity classes have to be disjunct at all times. In the following, we introduce two setups of data separation: homogeneous and heterogeneous. The homogeneous setup learns the transformation matrix on $1/3$ samples of C_L identities and is evaluated on templates derived from the other $2/3$ samples of the same $C_E = C_L$ identities. The heterogeneous setup learns the transform on all samples in C_L identities and is evaluated on all templates derived from other C_E identities. An abstraction of this concept is depicted in Fig. 2. Note that unlike in the homogeneous setup, no walker identity is ever used for both learning and evaluation at the same time in the heterogeneous setup.

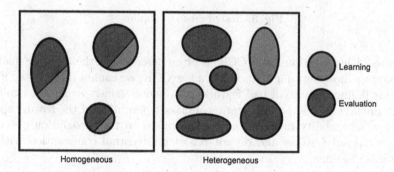

Fig. 2. Data separation for the homogeneous setup of $C_L = C_E = 3$ learning-and-evaluation classes (left) and for the heterogeneous setup of $C_L = 2$ learning classes and $C_E = 4$ evaluation classes (right). The black square represents a database and the ellipses are the identity classes.

The homogeneous setup is parametrized by a single number $C_L = C_E$ of learning-and-evaluation identity classes, whereas the heterogeneous setup has the form (C_L, C_E) specifying how many learning and how many evaluation identity classes are randomly selected from the database. The evaluation of each setup is repeated 3 times, selecting new random C_L and C_E identity classes each time and reporting the average result.

In the homogeneous setup, all results are estimated with nested cross-validation (see Fig. 3) that involves the outer 3-fold cross-validation loop where templates in one fold are used for learning the features, while templates in the remaining two folds are used for evaluations. In the heterogeneous setup, the learning and evaluation parts are selected at random based on the given C_L and C_E, respectively. For both setups, this model is frozen and ready to be evaluated for class separability coefficients. Evaluation of rank-based classifier performance metrics advances to the inner 10-fold cross-validation loop taking one dis-labeled fold as a testing set and the other nine labeled folds as gallery. Test templates are classified by the winner-takes-all strategy, in which a test template $\widehat{\mathbf{g}}^{\text{test}}$ gets assigned with the label $\ell_{\arg\min_l \widehat{\delta}(\widehat{\mathbf{g}}^{\text{test}}, \widehat{\mathbf{g}}_l^{\text{gallery}})}$ of the gallery's closest identity class.

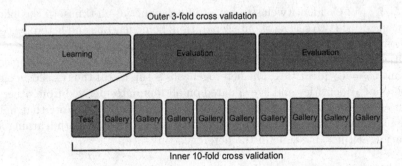

Fig. 3. Nested cross-validation.

Correct Classification Rate (CCR) is often perceived as the ultimate qualitative measure, however, if a method has a low CCR, we cannot directly say if the system is failing because of bad features or a bad classifier. It is more explanatory to provide an evaluation in terms of class separability of the feature space. The class separability measures give an estimate on the recognition potential of the extracted features and do not reflect an eventual combination with an unsuitable classifier:

- *Davies-Bouldin Index:* **(DBI)**

$$\text{DBI} = \frac{1}{C_E} \sum_{c=1}^{C_E} \max_{1 \le c' \le C_E, c' \ne c} \frac{\sigma_c + \sigma_{c'}}{\widehat{\delta}(\widehat{\mu}_c, \widehat{\mu}_{c'})} \tag{1}$$

where $\sigma_c = \frac{1}{N_c} \sum_{n=1}^{N_c} \widehat{\delta}(\widehat{\mathbf{g}}_n, \widehat{\mu}_c)$ is the average distance of all elements in identity class $\mathcal{I}_c$ to its centroid, and analogically for $\sigma_{c'}$. Templates of low intra-class distances and of high inter-class distances have a low DBI.

- *Dunn Index:* **(DI)**

$$\text{DI} = \frac{\min_{1 \le c < c' \le C_E} \widehat{\delta}(\widehat{\mu}_c, \widehat{\mu}_{c'})}{\max_{1 \le c \le C_E} \sigma_c} \tag{2}$$

with σ_c from the above DBI. Since this criterion seeks classes with high intra-class similarity and low inter-class similarity, a high DI is more desirable.

- *Silhouette Coefficient:* **(SC)**

$$SC = \frac{1}{N_E} \sum_{n=1}^{N_E} \frac{b(\widehat{\mathbf{g}}_n) - a(\widehat{\mathbf{g}}_n)}{\max\left\{a(\widehat{\mathbf{g}}_n), b(\widehat{\mathbf{g}}_n)\right\}} \tag{3}$$

where $a(\widehat{\mathbf{g}}_n) = \frac{1}{N_c} \sum_{n'=1}^{N_c} \widehat{\delta}(\widehat{\mathbf{g}}_n, \widehat{\mathbf{g}}_{n'})$ is the average distance from $\widehat{\mathbf{g}}_n$ to other samples within the same identity class and $b(\widehat{\mathbf{g}}_n) = \min_{1 \le c' \le C_E,\, c' \ne c} \frac{1}{N_{c'}} \sum_{n'=1}^{N_{c'}} \widehat{\delta}(\widehat{\mathbf{g}}_n, \widehat{\mathbf{g}}_{n'})$ is the average distance of $\widehat{\mathbf{g}}_n$ to the samples in the closest class. It is clear that $-1 \le SC \le 1$ and SC close to one means that classes are appropriately separated.

- *Fisher's Discriminant Ratio:* **(FDR)**

$$FDR = \frac{\frac{1}{C} \sum_{c=1}^{C_E} \widehat{\delta}(\widehat{\mu}_c, \widehat{\mu})}{\frac{1}{N_E} \sum_{c=1}^{C_E} \sum_{n=1}^{N_c} \widehat{\delta}(\widehat{\mathbf{g}}_n, \widehat{\mu}_c)}. \tag{4}$$

High FDR is preferred for classes of low intra-class sparsity and high inter-class sparsity.

Apart from analyzing the distribution of templates in the feature space, it is schematic to combine the features with a rank-based classifier and to evaluate the system based on distance distribution with respect to a probe. For obtaining a more applied performance evaluation, we evaluate:

- *Cumulative Match Characteristic:* **(CMC)**
  Sequence of Rank-k (for k on X axis from 1 up to C_E) recognition rates (Y axis) for measuring ranking capabilities of a recognition method. Its headline Rank-1 is the well-known **CCR**.
- *False Accept Rate vs. False Reject Rate:* **(FAR/FRR)**
  Two sequences of the error rates (Y axis) as functions of discrimination threshold (X axis). Each method has a value e of this threshold giving Equal Error Rate (**EER** = FAR = FRR).
- *Receiver Operating Characteristic:* **(ROC)**
  Sequence of True Accept Rate (**TAR**) and False Accept Rate (**FAR**) with a varied discrimination threshold. For a given threshold the system signals both TAR (Y axis) and FAR (X axis). Area Under Curve (**AUC**) is computed as the integral of the ROC curve.
- *Recall vs. Precision:* **(RCL/PCN)**
  Sequence of rates with a varied discrimination threshold. For a given threshold the system signalizes both RCL (X axis) and PCN (Y axis). The value of Mean Average Precision (**MAP**) is computed as the area under RCL/PCN curve.

These measures reflect how well the feature is class-separated and how much it takes to confuse the identities of two people. They do not, in fact, provide complementary information, however, a quality evaluation framework should be able to evaluate the most popular measures. Each measure is evaluated in the context of a particular application. For example, a hotel lobby authentication system could use a high Rank-3 at the CMC, while a city-level person tracking system is likely to need the ROC curve leaning towards the upper left corner.

5   Reproducing the Experiments

This section provides a description of the framework we implemented and the database we extracted. With this manual, a reader should be able to reproduce the evaluation and to use the implementation for recognizing people. All source codes including (1) database extraction drive, (2) implementations of the proposed and all relevant methods, (3) classifier learning and classification mechanisms and (4) evaluation mechanism and metrics, are available at our departmental Git repository [1]. The original CMU MoCap database and extracted databases are available online at our research group web page [2].

Executor.java is the main execution class. Set all parameters of evaluation and file locations and distanceThreshold, then select which actions to perform and finally, select the evaluation setups. The class contains the main(String[] args) method. It contains four methods to select for execution:

extractDatabase() for extracting an experimental database from the original CMU MoCap database —this is also available for download at our page as original.zip. To run this method, unzip to get the files gaitcycle.amc (exemplary gait cycle) and skeleton.asf (prototypical skeleton) and the directory amcOriginal (original AMC files). Extraction begins with normalization with respect to a person's position and walk direction as provided in the normalized.zip file. Clean gait cycles are then filtered out by the distance threshold (see last paragraph of Sect. 2) that numerically expresses how much extracted motions resemble gait cycles, that is, the lower the distance threshold, the fewer and cleaner the gait cycles. Set a value for distanceThreshold to produce a folder of the extracted database. Evaluations in [7,8] are set with 302.0, extracting a database of 54 identities and 3,843 gait cycles. A higher distance threshold will qualify some non-gait motions.

learnClassifiers() for learning classifiers of all implemented methods on a sub-database determined by the distance threshold. Set a value for distanceThreshold (such as 302.0) and provide the corresponding directory of the learning database (such as amc302.0 in extracted-302.0.zip) and the learned classifiers appear in the classifiers folder.

performClassification() for performing a classification of a custom probe/query on a custom gallery with a custom classifier. Set file locations for the classifier file customClassifier, the probe gait cycle customQueryFileAMC and the gallery directory customGalleryDirectory. Results are printed on the standard output.

evaluateMethods() for evaluating the implemented methods in homogeneous and heterogeneous setups. To skip database extraction, one could supply a provided extracted database (such as amc302.0 in extracted-302.0.zip) and a skeleton file (such as skeleton.asf in any extracted database ZIP file). Our page provides additional databases categorised according to various values of distanceThreshold. The results are set to be printed on the standard output but we suggest to redirect it to a CSV file. Results of individual evaluation attempts vary slightly as different learning, testing and gallery sets are randomly selected upon each attempt.

Compile to obtain `Gait.jar`. The main project location should also contain the `lib` directory and all necessary files and directories depending on which actions are to be executed. Run command `$ java -jar Gait.jar >` `output.csv`.

The output file (see structure in Table 1) contains the performance metrics as specified in Sect. 4 and the information about average distance computation time (**DCT**) in milliseconds and average template dimensionality (**TD**). The evaluation results are in the form of one value per coefficient (see results in Table 2) and the sequences CMC, FAR/FRR, ROC = TAR/FAR and RCL/PCN. The CMC sequence contains C_E values, one for each k in the Rank-k recognition rate. The other three pairs of sequences are normalized to 30 values by `method.setFineness(30)`. The FAR/FRR sequences of all methods are normalized to the discrimination threshold with respect to the first value of FAR = 0 and FRR = 1, and to the middle value that represents EER where all sequences cross. The ROC sequences are normalized with respect to the first value of TAR = FAR = 0 and to the last value of TAR = FAR = 1. Finally, the RCL/PCN sequences are normalized with respect to the first value of RCL = 0 and to the last value of RCL = 1.

Table 1. Structure of the output file.

{method name}, {distance threshold}
DBI DI SC FDR CCR EER AUC MAP DCT TD
{1 line – one value for each coefficient}
CMC
{C_E lines – the CMC sequence}
FAR FRR TAR FAR RCL PCN
{30 lines – all six sequences}

To reproduce the experiments in Table 2, follow the instructions in the README file at [1] in the `reproduce` folder. Please note that some methods are slow even on a leading edge hardware. Learning and evaluation times in Table 3 were measured on a computer with Intel® Xeon® CPU E5-2650 v2 @ 2.60 GHz and 256 GB RAM.

The goal of the MMC-based learning is to find a linear discriminant that maximizes the misclassification margin. This optimization technique appears to be more effective than designing geometric gait features. Table 2 indicates the best results for the MMC on bone rotational data: highest SC, EER and AUC, and competitive DBI, DI, FDR, CCR and MAP. In terms of the Correct Classification Rate metric, our MMC method was only outperformed by the Raw method, which is implemented here as a form of baseline. We interpret the high scores as a sign of robustness.

Table 2. First line results of all 20 implemented methods on the 302.0 database.

Method	Class separability coefficients				Classification based metrics				Scalability	
	DBI	DI	SC	FDR	CCR	EER	AUC	MAP	DCT	TD
Ahmed	216.2	0.842	−0.246	0.954	0.657	0.38	0.659	0.165	<1	24
Ali	501.5	0.26	−0.463	1.175	0.225	0.384	0.679	0.111	<1	2
Andersson	142.3	1.297	−0.102	1.127	0.84	0.343	0.715	0.251	<1	68
Ball	161	1.458	−0.163	1.117	0.75	0.346	0.711	0.231	<1	18
Dikovski	144.5	1.817	−0.135	**1.227**	0.881	0.363	0.695	0.254	<1	71
Gavrilova	185.8	1.708	−0.164	0.77	0.891	0.374	0.677	0.254	45	5,254
Jiang	206.6	1.802	−0.249	0.85	0.811	0.395	0.657	0.242	8	584
Krzeszowski	154.1	1.982	−0.147	0.874	0.915	0.392	0.662	0.275	35	3,795
Kumar	**118.6**	1.618	−0.086	1.09	0.801	0.459	0.631	0.217	8	13,950
Kwolek	150.9	1.348	−0.084	1.175	0.896	0.358	0.723	0.323	<1	660
Preis	1,980.6	0.055	−0.512	1.067	0.143	0.401	0.626	0.067	<1	13
Sedmidubsky	398.1	1.35	−0.425	0.811	0.543	0.388	0.657	0.149	<1	292
Sinha	214.8	1.112	−0.215	1.101	0.674	0.356	0.697	0.191	<1	45
_MMC$_{BR}$	154.2	1.638	**0.062**	1.173	0.925	**0.297**	**0.748**	0.353	<1	53
_MMC$_{JC}$	130.3	1.891	0.051	1.106	0.918	0.378	0.721	0.315	<1	51
_PCALDA$_{BR}$	182	1.596	−0.015	0.984	0.918	0.361	0.695	0.276	<1	54
_PCALDA$_{JC}$	174.4	1.309	−0.091	0.827	0.863	0.44	0.643	0.201	<1	54
_Random					0.042					0
_Raw$_{BR}$	163.7	**2.092**	0.011	0.948	**0.966**	0.315	0.743	**0.358**	70	8,229
_Raw$_{JC}$	155.1	1.954	−0.12	0.897	0.926	0.377	0.679	0.283	161	13,574

Table 3. Evaluation times of the methods in Table 2. Units: s seconds, m minutes, h hours, d days.

Method	Time	Method	Time	Method	Time	Method	Time
Ahmed	48.6 m	Gavrilova	10.3 d	Preis	48.7 m	_PCALDA$_{BR}$	4.7 h
Ali	40.9 m	Jiang	1.9 d	Sedmidubsky	1.4 d	_PCALDA$_{JC}$	10.9 h
Andersson	45.7 m	Krzeszowski	8.1 d	Sinha	49.6 m	_Random	27.9 m
Ball	48.5 m	Kumar	1.8 d	_MMC$_{BR}$	2.6 h	_Raw$_{BR}$	16.1 d
Dikovski	50.7 m	Kwolek	1.1 h	_MMC$_{JC}$	3.0 h	_Raw$_{JC}$	36.7 d

Apart from the performance merits, the MMC method is also efficient: relatively low-dimensional templates and Mahalanobis distance ensure fast distance computations and thus contribute to high scalability. Note that even if the Raw method has some of the best results, it can hardly be used in practice due to its extreme consumption of time and space resources. On the other hand, Random has no features but cannot be considered a serious recognition method. To illustrate the evaluation time, calculating the distance matrix (a matrix of distances between all evaluation templates) took a couple minutes for the MMC method, almost nothing for the Random method, and more than two weeks for the Raw method. To conclude, the MMC method on bone rotational data appears to be an optimal trade-off between effectiveness and efficiency, and thus the new state-of-the-art in feature extraction for MoCap-based gait recognition.

6   Summary and Future Work

As our contribution to reproducible research, we have provided implementation details and source codes [1] of our evaluation framework for gait recognition [7,8]. The software implements the proposed method as well as all related methods. We include the evaluation database [2] together with source codes for its extraction from the general CMU MoCap database. We also attach the description and portable software for evaluating class separability coefficients of extracted features and classifier performance metrics. Finally, we provide documentation and installation instructions for easy and straightforward reproducibility of the experiments.

As demonstrated by outperforming other methods in four class separability coefficients and four classification metrics, the proposed features learning mechanism has a strong potential in gait recognition applications. Even though we believe that MMC is the most suitable criterion for optimizing gait features, we continue to research further potential optimality criteria and machine learning approaches.

We hope that the evaluation framework and database presented here will contribute to smooth development and evaluation of further novel MoCap-based gait recognition methods. All used data and source codes have been made available [1,2] under the Creative Commons Attribution license (CC-BY) for database and the Apache 2.0 license for software, which grant free use and allow for experimental evaluation. We encourage all readers and developers of MoCap-based gait recognition methods to contribute to the framework with new algorithms, data and improvements.

Acknowledgments. The authors thank to the anonymous reviewers for their detailed commentary and suggestions. The data used in this project was created with funding from NSF EIA-0196217 and was obtained from http://mocap.cs.cmu.edu [11].

References

1. Evaluation framework for MoCap-based gait recognition methods. https://gitlab.fi.muni.cz/xbalazia/GaitRecognition. Commit hash 0ac9b0dd from 25th November 2016
2. Extracted MoCap Gait Database. Faculty of Informatics, Masaryk University, Brno. https://gait.fi.muni.cz/#database
3. Ahmed, F., Paul, P.P., Gavrilova, M.L.: DTW-based kernel and rank-level fusion for 3D Gait recognition using Kinect. Vis. Comput. **31**(6), 915–924 (2015). https://doi.org/10.1007/s00371-015-1092-0

4. Ahmed, M., Al-Jawad, N., Sabir, A.: Gait recognition based on Kinect sensor. In: Proceedings of SPIE 9139, pp. 91390B–91390B-10 (2014). https://doi.org/10.1117/12.2052588B

5. Ali, S., Wu, Z., Li, X., Saeed, N., Wang, D., Zhou, M.: Applying geometric function on sensors 3d gait data for human identification. In: Gavrilova, M.L., Tan, C.J.K., Iglesias, A., Shinya, M., Galvez, A., Sourin, A. (eds.) Transactions on Computational Science XXVI. LNCS, vol. 9550, pp. 125–141. Springer, Heidelberg (2016). doi:10.1007/978-3-662-49247-5_8

6. Andersson, V.O., Araujo, R.M.: Person identification using anthropometric and gait data from Kinect sensor. In: Proceedings of the Twenty-Ninth AAAI Conference on Artificial Intelligence (AAAI 2015), pp. 425–431. AAAI Press (2015). http://www.aaai.org/ocs/index.php/AAAI/AAAI15/paper/view/9680

7. Balazia, M., Sojka, P.: Learning robust features for gait recognition by maximum margin criterion. In: Proceedings of 23rd International Conference on Pattern Recognition (ICPR 2016), p. 6. IEEE (2016). arXiv:1609.04392

8. Balazia, M., Sojka, P.: Walker-independent features for gait recognition from motion capture data. In: Robles-Kelly, A., Loog, M., Biggio, B., Escolano, F., Wilson, R. (eds.) S+SSPR 2016. LNCS, vol. 10029, pp. 310–321. Springer, Cham (2016). doi:10.1007/978-3-319-49055-7_28

9. Ball, A., Rye, D., Ramos, F., Velonaki, M.: Unsupervised clustering of people from 'skeleton' data. In: Proceedings of the Seventh Annual ACM/IEEE International Conference on Human-Robot Interaction (HRI 2012), pp. 225–226. ACM, New York (2012). http://doi.acm.org/10.1145/2157689.2157767

10. Chen, X., Koskela, M.: Classification of RGB-D and motion capture sequences using extreme learning machine. In: Kämäräinen, J.-K., Koskela, M. (eds.) SCIA 2013. LNCS, vol. 7944, pp. 640–651. Springer, Heidelberg (2013). doi:10.1007/978-3-642-38886-6_60

11. CMU Graphics Lab: Carnegie-Mellon Motion Capture (MoCap) Database (2003). http://mocap.cs.cmu.edu

12. Dikovski, B., Madjarov, G., Gjorgjevikj, D.: Evaluation of different feature sets for gait recognition using skeletal data from Kinect. In: 37th International Convention on Information and Communication Technology, Electronics and Microelectronics, pp. 1304–1308 (2014). http://ieeexplore.ieee.org/stamp/stamp.jsp?arnumber=6859769

13. Fisher, R.A.: The use of multiple measurements in taxonomic problems. Ann. Eugenics 7(2), 179–188 (1936). https://doi.org/10.1111/j.1469-1809.1936.tb02137.x

14. Jiang, S., Wang, Y., Zhang, Y., Sun, J.: Real time gait recognition system based on kinect skeleton feature. In: Jawahar, C.V., Shan, S. (eds.) ACCV 2014. LNCS, vol. 9008, pp. 46–57. Springer, Cham (2015). doi:10.1007/978-3-319-16628-5_4

15. Kastaniotis, D., Theodorakopoulos, I., Theoharatos, C., Economou, G., Fotopoulos, S.: A framework for gait-based recognition using Kinect. Pattern Recognit. Lett. 68(Part 2), 327–335 (2015). Special Issue on "Soft Biometrics". http://www.sciencedirect.com/science/article/pii/S0167865515001920,

16. Krzeszowski, T., Switonski, A., Kwolek, B., Josinski, H., Wojciechowski, K.: DTW-based gait recognition from recovered 3-d joint angles and inter-ankle distance. In: Chmielewski, L.J., Kozera, R., Shin, B.-S., Wojciechowski, K. (eds.) ICCVG 2014. LNCS, vol. 8671, pp. 356–363. Springer, Cham (2014). doi:10.1007/978-3-319-11331-9_43

17. Kumar, M.S.N., Babu, R.V.: Human gait recognition using depth camera: a covariance based approach. In: Proceedings of the Eighth Indian Conference on Computer Vision, Graphics and Image Processing (ICVGIP 2012), NY, USA, pp. 20:1–20:6 (2012). http://doi.acm.org/10.1145/2425333.2425353

18. Kwolek, B., Krzeszowski, T., Michalczuk, A., Josinski, H.: 3D gait recognition using spatio-temporal motion descriptors. In: Nguyen, N.T., Attachoo, B., Trawiński, B., Somboonviwat, K. (eds.) ACIIDS 2014. LNCS (LNAI), vol. 8398, pp. 595–604. Springer, Cham (2014). doi:10.1007/978-3-319-05458-2_61

19. Preis, J., Kessel, M., Werner, M., Linnhoff-Popien, C.: Gait recognition with Kinect. In: 1st International Workshop on Kinect in Pervasive Computing, New Castle, UK, 18–22 June, pp. 1–4 (2012). https://www.researchgate.net/publication/239862819_Gait_Recognition_with_Kinect

20. Ramu Reddy, V., Chakravarty, K., Aniruddha, S.: Person identification in natural static postures using Kinect. In: Agapito, L., Bronstein, M.M., Rother, C. (eds.) ECCV 2014. LNCS, vol. 8926, pp. 793–808. Springer, Cham (2015). doi:10.1007/978-3-319-16181-5_60

21. Sedmidubsky, J., Valcik, J., Balazia, M., Zezula, P.: Gait recognition based on normalized walk cycles. In: Bebis, G., et al. (eds.) ISVC 2012. LNCS, vol. 7432, pp. 11–20. Springer, Heidelberg (2012). doi:10.1007/978-3-642-33191-6_2

22. Sinha, A., Chakravarty, K., Bhowmick, B.: Person identification using skeleton information from Kinect. In: Proceedings of the Sixth International Conference on Advances in CHI (ACHI 2013), pp. 101–108 (2013). https://www.thinkmind.org/index.php?view=article&articleid=achi_2013_4_0_20187

23. Su, H., Liao, Z.W., Chen, G.Y.: A gait recognition method using L1-PCA and LDA. In: Proceedings of the Eighth International Conference on Machine Learning and Cybernetics, vol. 6, pp. 3198–3203 (2009). https://doi.org/10.1109/ICMLC.2009.5212776

24. Valcik, J., Sedmidubsky, J., Zezula, P.: Assessing similarity models for human-motion retrieval applications. Comput. Anim. Virtual Worlds **27**(5), 484–500 (2016). http://dx.doi.org/10.1002/cav.1674

Reproducible Pattern Recognition Research: The Case of Optimistic SSL

Jesse H. Krijthe[1,2]([⊠]) and Marco Loog[1,3]

[1] Pattern Recognition Laboratory,
Delft University of Technology, Delft, Netherlands
jkrijthe@gmail.com
[2] Department of Molecular Epidemiology,
Leiden University Medical Center, Leiden, Netherlands
[3] The Image Section, University of Copenhagen, Copenhagen, Denmark

Abstract. In this paper, we discuss the approaches we took and trade-offs involved in making a paper on a conceptual topic in pattern recognition research fully reproducible. We discuss our definition of reproducibility, the tools used, how the analysis was set up, show some examples of alternative analyses the code enables and discuss our views on reproducibility.

Keywords: Reproducibility · Pattern recognition · Semi-supervised learning

1 Introduction

The goal of this work is to describe and discuss the choices involved in making the results of a conceptual work in pattern recognition fully reproducible. Conceptual, here, refers to the type and goal of the analysis that was done in that work: using simulations and experiments, it tries to improve our understanding of one or more methods, rather than apply an existing method to some new application or introduce supposedly novel approaches. The work in question is our paper on *Optimistic Semi-supervised Least Squares Classification* [7], which reports on two ways in which a supervised least squares classifier can be adapted to the semi-supervised setting, the connections between these two approaches and why one of these approaches often outperforms the other.

The conceptual nature of the work has particular advantages in making it reproducible: the data required to run experiments can easily be made available or, for simulated datasets, data are not required and the code to run the experiments is relatively self-contained, i.e. it has few dependencies on code outside this project. One could argue that for these types of projects, there is no reason *not* to make results reproducible. We notice, however, that in practice, trade-offs and problems still come up. We will discuss our experience in this paper and use it as a case study to discuss the uses of reproducibility in pattern recognition research.

© Springer International Publishing AG 2017
B. Kerautret et al. (Eds.): RRPR 2016, LNCS 10214, pp. 48–59, 2017.
DOI: 10.1007/978-3-319-56414-2_4

We will start by giving a short summary of the original paper on optimistic semi-supervised learning. We will then discuss what we mean by reproducibility and discuss the tools and strategies used here. After some examples of alternative analyses enabled by the reproducible nature of the work, we end with a discussion on the relevance of reproducibility in pattern recognition research.

2   Summary of Optimistic SSL

In supervised classification, classifiers are trained using a dataset of input/output pairs $\{(\mathbf{x}_i, y_i)\}_{i=1}^L$, where $\mathbf{x}_i$ is a d-dimensional input vector and y_i is a binary outcome encoded using some value m for one class and n for the other. In semi-supervised learning, one attempts to use an additional set of unlabeled data $\{(\mathbf{x}_j)\}_{j=1}^U$ to improve the construction of a classifier to solve the super-vised learning task. Semi-supervised learning is an active area of research due to its promise of improving classifiers in tasks where labeling objects is relatively expensive, or unlabeled data is inexpensive to come by.

The goal of the work in [7] is to study two different ways to adapt the supervised least squares classifier to the semi-supervised learning setting. The supervised least squares classifier for the two-class problem is defined as the linear classifier that minimizes the quadratic loss on the labeled objects or, equivalently, least squares regression applied to a numeric encoding of the labels, with the following objective function:

$$J_s(\mathbf{w}) = \|\mathbf{X}\mathbf{w} - \mathbf{y}\|^2 + \lambda\|\mathbf{w}\|^2,$$

where $\mathbf{X}$ is the $L \times d$ design matrix of the labeled objects, $\mathbf{w}$ refers to the weights of the linear classifier and λ is a regularization parameter. We now define two straightforward ways to include the unlabeled data in this objective function. The first we refer to as the *label based objective*, since it treats the missing labels of the unlabeled data as a vector $\mathbf{u}$ that we should minimize over:

$$J_l(\mathbf{w}, \mathbf{u}) = \left\|\mathbf{X}_e\mathbf{w} - \begin{bmatrix} \mathbf{y} \\ \mathbf{u} \end{bmatrix}\right\|^2 + \lambda\|\mathbf{w}\|^2,$$

where $\mathbf{X}_e$ is an $(L+U) \times d$ design matrix containing the d feature values for all, labeled and unlabeled, objects. A second way to include the data is to consider that each unlabeled object belongs to one of two classes, and we can assign each object a responsibility: a probability of belonging to each class. If the classes are encoded as m and n, for instance -1 and $+1$, this *responsibility based objective* is defined as:

$$J_r(\mathbf{w}, \mathbf{q}) = \|\mathbf{X}\mathbf{w} - \mathbf{y}\|^2 + \lambda\|\mathbf{w}\|^2 + \sum_{j=1}^U q_j(\mathbf{x}_j^\top\mathbf{w} - m)^2 + (1 - q_j)(\mathbf{x}_j^\top\mathbf{w} - n)^2.$$

The first result from the paper is that applying block coordinate descent to these objectives – where we alternate between minimizing over $\mathbf{w}$ and $\mathbf{u}$

respectively $\mathbf{q}$ – the second procedure turns out to be equivalent to the well-known *hard-label self-learning* approach applied to the least squares classifier, while the first approach is equivalent to a *soft-label self-learning*, similar to a method that was originally proposed for regression as early as the 1930s [4].

The second result from the paper [7] is that the soft-label variant typically outperforms the hard-label variant on a set of benchmark datasets. In the paper we showed these results in terms of the error rate on an unseen test set: the learning curves of the performance for different amounts of unlabeled data are typically lower for the soft-label variant than for the hard-label variant. We will revisit these results in Sect. 4, by showing how to adapt the code to not only consider the performance in terms of the error rate, but in terms of the quadratic loss used by the classifier as well.

The third result is a study of one reason for the performance difference by looking at the effect of local minima on the optimization problems posed by both approaches. We find that the label based objective corresponding to the soft-label variant has much fewer local minima for the optimization to get stuck in, compared to the hard-label variant, which often gets stuck in a bad local minimum, even though a better local minimum may be available.

3   Reproducibility

3.1   Definition of Reproducibility

Reproducibility and replicability of experiments has gained increasing interest both in science in general [3] and in pattern recognition/computer vision/machine learning as well [1,2]. Much of this interest can be attributed to what some call the "Reproducibility crisis" in science: many published results can not be replicated by others trying to verify these results. Perhaps the most visible and laudable effort to estimate the scale of this problem in one scientific discipline has been the Open Science Collaboration's efforts in Psychology [8] which finds that by some measures of replicability, the results of less than half of the 100 studies selected for replication could actually be replicated. A related, but different phenomenon is the "credibility crisis" [1] which refers to the decrease in the believability in computational scientific results caused by the increasing difficulty to understand exactly how results were obtained based on the textual description alone.

While "replicability is not reproducibility" [2], these terms on their own may already refer to different things. Reference [3] attempts to give clear definitions for different notions of reproducing a result. In this paper, we are mostly concerned with what they call *methods reproducibility*, meaning the ability of different researchers to reproduce exactly the same figures and tables of results based on the data, code and other artefacts provided by the original authors. Like [9], we will refer to this simply as *reproducibility*. Note that the moniker reproducibility does not say anything about the correctness of results, only that they can be obtained again by a different researcher.

Also like [9], we will use the word *replicability* to what [3] calls *results repro-ducibility*: the ability to obtain the results that support the same conclusion by an independent study. Here independent study is still vaguely defined to mean that we set up a new study, where we gather and analyse data using a procedure that "closely resembles" the procedures used in the original work. This is what the "reproducibility crisis" we mentioned at the start of this section refers to: not being able to obtain the same results by such studies. In the pattern recognition context, this definition could often come down to the exact same thing as reproducibility. The definition in [9] is slightly more explicit and considers a study to be a replication if the population, question, hypothesis, experimental design and the analysis plan remain fixed, but the analyst and the code, for instance, have been changed. For a proper definition of a replication in pattern recognition research, one aspect of a replication could be a re-implementation of methods. We will come back to this in the discussion.

The reason we attempt to be so explicit about our definitions here is that the meaning of the words reproducibility and replicability is sometimes interchanged by other authors. Note, for instance, that by our definitions, the reproducibility crisis is best referred to as the replicability crisis. Or consider [2] who refers to methods reproducibility as replicability, and uses reproducibility to mean obtaining the same result using an independent study.

While our definition of reproducibility only concerns the reproduction of the results in the original paper, we will illustrate that having reproducible results reduces the friction to make small changes to the code to explore alternative analyses. This allows one to explore, for instance, how sensitive the results are to particular parameter choices made by the original authors, or whether the method also works for slightly different datasets. In other words, like in a replication, where many things are changed at once to see whether a result can still be obtained, these small changes teach us something about the robustness of the results.

Even if we stick to our definition of 'reproduce exactly the results', there are several levels at which this can be interpreted for a pattern recognition study like ours. We could, for instance, consider the following levels:

- Final paper can be reproduced from the source text
- Figures and tables can be generated from results of computations
- Results of computations can be generated from experiment datasets
- Experiment datasets can be generated from raw data

All using steps for which open source code is available. Although we consider a paper reproducible when all these steps are fulfilled, in practice we will show that for many of the benefits of reproducibility, it may be useful to consider these as separate steps: to explore the effect of a different outcome measure, we may not want to redo the computations. Or for a particular experiment, the preprocessing applied to the raw data may not be particularly relevant, as long as we have the processed data.

3.2 Strategy for Reproducibility

All the code used to produce the results in [7] is written in the R programming language [10], while the paper itself is a combination of Latex and R code to generate the figures. The two are combined using the knitr package [12]. Knitr allows one to intersperse Latex with blocks of R code that get executed and turned into Latex expressions or figures before the Latex document is compiled. This allows for the code that generates the figures to be placed where one would usually place a figure environment in the Latex document, so that everything that visually becomes part of the paper is defined in a single document. One of the advantages of this approach is that the author can be sure that the figures and tables in the paper were actually generated by this code, i.e. the code did not inadvertently change in the meantime.

In principle, one could also include the code for the experiments itself in this document. We noticed, however, that even for projects of this relatively small size, and even though knitr is able to optionally cache results, we found it more convenient to place the code of the experiments in separate files, save the results to an R data file, and then load these result files to be used in the generation of the figures in the knitr document.

The advantage of this particular approach to splitting the computations across files was that we could easily transfer the experiment code to a compute server to run the experiments, while writing the document. A disadvantage of not including the experiment code in the final document is that it increases the possibility that the chain of reproducibility is broken: for instance, we could apply some transformation to the data between the time the experiments where run and the figures are generated and forget, or accidentally save or load an old result file.

Another trade-off was between writing code for this particular analysis project or splitting code off into separate packages. For instance, for the implementations of the classifiers, we decided to make these part of a larger package of methods for semi-supervised learning [6]. This makes the methods and some code used to run experiments available for other applications. It also made sense here, since this project was part of a larger research programme into semi-supervised learning. The downside is that it introduces dependencies between projects. The main practical lesson we learned here is to save the reference to the particular version that was used to generate the results in the paper in the version control system, so that future changes do not effect one's ability to reproduce the results.

Similar to the implementations of the methods, we split the code used to load the datasets into a separate project, to be used for other projects. These scripts download the data and save them locally, unless this is already done previously.

4 Examples

In this section we will show some additional analyses that are possible by changing the original code from [7] and that lead to some additional insights into the methods covered in the paper. The examples shown here are meant to illustrate that reproducible results have utility beyond the mere fact that we are sure how the results were produced: it allows for small changes by readers that can lead to additional insights. We order the examples by the size of the changes to the code required to obtain the results.

4.1   Changing an Example Figure

We start with the simplest case where small changes to the code that generates a figure can help illustrate a point. In the original paper we give an example why the soft-label self-learning variant would update the decision boundary using the unlabeled objects, and that this updating depends on the location of the unlabeled objects. Here we change the location of the unlabeled objects, by changing the line X_u <- matrix(c(-1, 4), 2, 1) to X_u <- matrix(c(-1, 0.5), 2, 1) to show that when the decision values for all unlabeled objects are within $[-1, 1]$, the soft-label self-learning is no different than the supervised solution. The result is shown in Fig. 1. Note that this would be a case where an interactive version of the plot could be illustrative, instead of manually changing values and regenerating the plot.

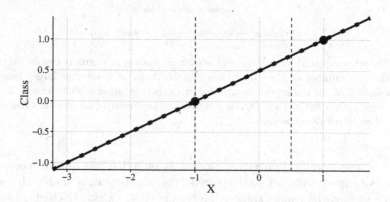

Fig. 1. Example of the first step of soft-label self-learning. The circles indicate two labeled objects, while the dashed vertical lines indicate the location of two unlabeled objects. The solid line is the supervised decision function. A dotted line indicates the updated decision function after finding the labels that minimize the loss of the supervised solution and using these labels as the labels for the unlabeled data in the next iteration. This last line is barely visible because the unlabeled data do not cause an update of the decision function in this case.

4.2   Changing the Outcome Quantity for the Learning Curves

In the original paper, we report the error rate on a test set, for a fixed number of labeled training examples and an increasing amount of unlabeled examples. Alternatively, one might be interested in the performance in terms of the loss,

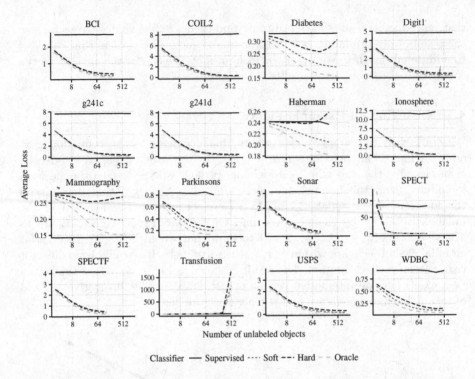

Fig. 2. Average squared loss on the test set for increasing amounts of unlabeled training data. The number of labeled objects remains fixed at a number larger than the dimensionality of the dataset to ensure the supervised solution is well-defined. Results are averaged over 1000 repeats. Oracle refers to the supervised classifier that has access to the labels of all the objects.

instead of the classification error. Since this quantity was already computed during the experiment, we need not redo the experiment: a simple change in the code to plot the results suffices. More explicitly, we simply change the line `filter(Measure=="Error")` to `filter(Measure=="Average Loss Test")`.

The results in Fig. 2 show an interesting discrepancy when compared to the results in terms of the error rate: here in all cases the soft-label variant outperforms the hard-label variant, even on the dataset (Haberman) where it did not in terms of the error rate. Additionally, the loss starts increasing in more cases than for the error rate, especially for the hard-label variant.

4.3 Sensitivity to Random Seed

In the original work, we gave an example of a dataset where the hard-label self-learner is clearly outperformed by the soft-label self-learner. One might wonder how sensitive this dataset is to slight perturbations: is hard-label self-learning always much worse in this type of dataset or does it depend on the particular seed that was chosen when generating the data? This can be easily checked by changing the random seed and computing the classifiers.

In Fig. 3 we show two common configurations we find when we change the random seed. These configurations are qualitatively different from the result reported in the paper. In one case, there is no big difference between the two classifiers, unlike the result in the original work, while in the other, the hard-label self-learner gives deteriorated performance for a different reason: it assigns all objects to a single class.

These results show that the original example is not stable to changes in the random seed. However, the conclusion that soft-label self-learning does not suffer from as severe a deterioration in performance as hard-label self-learning still holds. Our experience generating these additional examples does indicate, though, that other configurations than the prototypical example given in the paper are just as likely, if not or more likely, to occur.

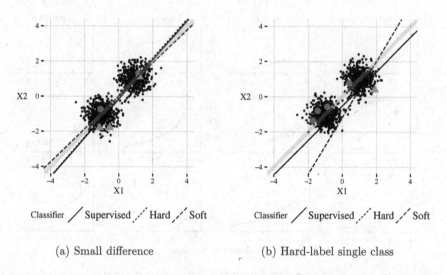

(a) Small difference   (b) Hard-label single class

Fig. 3. Additional examples of the behaviour of hard-label and soft-label self-learning. Light-grey line indicates true decision boundary. In (a), there is only a minor difference between soft-label and hard-label self-learning. In (b), the hard-label self-learner is not visible and assigns all objects to one class.

4.4   Different Type of Learning Curve

For a more involved example, we use the code to generate a different type of learning curve. While we reported the learning curves for a fixed number of labeled samples and an increasing number of unlabeled samples, alternatively one could consider learning curves where the total number of training objects remains fixed, while the fraction of labeled objects is increased. Since the datasets are already available, we can easily set up these experiments by making some changes to the code that generates the other learning curves. We report these results in Fig. 4.

Although the ordering, in terms of performance, is similar in these curves as in the learning curves we originally reported, in many more cases the semi-supervised learners perform worse than the supervised learner. This indicates that as more labeled data becomes available, it is harder to outperform the supervised learner, especially since in these experiments, the amount of unlabeled data shrinks as we add more labeled data. Again, hard-label self-learning suffers more from degradation in performance than soft-label self-learning.

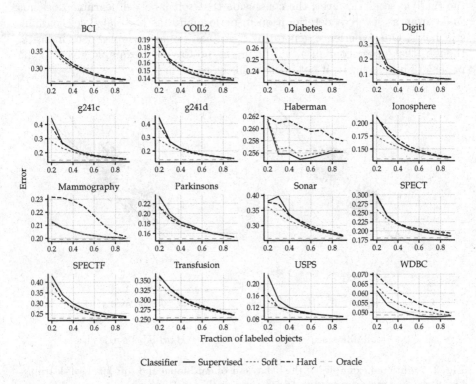

Fig. 4. Classification accuracy when different fractions of the training set are labeled. 20% of the data is left out as test data, the fractions indicate the fraction of objects of the remaining data that was labeled. Oracle refers to the supervised classifier that has access to the labels of all the objects.

5   Discussion

While reproducible research is sometimes framed as being a requirement for a result to be believable [1,3], we think it is important to emphasize that it does not just benefit scientific discourse, but has advantages for the researchers carrying out the original work as well. We elaborate in what follows.

5.1   Advantages to the Researcher

Every research project is a collaboration. Sometimes with other individuals, but at the very least, a collaboration with yourself at some point in the future [11, Chap. 13]. It is rare that one does not have to revisit results after they were originally generated. Making results reproducible ensures that collaborators and you yourself in the future can easily get back into old results and make changes.

Secondly, although reproducibility does not eliminate all errors, it makes it easier to catch some type of errors. For instance, errors introduced by copying and pasting results from one document to another. At the very least, it makes it easier to fix them.

On the whole, for the individual researcher, reproducibility reduces friction: it makes it easy to make changes to figures and experiments even after the whole analysis is done since the later steps in an analysis can be reused if they are implemented in a reproducible way.

5.2   Advantages to Scientific Communication

The Case for Reproducibility. Unlike the claim by [9], the requirement of reproducibility is not something "everybody agrees" on. In this respect, Drummond [2] argues that replicating results is an important part of scientific progress, yet exactly reproducing results is a poor substitute that does not add much other than counter outright fraud, and reproducibility can become a distraction. It may, in other words, not be worthwhile to spend much resources on.

This is perhaps a bit too pessimistic, for two reasons.

First, while reproducibility says nothing about the correctness of a result, it does allow apparent mistakes to be more easily checked than if the code was not available. Consider, for instance, the well-known case of the finding of [5], after much work, that the conclusions in a highly influential study on the effect of government debt on economic growth depended on a data coding error and were very sensitive to particular choices in the analysis. While reproducibility does not eliminate these errors, nor was it required to finally spot them, it would likely have sped up the efforts to uncover these errors. As this case shows, this can have real world consequences, since the original conclusions had been used as an argument around the world by proponents of austerity measures during the recent economic crisis.

Secondly, Drummond's main concern is that reproducibility only deals with keeping steps in an analysis pipeline fixed, while replicability is about changing things. However, as the case study in this paper has hopefully shown, an important side effect from exactly reproducing results is that it removes friction for both the original researchers and the community to make changes and build on the code. We have seen this has two advantages: it aids in communicating results and insights and it provides a stepping stone for others to build new results on.

Replicability in Pattern Recognition. One way to define replicability is to consider a study where the "same procedures are followed but new data are

collected" [3], where this data is sampled from the same population. Is this definition of replicability then a useful construct in methodological pattern recognition
research? In the pattern recognition context, data from the same population may
be hard to define, if your population is a set of benchmark datasets. One could
wonder whether results generalize to other problems. This however, does not
fall under the conventional definition of replicability, but rather under the term
generalizability. In most sciences, one of the things we learn from a replication
is what the essential conditions are that are necessary for a result to hold. Anal-
ogously, we argue one aspect of replicability in pattern recognition research is
the implementation of the methods. As we have noticed in our own work, it is
an under appreciated point how difficult or easy it is for another programmer
or analyst to replicate the results of a method. It teaches us not just something
about the competence of the programmer (a point that is often overstated)
but also of the elegance of the method and its sensitivity to particular implementation choices that may have gone unnoticed and even unreported in the
original work.

Practicalities. There is still a technical problem with reproducible results:
how do we make sure they are still reproducible after programming languages,
toolboxes and online platforms change or cease to exist? For centuries, the unit
of the paper as the narrative artefact has proven to be a format that stands the
test of time and changes in technology. In the work considered here, we refer
to papers from the 1950s, which we where able to recover and which got its
authors' point across perfectly well. We need to ensure this is still the case for
the work produced today. The only proposal we have towards this is that, at the
very least, the software used to produce results is produced using open source
software. This both allows one to dig into every level of the implementation if
this is required to answer a particular question, but also provides some chance of
ensuring software is still available in a future where a particular software vendor
may have ceased to exist.

Going Forward. While we still consider reproducibility a worthwhile goal,
there is a danger it leads to a false sense of security. Reproducibility is not
replicability and it is replicability that constitutes progress in science. And reproducibility is not free: it requires effort on the part of the authors and reviewers
of a manuscript. In the case covered in this paper, which is relatively easy to
make reproducible, the advantages to the authors and the advantages to the
community easily outweigh this effort. We should avoid dogmatism by realizing
this trade-off might be different for other works.

6   Conclusion

We covered our approach to reproducing our paper on optimistic semi-supervised
learning and showed some additional interesting, and nontrivial results by making slight adjustments to the figures and experiments which the reproducible

nature of the paper allows. We argue that the advantages of reproducibility start during the research itself and extend to scientific communication. We need to realize, however, that reproducing results is not the same as replicating experiments, it primarily offers a poor but useful substitute.

Acknowledgement. This work was funded by project P23 of the Dutch public/private research network COMMIT.

References

1. Donoho, D.L., Maleki, A., Rahman, I.U., Shahram, M., Stodden, V.: Reproducible research in computational harmonic analysis. Comput. Sci. Eng. **11**(1), 8–18 (2009)
2. Drummond, C.: Replicability is not reproducibility: nor is it good science. In: Proceedings of the Evaluation Methods for Machine Learning Workshop at the 26th ICML (2009)
3. Goodman, S.N., Fanelli, D., Ioannidis, J.P.A.: What does research reproducibility mean? Sci. Transl. Med. **8**(341), 341ps12 (2016)
4. Healy, M., Westmacott, M.: Missing values in experiments analysed on automatic computers. J. Roy. Stat. Soc. **5**(3), 203–206 (1956)
5. Herndon, T., Ash, M., Pollin, R.: Does high public debt consistently stifle economic growth? A critique of reinhart and rogoff. Cambridge J. Econ. **38**(2), 257–279 (2014)
6. Krijthe, J.H.: RSSL: semi-supervised Learning in R (2016). https://github.com/jkrijthe/RSSL
7. Krijthe, J.H., Loog, M.: Optimistic semi-supervised least squares classification. In: Proceedings of the 23rd International Conference on Pattern Recognition (2016)
8. Open Science Collaboration: Estimating the reproducibility of psychological science. Science **349**(6251) (2015). http://www.sciencemag.org/cgi/doi/10.1126/science.aac4716
9. Patil, P., Peng, R.D., Leek, J.T.: A statistical definition for reproducibility and replicability. Biorxiv (2016). http://dx.doi.org/10.1101/066803
10. R Core Team: A Language and Environment for Statistical Computing. R Foundation for Statistical Computing, Vienna, Austria (2016). https://www.r-project.org/
11. Wickham, H.: R Packages. O'Reilly Media, Sebastopol (2015)
12. Xie, Y.: knitr: a comprehensive tool for reproducible research in R. In: Stodden, V., Leisch, F., Peng, R.D. (eds.) Implementing Reproducible Research. CRC Press, Boca Raton (2014)

OpenMVG: Open Multiple View Geometry

Pierre Moulon[1](✉), Pascal Monasse[2], Romuald Perrot[3], and Renaud Marlet[2]

[1] Zillow Group, Seattle, USA
pierrem@zillowgroup.com
[2] LIGM, UMR 8049, École des Ponts, UPE, Champs-sur-Marne, France
{pascal.monasse,renaud.marlet}@enpc.fr
[3] Université de Poitiers - Laboratoire XLIM, UMR CNRS 7252, Futuroscope,
Poitiers, France
romuald.perrot@univ-poitiers.fr

Abstract. The OpenMVG C++ library provides a vast collection of multiple-view geometry tools and algorithms to spread the usage of computer vision and structure-from-motion techniques. Close to the state-of-the-art in its domain, it provides an easy access to common tools used in 3D reconstruction from images. Following the credo "Keep it simple, keep it maintainable" the library is designed as a modular collection of algorithms, libraries and binaries that can be used independently or as bricks to build larger systems. Thanks to its strict test driven development, the library is packaged with unit-test code samples that make the library easy to learn, modify and use. Since its first release in 2013 under the MPL2 license, OpenMVG has gathered an active community of users and contributors from many fields, spanning hobbyists, students, computer vision experts, and industry members.

Keywords: Reproducible research · Computer vision · Multiple-view geometry · 3D reconstruction · Structure from Motion · C++ · Open source

1 Introduction

Computer vision is used extensively nowadays, even by our pocket devices thanks to our smartphones. Some of the computer visions tasks they perform include stitching images to create a planar mosaic and a spherical panorama, using image content-based search retrieval (bar codes, similar product search), and performing 3D reconstruction from photographs. Moreover, 3D content creation from images is more and more used: *e.g.*, digitizing our world for offline (surveying, cartography, VFX) or for online applications (gaming, AR/VR), digitizing dynamic elements for gaming (Kinect), and autonomous navigation of vehicles are all trendy topics.

Regarding the large scope of applications and the diverse needs of computer vision techniques relating to 3D reconstruction, it is clear that the community can have a major gain if a common framework can be used to communicate, make

© Springer International Publishing AG 2017
B. Kerautret et al. (Eds.): RRPR 2016, LNCS 10214, pp. 60–74, 2017.
DOI: 10.1007/978-3-319-56414-2_5

experiments, and build new prototypes. Often, high level and general purpose tools like Matlab or Intel IPP[1] are used, but they are not the best choice, since beside being costly they do not have all the needed algorithms implemented. They include only a subset of the major Multiple-View-Geometry (MVG) algorithms and are not specialized for Structure from Motion (SfM). Other alternatives like OpenCV can be compelling, but again, only partial implementations exist. Since these alternatives want to cover a large scope of applications they do not focus on multiple view geometry and 3D reconstruction from images in an efficient way.

2   Photogrammetry Software Alternatives

Photogrammetry is the science of making measurements from photographs, especially for recovering the exact positions of surface points. The domain is mature; as witnessed on the internet[2], more than 80 software solutions (commercial, free or open source) are listed. 3D reconstruction from images knows a second breath nowadays, since the emergence of UAV is making a true revolution in land surveying, the acquisition of low altitude images being now a cheap and simple task.

We make here a distinction between multiple view geometry (MVG) and multiple view stereovision (MVS) software. The former is concerned with recovering camera locations and orientations from the data (images and camera intrinsics); it delivers also a sparse set of 3D points, built by triangulation from the feature points observed in the photographs. The latter deals with the dense 3D reconstruction; its output can be a dense point cloud, a faceted surface (mesh), or a set of planes, which can be visualized as a realistic 3D rendering of the scene. It relies on MVG to achieve that.

Commercial Software. The solutions, integrating MVG and MVS in single products, are clustered around the markets they are addressing: UAV land surveying is addressed by the Pix4D products[3] and by DroneDeploy software[4], while the large scale close range photogrammetry market is mostly addressed by the Bentley ContextCapture[5] and CapturingReality[6] software.

Free Software. Visual SfM (VSfM [13]) is a solution that is largely used. The main point that eases its usage is due to the fact the software is delivered with a graphical user interface (GUI) and that it uses multi-threading on CPU and GPU for high efficiency.

---

[1] Intel Integrated Performance Primitives https://software.intel.com/en-us/intel-ipp/.

[2] https://en.wikipedia.org/wiki/Comparison_of_photogrammetry_software#Comparison.

[3] https://pix4d.com/.

[4] https://www.dronedeploy.com/.

[5] https://www.bentley.com/en/products/brands/contextcapture.

[6] https://www.capturingreality.com/.

Open Source Solutions. While some solutions deliver a software program (Bundler [1], ColMap [39], MicMac [40], PMVS [35], CMVS [34]), others deliver both a collection of libraries and softwares (MVE [37], OpenMVG, OpenSfM [41], OpenMVS [42], TheiaSfM [38])[7]. Combining OpenMVG with OpenMVS or MVE provides an end-to-end open-source photogrammetry pipeline.

From a user point of view, commercial and freeware solutions are like black boxes that cannot be tuned or modified for the user needs, while open source solutions provide complete pipelines and interface to multiple view geometry algorithms that can be modified and customized.

Regarding the reproducible research side, open-source alternatives are interesting since they deliver a transparent implementation of some algorithms that anyone can test, use, check, and modify. While it is not easy to implement an algorithm in the right way, some software guidelines rules can help to provide transparency and fairness to the respective algorithm or paper implementation.

It is interesting to note that Bundler (more than 2000 citations) and VSfM (more than 200 citations) projects have helped spreading the usage of Structure from Motion into the computer vision community. Bundler was released as a PhD code dump under an open-source license. It caught a lot of attraction since it offers an easy to use command line software. Unfortunately, it did not receive any major evolution, cleanup or updates since its initial release. Although also initially developed during a PhD preparation [2], OpenMVG was designed from the start with the idea of providing a collection of tools, a test driven high quality library, a regular support and up to date features.

3   OpenMVG Design

This section gives an overview of OpenMVG[8] functionality and design. OpenMVG goals are multiple, providing the computer vision community with: (i) an easy access to accurate implementation of multiple view geometry algorithms; (ii) an understandable source code library; (iii) a set of tools used to build complete applications such as SfM pipelines. OpenMVG includes functionalities for image loading and processing, feature detection and matching, multi-view geometry solvers and provides an easy access to linear algebra and optimization frameworks. It delivers a collection of modular core features arranged in small libraries (Table 1) that can be used independently or as building blocks in an entire pipeline in order to perform 3D reconstruction from images (SfM) or localize images into an existing 3D reconstruction.

OpenMVG is written in standard C++11 and uses the CMake build system bringing portable builds on x86, x86_64 and ARM targets. It relies on the Eigen [10] library to perform high performance linear algebra manipulations, the Ceres-solver [9] to solve large scale non-linear minimization such as bundle adjustment, and OSI-CLP [14] as a linear programming solver. Thanks to well

---

[7] See https://github.com/openMVG/awesome_3DReconstruction_list.
[8] https://github.com/openMVG/openMVG/.

documented and transparent interfaces, OpenMVG can be extended or inter-
faced with other software and even use custom data in a few easy steps.

OpenMVG Goals. OpenMVG goals are twofold:

- an educational side: to provide easy to read and accurate implementation of
  state of the art "classic algorithms" that the community considers as "common
  knowledge".
- a knowledge diffusion side: to spread the usage of the computer vision techniques to the community by delivering easy to use code, libraries, samples,
  and pipelines.

OpenMVG Philosophy. In order to complete its vision in the best way, Open-
MVG follows as guidelines the credo **"Keep it simple, keep it maintainable"**. OpenMVG authors believe that it is more important for the reproducible
research side to have a code that is easy to read and use than a code that is fast
but difficult to edit due to cumbersome optimization.

Beside the readability criteria, algorithm effectiveness must be also demonstrated. This goal is achieved using Test Driven Development. The main motivations for using unit testing is that it helps:

- to assert that algorithm and code are working as expected;
- to perform non regression tests following code updates;
- to provide usage examples in real context;
- people to implement new things.

Thanks to its large collection of unit test, external users can integrate their
new method, test if it works as expected, and use it later in a larger context
with no new code requirements.

OpenMVG License. OpenMVG is licensed under the MPL2 (*Mozilla Public
License 2*). The choice has been made to maximize its usage, even by industry partners, but force somehow contribution back to the existing library files.
This license is similar to the well-known LGPL, but it has a file extent: a modification or a bug fix inside an existing file must be shared under the same license.
However the license allows a larger work to be released under different terms and
so enables the usage of OpenMVG powered code in a commercial application. As
shown by the number of external contributions, the community is comfortable
with this license (31 contributors, 100 Pull Requests, 500 issues handled).

4 OpenMVG Functionalities

OpenMVG provides algorithms that perform tasks like image loading and
processing, feature detection and matching, multi-view geometry solvers and
an easy access to linear algebra and optimization frameworks. The different
modules/libraries are listed in Table 1.

Table 1. Set of OpenMVG modules

Module name	Usage
cameras	Abstract camera model
features	Abstract region description (point position, descriptors)
geometry	3D transformation (similarity, 3D pose)
matching	Abstract nearest neighbour interface
multiview	Multiple view geometry solvers
robust_estimation	Robust estimation framework
stl	C++ STL extensions
tracks	Un-ordered feature tracking
exif	Exif data parsing
geodesy	Geodesy transformation
graph	Graph analysis tools
linearProgramming	Abstract linear programming interface
matching_image_collection	Abstract interface to match image collection
numeric	Linear algebra tools
sfm	reconstruction pipeline (SfM & localization)
system	Benchmarking tools

4.1 Generic Photogrammetry Data Description

The OpenMVG processing pipeline is articulated around the SfM_Data, container. It acts as a spine and allows to have a smooth communication between the tools during the whole process. This data container stores relations between images and their related data: *abstract views* (image metadata, IDs to the camera model and pose), *abstract camera models, camera poses, structure landmarks and image observations IDs*. Thanks to a generic I/O interface this container can be saved in binary (for compactness and fast reading/saving) or in JSON/XML (for easy transfer to third party projects). Thanks to this container an effective pipeline can be built for different purposes, like 3D reconstruction from images.

4.2 Image Processing

OpenMVG provides a simple image handling module. The generic image class acts as a 2D template pixel container based on the Eigen matrix structure. It allows to have all Eigen optimizations available to perform efficient image processing operations. Built on top of this class, the user can have access to:

- Image I/O (png, jpeg, tiff);
- Image sampling (nearest, linear, cubic, spline) and warping;
- Primitive drawing (line, circle, ellipse);

- Color space conversion;
- Image filtering (gradient computation, linear convolution, non-Linear diffusion [22]).

4.3 Feature Extraction and Description

Detecting distinctive, repeatable image points and descriptors is a fundamental aspect of computer vision. This is a key step for object detection, image recognition and multi-view stereovision applications. OpenMVG allows to describe an image by a collection of regions. Since the region concept in OpenMVG is abstract freely chosen attributes can be embedded in the point description (*e.g.*, such as a point location, scale and orientation) and a binary descriptor of arbitrary length. The current implementation allows to detect and describe:

- Blob regions (Scale invariant points): SIFT [11] (based on VlFeat [20] and Sift Anatomy [12]), AKAZE [22].
- Corner regions: FAST keypoints [25].
- Affine invariant regions: Tree-Based Morse Regions (TBMR) [23], Maximally Stable Extremal Regions (MSER) [24].

4.4 Feature and Image Collection Matching

OpenMVG provides an abstract nearest neighbor search framework that could be used with any vector dimension. The concrete implementations are: (i) Brute-Force; (ii) ANN-kD trees [19]; (iii) Cascade hashing [21]. They can be used to compute nearest 3D points or to find corresponding points of a scene by matching features across a series of image pairs.

The image collection matching can be customized by: (i) choosing the appropriate nearest neighbor method; (ii) sending a custom pair list. Thanks to this customization the user can control the accuracy *vs.* time of the retrieval task or easily configure an exhaustive, a sliding window, a loop matching or even a custom matching (*i.e.*, selection of pair by similarity search based on vocabulary tree [33]).

Then the "photo-metric" putatives matches are filtered as geometric coherent matches using an interface to fit robustly multiple-view geometric models.

In order to better understand and visualize the relationship between the images and the computed data (features, matches), OpenMVG exports some SVG data, Fig. 1. Using the SVG format allows to preserve details when zooming thanks to its vectorial nature; it is really useful to see the pairwise matches, since the user can click on a match and see the matching features.

4.5 Multiple View Geometry

On top of matching pairs, some multiple view geometric constraints can be checked. This can, for example, be employed to filter the set of matching feature points between images. OpenMVG provides various models and solvers, illustrated Fig. 2:

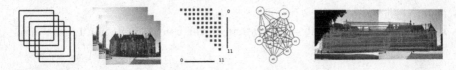

Fig. 1. OpenMVG SVG files exported during the image collection matching task (from Left to Right): image collection, computed features, adjacency matrix, visibility graph [36], pair matches.

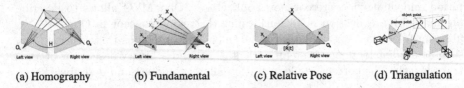

(a) Homography   (b) Fundamental   (c) Relative Pose   (d) Triangulation

Fig. 2. Multiple view geometry model estimation.

- **Relative pose** from pairs of image-image matching points, such as homography (4-point algorithm [6] for transform of planar scene or scene viewed under pure rotation), fundamental matrix (7/8-point algorithm [6], in case of ignorance of camera internal parameters), essential matrix (5-point [8], in case of known camera internal parameters).
- **Absolute pose** from pairs of 3D-2D matching points by different algorithms, P3P (Perspective from 3 Points) [16], DLT (Direct Linear Transform) [6] (6 pairs), ePnP [15] (n pairs).
- **Similarity transformation** from 3D-3D matching space points, model with 7 degrees of freedom.
- **Triangulation** of 3D point from two view projections through linear method [6], non linear, and L_∞ distance [7].
- **Structure and Motion** with L_∞ norm [7].

For each model, OpenMVG provides a simple and direct method to compute the resulting pose. For example, estimating the homography between two corresponding point sets xLeft and xRight can be performed in a few lines of code:

```
// Setup left, right corresponding points and solve for H
openMVG::Mat xLeft(2,4), xRight(2,4);
// Instantiation of homography solver
using H_Solver=openMVG::homography::kernel::FourPointSolver;
// Perform model solving
std::vector<openMVG::Mat3> Hs; //Multi. sol. for some solvers
openMVG::H_Solver::Solve(xLeft, xRight, &Hs);
```

Multiple View Geometry also deals with motion averaging. It consists in computing global motions from relative motions, that is, putting all viewpoints and orientations in a common coordinate system. OpenMVG implements rotation and translation averaging algorithms using various metrics:

- **Rotation averaging** with L_2 norm, non linear L_2 and L_1 [18].
- **Translation averaging** with L_2 norm [17], L_1, and L_∞ [5].

4.6 Robust Estimation

Real world data is corrupted by noise and corresponding point pairs may contain outliers. Therefore it is mandatory to use a *robust* model estimation method. OpenMVG proposes various methods to perform robust estimation. Some are based on user-defined thresholds while the others estimate automatically the best model based on a statistical balance between the tight fitting of the data to the model and the number of inlier data. OpenMVG implements these methods:

- **Threshold priors** through MaxConsensus and RANSAC (RANdom SAmple Consensus) [26]
- **Threshold free** with Least Median of Squares and *a contrario*-RANSAC [27,28].

Fig. 3. An *a contrario*-RANSAC unit test example: Automatic threshold adaptivity for line estimation. On the right: no detected model is hallucinated in pure noise data.

An example of robust line regression to 2D points is illustrated in Fig. 3. The robust estimation framework uses a kernel concept to keep genericity. The kernel is a template object that embeds the model solver and the error metrics (*i.e.*, a measure of the fitting error between the model and the data).

4.7 Camera Models

OpenMVG provides an abstract camera interface that can be used seamlessly along the library with the following concrete implementations: pure pinhole [6], pinhole with 1 to 3 radial distortion coefficients [31], pinhole with 5 distortion coefficients (3 radial + 2 tangential) (aka. Brown-Conrady) [29,30], and fish-eye [32]. The abstract camera model allows easy computation of bearing vectors from 2D points, 3D point projection to camera and application or correction of lens distortion.

4.8   Structure from Motion

Using all previous modules, an incremental [3] and a global [5] 3D-reconstruction pipelines are implemented in OpenMVG. The first is more adapted for images with low cross-coverage, but it suffers from drift effects and low scalability due to its sequential nature. The second is fast for datasets with large image overlap and offers a good scalability. The two pipelines have been demonstrated to be very accurate compared to the other existing open solutions [1,13]. Ready to use Python scripts are delivered with the library in order to ease the usage of this tool-chain.

Bundle Adjustment. All SfM pipelines rely on a generic bundle adjustment module that allows to perform non linear refinement of the SfM scene by minimizing the structure reprojection in the images (residual error). It consists of a non-linear minimization in a high-dimensional space. This module provides a fine grain control of which parameters (intrinsic (principal point, focal, distortion), extrinsic (rotation, translation), structure landmarks) will be held as constants or variable during the minimization. This fine grain control interface is done using bitwise operator that make the code compact and very expressive. An efficient multi-thread concrete implementation is provided through the Ceres-solver interface [9].

4.9   Localization

This module allows to find the camera pose and orientation of a collection of images in an existing reconstruction. Such a problem is common in virtual/augmented reality setup where one wants to localize the user in a known 3D world in order to display virtual elements at the right place, or when one wants to localize video frames in an existing map/asset for VFX issues (virtual camera system).

4.10   Geodesy

This module provides tools to use known 3D priors to fit the 3D reconstruction to a given user Spatial Reference System (SRS), such as ECEF, for geo-localization. Registration can be performed using Ground Control Points (GCP), and GPS data (pose center position prior) for (i) rigid transformation or (ii) non rigid constraints used in the bundle adjustment framework. Pose priors can also be useful in order to limit the number of pairs to match in a very large image collection in case of UAV/mobile mapping survey.

5   Reproducible Research

The project tries to follow the best practice of open source software development. It uses some strict guidelines in order to deliver a high quality code that allows the community to be involved in any work in progress.

5.1   OpenMVG Infrastructure

In order to build a project for a community it is necessary to maximize its accessibility and provide tools for feedback about the status of the library. To do so OpenMVG eco-system relies on free tools that allow to perform online version control system, continuous integration and documentation. Here is the list of the different tools used and their purpose:

- **Project management:** https://github.com/openMVG/openMVG

 - Github (version control system) for easy access and collaboration, issue tracking, milestones, fork, pull request, code review.

- **Documentation:**

 - reStructuredText for Github integration (visible as a formatted document and not as code), online doc generation & hosting, http://openmvg.readthedocs. io/en/latest/.

- **Continuous integration:**

 - Travis-CI for Unix (Linux, OsX).
 - AppVeyor for Windows (Visual Studio).
 - Docker for container based deployment.

5.2   Development Principles

Updates rely on the simple rule that they must not break any existing code. Releases are pushed in the *master* branch with tagging; Each time a new release is planned, a new branch *develop* is started. Each *new feature development (X)* happens in a new branch. (i) A Github issue is created with a comprehensive step by step explanation that is required for completion of the feature; (ii) a branch *develop_X* is created from *develop*; (iii) each commit is linked to the Github issue; (iv) once validated, *develop_X* is merged to *develop*.

Github Pull Request (external contribution) are handled by a code review from the community (code style, check the code is easy to use, readable and understandable with comprehensive code comments and paper references), suggestion of an enhanced API or usage of existing functionalities, suggestion of unit test or samples if missing, suggestion to complete the documentation, continuous integration test and non regression, merge once tested and validated by the community to *develop* branch.

Creation of a new release follows these steps: (i) modify *develop* branch API internal version number; (ii) merge from *develop* to *master*; (iii) create a release tag; (iv) edit the Github release tag with a complete CHANGELOG; (v) advertise the new version and features to the community.

Thanks to this set of rules the quality of any modified line of code OpenMVG can be followed by the community and open to comments, tests and critics. People can join effort to develop a feature by using the fork mechanism and contribute actively.

5.3   Future Development

The OpenMVG developers hope to continue improving its database of algorithms to follow the state of the art, extend the scope of its users, provide best in class "easy to read and use" code, hoping to seduce some real time oriented users to add some SLAM algorithms.

Another aim could be to build an open format inspired by the modular SfM_Data OpenMVG scene description for 3D photogrammetry purpose, to seamlessly connect projects between existing and upcoming products.

Beside this project, some OpenMVG authors started a new project called "Awesome 3DReconstruction list" that collects the papers (tutorials, conference papers) and open-source resources related to 3D reconstruction from images (more than 120 references are collected) (see Footnote 7).

6   Community Adoption

One difference to the other existing framework is that OpenMVG is trying to initiate a real exchange with its community. Some Github statistics give an idea of the community size:

Project name	Year of creation	Contributors	Watchers	Stars	Fork
bundler_sfm	2008	8	108	530	245
COLMAP	2016	5	14	82	34
MVE	2012	13	61	188	131
OpenMVG	2013	**31**	**156**	**802**	**392**
THEIASfM	2015	15	43	165	80

Despite it is hard to compare the statistics due to the differing year of creation of each project, note that OpenMVG has an active community (OpenMVG is neither the oldest nor the most recent project). Moreover, OpenMVG is used by professionals and laboratories for real application, for example:

Arc-Team[9] (a professional company operating in different branches of archaeology, from fieldwork to research, and specialized in the use and development of open source software and hardware for cultural heritage projects) uses Open-MVG softwares for 3D archaeological and architectural documentations in different logistical conditions: ordinary excavations, underwater contexts, remote sensing, underground environments, glacial archaeological researches and abroad missions, see Fig. 4.

Ebrafol[10] provides an independent alternative to judicial expertise and technical assistance in forensic dentistry and forensic anthropology). It uses OpenMVG

---

[9] http://www.arc-team.com/.
[10] Brazilian Team of Forensic Anthropology and Legal Dentistry http://ebrafol.org/.

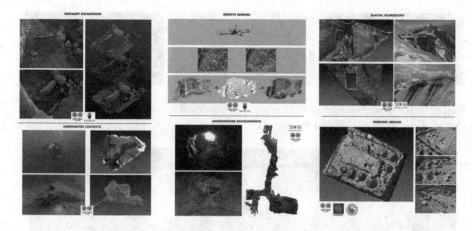

Fig. 4. Arc-Team reconstructions for archaeology.

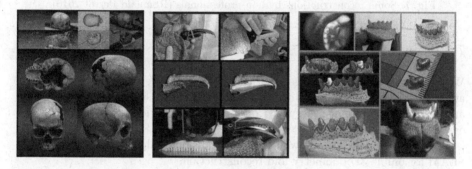

Fig. 5. EBRAFOL sample usage of OpenMVG reconstruction for skull reconstruction and accurate animal prothesis reconstruction and printing.

and its connection to multiple view stereo tools to build 3D models of skull for 3D face reconstruction and to help injured animals by building accurate prostheses, see Fig. 5.

Digital Humanities Laboratory DHLAB[11] (an EPFL laboratory team that conducts research in historical and geographical information systems. The team is creating a web based service, through the development of a 3D historic GIS server, allowing to view, explore and compare SfM, LIDAR and historical hand-made models). It uses OpenMVG to develop a reliable and powerful SfM pipeline in order to compute sparse and dense reconstructions of cities (taking advantage of existing aerial photography database and specific ground-based acquisitions), see Fig. 6.

The community also uses OpenMVG for non-professional work (Fig. 7).

---

[11] http://dhlab.epfl.ch/.

Fig. 6. DHLAB reconstructions of Paris (1945 historical aerial images, IGN) and Venice (aerial, UAV + ground-based images, DHLAB).

Fig. 7. Some reconstructions by non-professionals (Romuald Perrot 2016).

7   Conclusion

We presented OpenMVG, a generic library for multiple view geometry aimed at providing the community with a reference tool. Its insistence on code quality and readability does not prevent it from aiming at genericity without sacrificing ease of use and simplicity.

Interesting enhancements would be the addition of algorithms specialized in SLAM for online 3D odometry and reconstruction.

More generally, OpenMVG developers are willing to attract users that could eventually participate in its development. For that, they offered tutorials at the OpenWorld Forum in Paris in 2014, at the CVPR Boston conference in 2015 and at the SFPT Paris meeting in 2016.

Thanks to its strong connection to a state of the art solution for computing detailed models, the OpenMVS [42] open source project, OpenMVG and Open-MVS offer together a strong end-to-end collection of open source algorithms to the community to compute sparse and dense detailed models (see some dense reconstructions from Fig. 7).

Acknowledgements. The authors thank the Imagine project of École des Ponts ParisTech, MikrosImage, Foxel, Auxilium entity partners and all the OpenMVG community for its support and contributions.

References

1. Snavely, N., Seitz, S.M., Szeliski, R.: Photo tourism: exploring photo collections in 3D. ACM Trans. Graph. (TOG) **25**(3), 835–846 (2006)
2. Moulon, P.: Robust and accurate calibration of camera networks. Ph.D., Université Paris-Est (2014)

3. Moulon, P., Monasse, P., Marlet, R.: Adaptive structure from motion with *a contrario* model estimation. In: Lee, K.M., Matsushita, Y., Rehg, J.M., Hu, Z. (eds.) ACCV 2012. LNCS, vol. 7727, pp. 257–270. Springer, Heidelberg (2013). doi:10.1007/978-3-642-37447-0_20

4. Moulon, P., Monasse, P.: Unordered feature tracking made fast and easy. In: CVMP (2012)

5. Moulon, P., Monasse, P., Marlet, R.: Global fusion of relative motions for robust, accurate and scalable structure from motion. In: ICCV (2013)

6. Hartley, R.I., Zisserman, A.: Multiple View Geometry in Computer Vision, 2nd edn. Cambridge University Press, Cambridge (2004). ISBN: 0521540518

7. Kahl, F., Hartley, R.I.: Multiple-view geometry under the L_∞-norm. IEEE Trans. PAMI **30**, 1603–1617 (2008)

8. Nistér, D.: An efficient solution to the five-point relative pose problem. In: CVPR (2003)

9. Agarwal, S., Mierle, K., et al.: Ceres Solver. http://ceres-solver.org

10. Guennebaud, G., Jacob, B., et al.: Eigen v3 (2010). http://eigen.tuxfamily.org

11. Lowe, D.G.: Distinctive image features from scale-invariant keypoints. IJCV **60**(2), 91–110 (2004)

12. Otero, I.R., Delbracio, M.: Anatomy of the SIFT method. Image Process. On Line (2014). https://doi.org/10.5201/ipol.2014.82

13. Wu, C.: Towards linear-time incremental structure from motion. In: 3DV (2013)

14. Forrest, J., Hall, J. et al.: CLP (coin-or linear programming). https://projects.coin-or.org/Clp

15. Lepetit, V., Moreno-Noguer, F., Fua, P.: EPnP: an accurate o(n) solution to the PnP problem. IJCV **81**, 155 (2009). https://link.springer.com/article/10.1007/s11263-008-0152-6

16. Kneip, L., Furgale, P.: OpenGV: a unified and generalized approach to real-time calibrated geometric vision. In: ICRA (2014)

17. Wilson, K., Snavely, N.: Robust global translations with 1DSfM. In: Fleet, D., Pajdla, T., Schiele, B., Tuytelaars, T. (eds.) ECCV 2014. LNCS, vol. 8691, pp. 61–75. Springer, Cham (2014). doi:10.1007/978-3-319-10578-9_5

18. Chatterjee, A., Govindu, V.M.: Efficient and robust large-scale rotation averaging. In: ICCV (2013)

19. Muja, M., Lowe, D.G.: Fast approximate nearest neighbors with automatic algorithm configuration. In: VISAPP (2009)

20. Vedaldi, A., Fulkerson, B.: VLFeat: an open and portable library of computer vision algorithms. In: Proceedings of the ACM International Conference on Multimedia (2010)

21. Cheng, J., Leng, C., Wu, J., Cui, H., Lu, H.: Fast and accurate image matching with cascade hashing for 3D reconstruction. In: CVPR (2014)

22. Alcantarilla, P.F., Nuevo, J., Bartoli, A.: Fast explicit diffusion for accelerated features in nonlinear scale spaces. BMVC **34**(7), 1281–1298 (2013)

23. Xu, Y., Monasse, P., Géraud, T., Najman, L.: Tree-based morse regions: a topological approach to local feature detection. IEEE Trans. Image Process. **23**(12), 5612–5625 (2014)

24. Nistér, D., Stewénius, H.: Linear time maximally stable extremal regions. In: Forsyth, D., Torr, P., Zisserman, A. (eds.) ECCV 2008. LNCS, vol. 5303, pp. 183–196. Springer, Heidelberg (2008). doi:10.1007/978-3-540-88688-4_14

25. Rosten, E., Drummond, T.: Machine learning for high-speed corner detection. In: Leonardis, A., Bischof, H., Pinz, A. (eds.) ECCV 2006. LNCS, vol. 3951, pp. 430–443. Springer, Heidelberg (2006). doi:10.1007/11744023_34

26. Fischler, M.A., Bolles, R.C., Consensus, R.S.: A paradigm for model fitting with applications to image analysis and automated cartography. ACM (1981)

27. Moisan, L., Moulon, P., Monasse, P.: Automatic homographic registration of a pair of images, with a contrario elimination of outliers. Image Process. On Line (2012). http://dx.doi.org/10.5201/ipol.2012.mmm-oh

28. Moisan, L., Moulon, P., Monasse, P.: Fundamental matrix of a stereo pair, with a contrario elimination of outliers. Image Process. On Line (2016). http://dx.doi.org/10.5201/ipol.2016.147

29. Brown, D.C.: Decentering distortion of lenses. Photogramm. Eng. **32**, 444–462 (1966)

30. Conrady, A.E.: Decentred lens-systems. Mon. Not. R. Astron. Soc. **79**, 384–390 (1919)

31. de Villiers, J.-P., Leuschner, F. W., Geldenhuys, R.: Centi-pixel accurate real-time inverse distortion correction. In: International Symposium on Optomechatronic Technologies (2008)

32. Sturm, P., Ramalingam, S., Tardif, J.-P., Gasparini, S., Barreto, J.: Camera models and fundamental concepts used in geometric computer vision. Found. Trends Comput. Graph. Vis. **6**(1–2), 1–183 (2011)

33. Nistér, D., Stewenius, H.: Scalable recognition with a vocabulary tree. In: CVPR (2006)

34. Furukawa, Y., Curless, B., Seitz, S., Szeliski, R.: Towards internet-scale multi-view stereo. In: CVPR (2010)

35. Furukawa, Y., Ponce, J.: Accurate, dense, and robust multi-view stereopsis. In: PAMI (2010)

36. North, S.C.: Drawing graphs with NEATO. NEATO Users Manual (2004)

37. Fuhrmann, S., Langguth, F., Goesele, M.: MVE - a multi-view reconstruction environment. In: Proceedings of the Eurographics Workshop on Graphics and Cultural Heritage (2014)

38. Sweeney, C., Hollerer, T., Turk, M.: Theia: a fast and scalable structure-from-motion library. In: Proceedings of the 23rd ACM International Conference on Multimedia (2015)

39. Schönberger, J.L., Frahm, J.-M.: Structure-from-motion revisited. In: CVPR (2016)

40. Deseilligny, M.P., Clery, I.: APERO, an open source bundle adjustment software for automatic calibration and orientation of set of images. In: ISPRS (2011)

41. Mapillary: OpenSfM (2013). https://github.com/mapillary/OpenSfM

42. Cernea, D.: OpenMVS: open multiple view stereovision (2015). https://github.com/cdcseacave/openMVS/

A Novel Definition of Robustness for Image Processing Algorithms

Antoine Vacavant[✉]

Institut Pascal, Université Clermont Auvergne,
UMR 6602 UCA/SIGMA/CNRS, 63171 Aubière, France
antoine.vacavant@uca.fr
http://isit.u-clermont1.fr/~anvacava/index.html

Abstract. As image gains much wider importance in our society, image processing has found various applications since the 60's: biomedical imagery, security and many more. A highly common issue in those processes is the presence of an uncontrolled and destructive perturbation generally referred to "noise". The ability of an algorithm to resist to this noise has been referred to as "robustness"; but this notion has never been clearly defined for image processing techniques. A wide bibliographic study showed that this term "robustness" is largely mixed up with others as efficiency, quality, *etc.*, leading to a disturbing confusion. In this article, we propose a completely new framework to define the robustness of image processing algorithms, by considering multiple scales of additive noise. We show the relevance of our proposition by evaluating and by comparing the robustness of recent and more classic algorithms designed to two tasks: still image denoising and background subtraction in videos.

1 Introduction

As image gains much wider importance in our society, image processing has found various applications since the 60's [1]: visual inspection systems, remote satellite image interpretation, biomedical imagery, surveillance and security, astronomy, *etc.* As well established in many fields of research [31,32], image processing is carried out thanks to a series of algorithms applied on the input image after acquisition, sampling and quantization. It consists of two major steps: improvement by pre-processing treatments, as denoising filtering for example, and segmentation. More complex operations are driven afterwards on the image, such as object recognition, people identification, *etc.*, addressed as computer vision techniques.

A highly common issue in those processes, whatever the field, is the presence of an uncontrolled and destructive perturbation on the image, coming from diverse sources (medical images perturbed by artefacts coming from the acquisition system, videos jittered by the camera movement due to the wind, *etc.*), which is generally referred to *noise.*

The ability of an algorithm to resist to this noise (*i.e.* that the algorithm's output has been experimentally or theoretically approved to be independent

B. Kerautret et al. (Eds.): RRPR 2016, LNCS 10214, pp. 75–87, 2017.
DOI: 10.1007/978-3-319-56414-2_6

to this noise) has been referred as *robustness*. This robustness is a key issue in image processing, since it ensures that the developed algorithm satisfies the final user of the application. A wide bibliographic study around "robustness" in image processing demonstrated that it is largely mixed up with other terms as efficiency, quality, performance, persistence, *etc.*, leading to a highly disturbing confusion [3,14,23]. This lack of model for the robustness thus blocks its formal integration in algorithms designed for image processing tasks as filtering, segmentation, or even compression.

The formal definition of a robust algorithm in the field of computer vision comes initially from the researches and formulations of Peter Meer [26,27]. In this work, robust techniques, as RANSAC [13] or the Hough transform [17], are based on robust statistics tools [33]. Noise is considered as an additive perturbation of the input data, under a known or estimated scale. This can be summarized as follows: *"Robustness in computer vision cannot be achieved without having access to a reasonably correct value of the scale [of the noise]".* This work has a large impact upon computer vision tasks, which are machine learning algorithms [7] using robust statistical tools [6,8,29] and devoted to character recognition, object classification, people tracking, *etc.* When the targeted noise cannot be represented theoretically or do not fit into a statistical model, the challenge is to gather a sufficient amount of data to test, to evaluate the computer vision algorithms, and to increase their robustness: this data gathering is a key of *Big Data* [35].

Unfortunately, in the particular field of image processing, this definition of robustness, and also its evaluation, has not been further modelled in such a way. In this article, concurrently with these works in machine learning, we propose to solve the problem of robustness assessment in image processing tasks, thanks to a novel definition introduced in Sect. 2, based on multiple scales of noises. To the best of our knowledge, no formal definition of the robustness has been designed in the literature to evaluate image processing algorithms with such a formulation. We then propose to employ this measure, called α-robustness, to evaluate the robustness of algorithms devoted to two tasks in Sect. 3.1: image denoising filtering and background subtraction in videos. As a future prospect, we hope that this generic measure will be employed to evaluate the robustness of novel contributions in image processing and that related research communities will seize this scientific bottleneck.

2   A Novel Definition of Robustness

We first consider that an algorithm designed in image processing may be perturbed, because of an input data altered with an additive noise. With similar notations as the work of Peter Meer [26], we have:

$$\widehat{y_i} = y_i^0 + \delta y_i, \; y_i \in \mathbb{R}^q, \; i = 1, \ldots, n, \tag{1}$$

which will be shortened by $\widehat{\mathbf{Y}} = \mathbf{Y}^0 + \delta\mathbf{Y}$ when the context allows it, *i.e.* when the subscripts are not necessary. In this equation, the measurement $\widehat{\mathbf{Y}}$ is obtained from a true (and generally unknown) value $\mathbf{Y^0}$, corrupted by the noise $\delta\mathbf{Y}$. In robust statistics, the objective of an algorithm is to compute and minimize an error between (i) the estimated parameters $\widehat{\theta}$ of the measurements $\widehat{\mathbf{Y}}$, *e.g.* a set of lines constructed with a Hough transform through a cloud of noisy points, (ii) the true parameters of the model, θ, obtained from $\mathbf{Y^0}$, *e.g.* the true line that we should obtain (the underlying line represented by the points). In this case, we may assume that the noise is independent and identically distributed (iid):

$$\delta y_i \simeq GI(0, \sigma^2 C_y), \tag{2}$$

where $\sigma^2 C_y$ is the covariance of the errors at the known scale σ. This formulation leads to the definition of robustness by Peter Meer as *"An estimator is considered robust only when the estimation error is guaranteed to be less than what can be tolerated in the application"*.

As a summary, a statistical algorithm may be considered as robust if the error generated by the constructed parameters θ is less than a given threshold, depending on the final application and on the knowledge of the noise (scale σ in Eq. 2). This formulation represents the current challenges of designing robust computer vision algorithms in a large amount of data. We propose now to study further these notions of robustness and noise for the development of robust image processing.

In this article, we assume that the robustness must be assessed in a multi-scale approach, in order to appreciate the limitations of an algorithm, and what would even make it fail. Let A be an algorithm designed for a given image processing application, leading to a set of values $\mathbf{X} = \{x_i\}_{i=1,n}$ (generally the output image obtained by A). Let N be an additive noise (*i.e.* respecting Eq. 2) specific to the considered application, and $\{\sigma_k\}_{k=1,m}$ a set of scales of N. Let $Q(\mathbf{X_k}, \mathbf{Y_k^0})$ be a measure of the quality of A for the scale k of N (that is, σ_k),

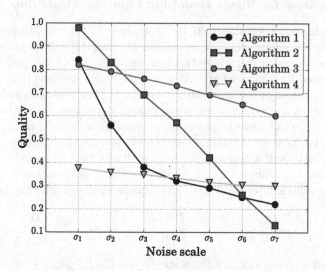

Fig. 1. Graphical illustration of our definition of robustness.

for example, the F-measure, combining both positive true and false detections versus negative ones in binary decisions (as in the case of binary segmentation).

The algorithm A may be considered as α-*robust* if the difference d_Y between the result $\mathbf{X}$ and the ground truth $\mathbf{Y^0}$ is bounded, w.r.t. the increase of noise scale d_X, by the Lipschitz continuity [5] of Q:

$$d_Y\left(Q(\mathbf{X_k}, \mathbf{Y_k^0}), Q(\mathbf{X_{k+1}}, \mathbf{Y_{k+1}^0})\right) \leq \alpha d_X(\sigma_{k+1} - \sigma_k),\ 1 \leq k < m. \tag{3}$$

Figure 1 is a synthetic illustration of the use of this definition, where we have indicated the quality score (*e.g.* the quality of an image segmentation algorithm by calculating a Dice coefficient) of four fictional algorithms for multiple scales of a given noise. In this figure, we can notice that Algorithm 2 has the best quality, at scale σ_1. We advocate that using this single scale is not sufficient to assess the robustness of this algorithm, *i.e.* to guarantee the error tolerated by the application for this algorithm, as P. Meer claimed. After increasing the impact of noise, Algorithm 4 has the best robustness (α-robust with $\alpha = 0.02$), and Algorithm 2 the worst ($\alpha = 0.30$). Finally, Algorithm 1's behaviour is not linear, implying a high α value, and Algorithm 3 is the best algorithm of this synthetic test, providing a very good robustness ($\alpha = 0.05$) and high performance in term of quality. Thanks to this synthetic study, we show the gap between classic quality assessment, as done currently in research in image processing when considering a single scale of noise, and this novel and original notion of robustness. We propose in the next section to compare image denoising and video background subtraction algorithms thanks to this framework.

3   Experimental Study

3.1   Application for Image Denoising Filtering Algorithms

Image denoising has been substantially dealt since 70's [21,22], from linear and simple non-linear algorithms such as median filtering [18] to more sophisticated approaches as block-matching based ones for example [25]. In the literature, algorithms are generally compared with some sample images to show their respective efficiency, without any peculiar strategy to evaluate their robustness. In this article, we will focus our attention on some classic algorithms, and others related to shock filters, which modify pixels by performing a dilation near local maxima and erosion near local minima [30]. The Laplacian of the image guides the choice of operations: if it is negative (resp. positive), then the pixel is judged to be located near a maximum (resp. minimum). Using an iterative discretization of a PDE, the shock filter produces local segmentations in inflection zones:

$$\begin{cases} \Delta f^{t-1}(p_i, q_j) < 0 \Rightarrow f^t(p_i, q_j) = f^{t-1}(p_i, q_j) \oplus D\ ; \\ \Delta f^{t-1}(p_i, q_j) > 0 \Rightarrow f^t(p_i, q_j) = f^{t-1}(p_i, q_j) \ominus D, \end{cases} \tag{4}$$

for each pixel $f^t(p_i, q_j)$ of a 2-D image $\{f^t(p_i, q_j)\}_{i=1,M;j=1,N}$ at iteration t, where $\Delta f^t(p_i, q_j)$ is the Laplacian computed at pixel (p_i, q_j), D is a disk-shaped structuring element of radius 1, and $\oplus$ and $\ominus$ are the symbols of classic dilation and erosion operators. Please also note that $f^0(p_i, q_j) = f(p_i, q_j)$, the first input image of the algorithm.

In [37], we have proposed to enhance this filter by using local smoothed histograms, which have the property to produce *smoothed dilations* and *smoothed erosions*, hence replacing the classic operators depicted in Eq. 4. The smoothed local histogram of the neighborhood $V_{ij} = \mathcal{V}((p_i, q_j))$ of a pixel $f(p_i, q_j)$ is modeled as:

$$h_{f(p_i, q_j)}(s_n) = \sum_{(p_k, q_l) \in V_{ij}} K(f(p_i, q_j) - s_k) W(\| (p_k, q_l) - (p_i, q_j) \|_2), \quad (5)$$

where $k \in \{1, n_b\}$, K, W are generally Gaussian kernels and s_n is the n-th bin of the histogram. We have also shown that this algorithm is capable of enhancing segmentation further processes in [38].

Fig. 2. Set of images used in our test.

We propose to show the application of our definition in comparing the robustness of our approach with several other related image denoising filtering algorithms of the literature. As depicted in Fig. 2, our material is a set of 13 classic images well-known in the field of image processing ($\widehat{\mathbf{Y}}$ in Eq. 1) perturbated by additive white Gaussian noises with increasing standard deviations, *i.e.* the scales $\{\sigma_k\}_{k=1,5} = \{5, 10, 15, 20, 25\}$. We compare our algorithm with the classic median filter [18]; the bilateral filter [36]; the original shock filter [30]; its complex extension proposed by [15]; the enhanced version from [4]; the coherence filter introduced by [40] and the smoothed median filter proposed by [21]. To do so, we employ the SSIM (Structural Similarity) quality measure [39], ranging between 0 and 1, which assesses the similarity between any output image and the original image without any noise (ground truth, $\mathbf{Y}^0$ in Eq. 1). Our study of robustness is illustrated in Fig. 3-a, wherein a plot represents the SSIM values obtained for all algorithms (averaged over all images), at each noise scale. The Gaussian noise alteration is also plotted as a reference with a black dotted line.

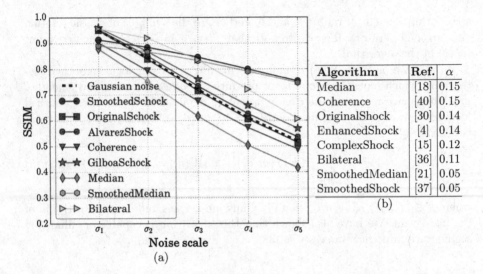

(a)

Algorithm	Ref.	α
Median	[18]	0.15
Coherence	[40]	0.15
OriginalShock	[30]	0.14
EnhancedShock	[4]	0.14
ComplexShock	[15]	0.12
Bilateral	[36]	0.11
SmoothedMedian	[21]	0.05
SmoothedShock	[37]	0.05

(b)

Fig. 3. (a) Graphical evaluation of robustness for image denoising filtering algorithms. (b) Evaluation of α-robustness for each algorithm.

For a clear comparison of numerical values obtained, evaluation of α-robustness is summarized in Fig. 3-b.

We can first observe that the original shock filtering method, the classic median filter and the coherence filter are not able to filter accurately the noisy images, since it even worsen the alteration originally impacted by the noise. At the first scale σ_1, several algorithms compete to achieve the first rank with high values of SSIM, but a further analysis of the α-robustness shows that our contribution, with smoothed median filtering are the most robust methods, being α-robust with $\alpha = 0.05$, while most of other algorithms achieve a higher value ($\alpha > 0.10$). We also show in Fig. 4 a visual comparison of the results obtained by means of several robust algorithms. This comparison confirms visually that our method enhances efficiently the structures in the image, as measured by the SSIM.

3.2 Application for Background Subtraction in Urban Videos

Background subtraction is a crucial step in many computer vision systems, and consists of detecting moving objects within videos by subtracting the background from the filmed scene, without any *a priori* knowledge about the foreground [10]. This technique has been widely investigated since the 90's, mainly for video-surveillance applications, but also for many others as compression, medecine, *etc.*

In [34], we have proposed a comprehensive review of background subtraction techniques, and compared classic and modern algorithms thanks to real and synthetic urban videos. The comparison of these approaches by averaging quality

Fig. 4. Outputs of some robust algorithms from this test for the *Lena* image.

measures upon a given data-set has shown some limitations, and it is difficult to separate them, when F-measure is always greater than 0.9 for the best methods in particular. To explore robustness evaluation in this article, we have kept the best algorithms of this survey (whose names afterwards are similar to those chosen in [34]): a simple adaptive background learning method explained in [34]; the fuzzy algorithm based on Choquet integral [12]; the single Gaussian distribution background model in [41]; the representation with mixture of Gaussian distributions from [19]; the type-2 fuzzy based approach [9]; the multi-layer algorithm employing color and texture [42]; the pixel based adaptive segmenter [16]; eigen values based background model introduced by [28] and a method that employs self-organizing maps [24].

A still open challenge of background subtraction is to take into account lighting variations in videos. Therefore, to compare those methods, we have generated synthetic videos with variable lighting perturbations by means of a real-time 3-D urban simulator produced by the 4D-Virtualiz company[1]. From a single scenario of 4500 frames long (*i.e.* 3 min) we have generated 4 videos, wherein an ambient light noise has been modeled in a multi-scale way, by perturbating lighting during the sequence. We have calculated this data-set by adapting ambient illumination in the rendering equation [20]. The lighting function is first modeled in a cloudy scene as a constant power during the whole sequence (first scale σ_1), which is then perturbed by sunny periods (in the following, such a period is denoted by S), with a higher lighting value. The probability that such periods

---

[1] http://www.4d-virtualiz.com/en/.

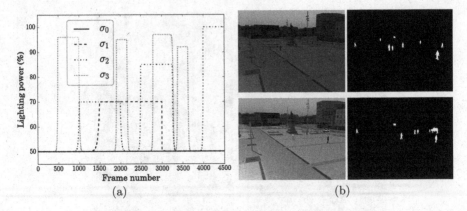

(a)   (b)

Fig. 5. (a) Lighting power during time for the 4 scales of noise we have generated upon a single scenario. (b) Two images with different lighting values, and associated ground truths.

occur during the sequence $P(S)$ increases, leading to 3 more scales of lighting noise. We also impose that the duration of S decreases and its associated lighting value increases while $P(S)$ increases, which models S as a function converging to a Dirac impulse and simulates fast lighting variations. Figure 5-a is a plot of the lighting value during the time of the 4 videos generated by the set of scales $\{\sigma_k\}_{k=1,4}$, with sample images obtained by the 3-D simulator. Moving objects in those scenes are automatically calculated, providing the ground truth for our tests as binary images (see Fig. 5-b). To evaluate the similarity between algorithms' outputs ($\mathbf{X_k}$ in our formalism) and ground truth ($\mathbf{Y_k^0}$) frames, we opt for a calculation of SSIM adapted to binary segmentation, as we proposed in [34].

The graphical evaluation of robustness for all tested algorithms is given in Fig. 6-a, wherein the plot represents the SSIM values obtained for all algorithms (averaged over all video frames), at each noise scale (lighting noise impact is plotted as a reference with a black dotted line). Values of α-robustness are presented in Fig. 6-b.

This experiment permits to separate the tested algorithms into two sets. A first one is composed of non-robust methods having high α values ($\alpha > 0.15$): PBAS, LBAdaptiveSOM and DPEigenBGS. The test failed for the two last methods of this group, considering the plot of Fig. 6-a. The other set contains the rest of the algorithms, the most α-robust method is MoGV1BGS with a α value of 0.01. We present in Fig. 7 the outputs obtained by means of the most robust algorithms of our test. The colors correspond to: black and yellow for true and false negative (background) detections, white and red for true and false positive (foreground) detections. Even if these are the best methods of our study, a lot of pixels are still wrongly classified (yellow and red pixels), which shows the complexity to take into account lighting variations in video background subtraction. Moreover, the calculations of those elements lead to

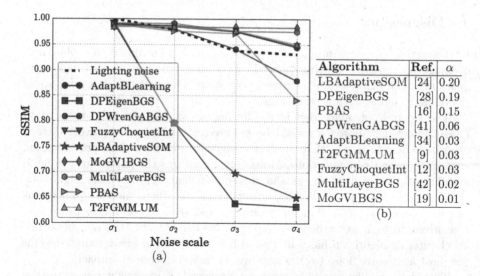

Algorithm	Ref.	α
LBAdaptiveSOM	[24]	0.20
DPEigenBGS	[28]	0.19
PBAS	[16]	0.15
DPWrenGABGS	[41]	0.06
AdaptBLearning	[34]	0.03
T2FGMM_UM	[9]	0.03
FuzzyChoquetInt	[12]	0.03
MultiLayerBGS	[42]	0.02
MoGV1BGS	[19]	0.01

(b)

(a)

Fig. 6. (a) Graphical evaluation of robustness for background subtraction algorithms. (b) Evaluation of α-robustness for each algorithm.

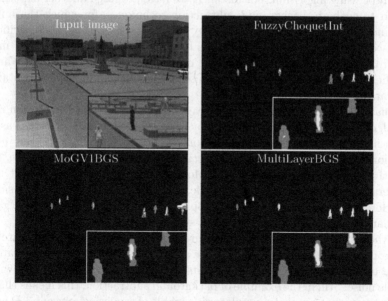

Fig. 7. Outputs of some robust background subtraction algorithms (see text for explanations). (Color figure online)

the same evaluation with F-measuring each algorithm. Most of the observations we have enumerated previously are confirmed with F-measure instead of SSIM measure (MoGV1BGS evaluated as the most α-robust methods, and PBAS, LBAdaptiveSOM and DPEigenBGS as the least ones).

4 Discussion

In this article, we have proposed a novel approach to evaluate the robustness of image processing algorithms, based on multiple scales of additive noises, to guarantee their error towards a given application. This first research work opens the doors to numerous investigations.

The example of image denoising filtering shows that the robustness of an image processing approach should be assessed at several noise powers instead of a single one, to ensure that the tested algorithm resists to this perturbation, even in the worst configurations. Moreover, it confirms the importance to build a sufficiently large data-set, as the current challenge of Big Data highlights. We have to propose more complex noises related to other concrete applications (medical image segmentation for example), and to confront image processing algorithms to high perturbances. In Fig. 3, we can remark that our smoothed shock filtering algorithm has still a good behaviour (SSIM greater than 0.8) for the most aggressive noise (σ_5), which invites us to increase its impact.

This first specific example we have proposed is obviously not a restriction for our definition of robustness, which can be used for any other kind of image processing algorithm. For instance, we have proposed another experiment devoted to evaluate background subtraction techniques, for which the impact of an increasing noise is not studied so far and robustness is not specifically addressed. Our α-robustness measure is a relevant way to compare new methods w.r.t. state-of-the-art, by employing quality measures as the SSIM. Various other fields can benefit from the α-robustness as medical image segmentation, large satellite image compression, etc.

Equations 1 and 2 refer to an additive Gaussian noise alteration upon data. Several complex noises can be assimilated to Gaussian distributions, as the Rician noise in medical MRI acquisition system for example [2]. But as an extension, various other noise impacts can be addressed, as Poisson noise, multiplicative Gaussian noise and so on. Moreover, it should be noted that noise is generally modeled at the pixel's scale, without any more global consideration. Here, our framework has been applied with the representation of global illumination changes in videos, which is still an open scientific challenge.

Gathering data to evaluate our measure of robustness implies that we are able to reproduce or to estimate a given noise at several scales. Hence, two strategies can be conducted. The first one consists of generating synthetic data with a variable noise. Still in the example of background subtraction, this means that we should ensure that a realistic simulator is capable of rendering relevant 3-D urban scenarios, incorporating complex noises. The second option is to collect data, and to estimate the target noise inside (δy_i in Eq. 1). In our illustrative example of medical image analysis, Rician noise can be estimated thanks to recent works as [11], which enables sorting MRI volumes by increasing noise order.

Finally, our definition of robustness can be compared with other formulations based on multiple instances of noises. Instead of using Lipschitz continuity (imposing local linearity under a given slope, α), we could consider an algorithm as robust by considering that the quality function Q is a linear function over the domain of noise σ. To compare those definitions, a supervised evaluation should be conducted, to decide which formalism induces the best robustness, regarding a given application (for example, counting people in urban scenes thanks to background subtracted videos).

Acknowledgement. The author would like to thank the 4D-Virtualiz company for providing realistic synthetic urban videos for this research work.

References

1. Acharya, T., Ray, A.: Image Processing - Principles and Applications. Wiley, New Jersey (2006)
2. Aja-Fernandez, S., Tristan-Vega, A.: A review on statistical noise models for magnetic resonance imaging. Technical report TECH-LPI2013-01, University of Valladolid (2013)
3. Al-Assaf, A., Vaudrey, T., Klette, R., Woo, Y.: An approach for evaluating robustness of edge operators using real-world driving scenes. In: International Conference on Image and Vision Computing, pp. 1–6 (2008)
4. Alvarez, L., Mazorra, L.: Signal and image restoration using shock filters and anisotropic diffusion. SIAM J. Numer. Anal. **31**(2), 590–605 (1994)
5. Ambrosio, L., Tilli, P.: Topics on Analysis in Metric Spaces. Oxford University Press, Oxford (2004)
6. Basiri, S., Ollila, E., Koivunen, V.: Robust, scalable and fast bootstrap method for analyzing large scale data. IEEE Trans. Signal Process. **64**, 1007–1017 (2015)
7. Bishop, C.: Pattern Recognition and Machine Learning. Springer, New York (2006)
8. Bouveyron, C., Girard, S.: Robust supervised classification with mixture models: learning from data with uncertain labels. Pattern Recogn. **42**(11), 2649–2658 (2009)
9. Bouwmans, T., El Baf, F.: Modeling of dynamic backgrounds by type-2 fuzzy Gaussian mixture models. MASAUM J. Basic Appl. Sci. **1**(2), 265–276 (2010)
10. Bouwmans, T., Porikli, F., Hörferlin, B., Vacavant, A.: Background Modeling and Foreground Detection for Video Surveillance. Chapman and Hall/CRC, Boca Raton (2014). ISBN: 1482205386
11. Coupé, P., Manjón, J., Gedamu, E., Arnold, D., Robles, M., Collins, D.: Robust Rician noise estimation for MR images. Med. Image Anal. **14**(4), 483–493 (2010)
12. El Baf, F., Bouwmans, T., Vachon, B.: Fuzzy integral for moving object detection. In: IEEE International Conference on Fuzzy Systems, Istanbul (2008)
13. Fischler, M., Bolles, R.C.: Random sample consensus: a paradigm for model fitting with applications to image analysis and automated cartography. In: DARPA Image Understanding Workshop, pp. 71–88 (1980)
14. Fridrich, J., Goljan, M.: Comparing robustness of watermarking techniques. In: SPIE Security and Watermarking of Multimedia Contents (1999)
15. Gilboa, G., Sochen, N., Zeevi, Y.: Regularized shock filters and complex diffusion. In: European Conference on Computer Vision, pp. 399–313 (2004)
16. Hofmann, M., Tiefenbacher, P., Rigoll, G.: Background segmentation with feedback: the pixel-based adaptive segmenter. In: IEEE Conference on Computer Vision and Pattern Recognition Work, Providence (2012)
17. Hough, P.: Method and means for recognizing complex patterns (1962)

18. Huang, T., Yang, G., Tang, G.: A fast two-dimensional median filtering algorithm. IEEE Trans. Acous. Speech Signal Process. **27**(1), 13–18 (1979)
19. Kaewtrakulpong, P., Bowden, R.: An improved adaptive background mixture model for realtime tracking with shadow detection. In: IEEE European Workshop on Advanced Video Based Surveillance Systems, London (2001)
20. Kajiya, J.: The rendering equation. ACM SIGGRAPH Comput. Graph. **20**(4), 143–150 (1986)
21. Kass, M., Solomon, J.: Smoothed local histogram filters. ACM Trans. Graph. **29**(4), 100:1–100:10 (2010)
22. Lebrun, M., Colom, M., Buades, A., Morel, J.: Secrets of image denoising cuisine. Acta Num. **21**, 475–576 (2012)
23. Liu, Z., Klette, R.: Performance evaluation of stereo and motion analysis on rectified image sequences. CITR, The University of Auckland, Technical report (2007)
24. Maddalena, L., Petrosino, A.: A self-organizing approach to background subtraction for visual surveillance applications. IEEE Trans. Image Process. **17**(7), 1168–1177 (2008)
25. Maggioni, M., Boracchi, G., Foi, A., Egiazarian, K.: Video denoising, deblocking and enhancement through separable 4-D nonlocal spatiotemporal transforms. IEEE Trans. Image Process. **21**(9), 3952–3966 (2012)
26. Meer, P.: From a robust hierarchy to a hierarchy of robustness. In: Foundations of Image Analysis, pp. 323–347. Kluwer (2001)
27. Meer, P.: Robust techniques for computer vision. In: Emerging Topics in Computer Vision, pp. 107–190. Prentice Hall, Boston (2004)
28. Oliver, N., Rosario, B., Pentland, A.: A Bayesian computer vision system for modeling human interactions. IEEE Trans. Pattern Anal. Mach. Intell. **22**(8), 831–843 (2000)
29. Ordonez, C., Omiecinski, E.: FREM: Fast and robust EM clustering for large data sets. In: International Conference on Systems, Man, and Cybernetics, pp. 590–599 (2012)
30. Osher, S., Rudin, L.: Feature-oriented image enhancement using shock filters. SIAM J. Numer. Anal. **27**, 919–940 (1990)
31. Pun, G., Ratib, O.: Image analysis and computer vision in medicine. Comput. Med. Imaging Graph. **18**(2), 85–96 (1994)
32. Qureshi, S.: Computer vision acceleration using GPUs. Talk presented at the AMD Fusion Developer Summit, Bellevue (2011)
33. Rampel, R., Ronchetti, E., Rousseeuw, P., Stahel, W.A.: Robust Statistics. The Approach Based on Influence Function. Wiley, New York (1986)
34. Sobral, A., Vacavant, A.: A comprehensive review of background subtraction algorithms evaluated with synthetic and real videos. Comput. Vis. Image Underst. **122**, 4–21 (2014)
35. Thomas, R., McSharry, P.: Big Data Revolution: What Farmers, Doctors and Insurance Agents Teach Us About Discovering Big Data Patterns. Wiley, New York (2015)
36. Tomasi, C., Manduchi, R.: Bilateral filtering for gray and color images. In: International Conference on Computer Vision, Bombay (1998)
37. Vacavant, A., Albouy-Kissi, A., Menguy, P., Solomon, J.: Fast smoothed shock filtering. In: IEEE International Conference on Pattern Recognition, Tsukuba (2012)
38. Vacavant, A., Ali, A., Grand-Brochier, M., Albouy-Kissi, A., Boire, J., Alfidja, A., Chabrot, P.: Smoothed shock filtered defuzzification with Zernike moments for liver tumor extraction in MR images. In: IEEE International Conference on Image Processing Tools and Applications, Orléans (2015)

39. Wang, Z., Bovik, A., Sheikh, H., Simoncelli, E.: Image quality assessment: from error visibility to structural similarity. IEEE Trans. Image Process. **13**(4), 600–612 (2004)
40. Weickert, J.: Coherence-enhancing shock filters. In: Michaelis, B., Krell, G. (eds.) DAGM 2003. LNCS, vol. 2781, pp. 1–8. Springer, Heidelberg (2003). doi:10.1007/978-3-540-45243-0_1
41. Wren, C., Azarbayejani, A., Darrell, T., Pentland, A.: Pfinder: real-time tracking of the human body. IEEE Trans. Pattern Anal. Mach. Intell. **19**(7), 780–785 (1997)
42. Yao, J., Odobez, J.: Multi-layer background subtraction based on color and texture. In: IEEE Conference on Computer Vision and Pattern Recognition, Minneapolis (2007)

Reproducible Research Results

Numerical Implementation of the Ambrosio-Tortorelli Functional Using Discrete Calculus and Application to Image Restoration and Inpainting

Marion Foare[1], Jacques-Olivier Lachaud[1(✉)], and Hugues Talbot[2]

[1] Laboratoire de Mathématiques, Université Savoie Mont Blanc,
73376 Chambéry, France
{marion.foare,jacques-olivier.lachaud}@univ-smb.fr
[2] Laboratoire d'Informatique Gaspard-Monge, Université Paris-Est – ESIEE,
Champs-sur-Marne, France
hugues.talbot@univ-paris-est.fr

Abstract. The Mumford-Shah (MS) functional is one of the most influential variational model in image segmentation, restoration, and cartooning. Difficult to solve, the Ambrosio-Tortorelli (AT) functional is of particular interest, because minimizers of AT can be shown to converge to a minimizer of MS. This paper takes an interest in a new method for numerically solving the AT model [11]. This method formulates the AT functional in a discrete calculus setting, and by this way is able to capture the set of discontinuities as a one-dimensional set. It is also shown that this model is competitive with total variation restoration methods. We present here the discrete AT models in details, and compare its merit with recent convex relaxations of AT and MS functionals. We also examine the potential of this model for inpainting, and describe its implementation in the DGtal library, an open-source project.

Keywords: Image denoising and restoration · Mumford-shah functional · Variational model · Optimization · Inverse problems · Discrete calculus · Ambrosio-Tortorelli functional · Image inpaiting

1 Introduction

This paper takes an interest in a new numerical method to solve the Ambrosio-Tortorelli (AT) functional [1]. This functional is a well known non-convex relaxation of the famous Mumford-Shah (MS) functional [17], which has many applications in image segmentation [2,6,18], restoration [2,4,5,8,12,19,23], cartooning [20] or inpainting [10]. This new method for solving AT redefines this functional into a discrete calculus setting and is presented in details in [11].

This work has been partly funded by CoMeDiC ANR-15-CE40-0006 research grant.

© Springer International Publishing AG 2017
B. Kerautret et al. (Eds.): RRPR 2016, LNCS 10214, pp. 91–103, 2017.
DOI: 10.1007/978-3-319-56414-2_7

Contributions. The present paper is a companion to the original paper [11], and complements it on several points. First of all, the possible formulations of AT in discrete calculus are discussed and compared in more details. Secondly, we examine other convex relaxations of the Ambrosio-Tortorelli and Mumford-Shah functionals (Kee and Kim [15], Strekalovskiy and Cremers [20]) and we compare our approach to them. Third, we study the influence of parameters in the method, as well as the possible scale spaces induced by the model. Fourth, we test the possible application of our discrete AT model to inpainting problems and discuss its potential and drawbacks. Last, we describe its implementation in the DGtal library [22], which is an open source C++ library for image and geometry processing of digital data.

Outline. The paper is organized as follows. We first briefly introduce the MS and AT functionals as well as the many variants and discretizations proposed in the literature (Sect. 2). We then present our discrete formulations of the AT functional, which is expressed in a discrete calculus framework, and the algorithm for its numerical optimization (Sect. 3). Our approach is compared to several state-of-the-art convex relaxations of MS or AT in Sect. 4. Parameters and their associated scale spaces are discussed in Sect. 5. The potential of our discrete AT for inpainting is encompassed in Sect. 6. Section 7 concludes by describing the implementation of our AT models in the DGtal library.

2   The Mumford-Shah and Ambrosio-Tortorelli Functionals

The Mumford-Shah (MS) model was introduced in [17] to solve image segmentation and restoration problems. This model was seminal to many important contributions in image processing and analysis, such as the Rudin-Osher-Fatemi (ROF) restoration method, the total variation (TV) denoising, Chan-Vese or Boykov-Jolly segmentation methods. The main idea is to see the input grey-level image as a function $g \in L^\infty(\Omega)$ where Ω is some domain of $\mathbb{R}^2$, and to seek the solution as a piecewise smooth function u that approaches g. The loci of discontinuities K is also a variable of the problem. Another strong idea is that the "size" of K is penalized. So the MS model is the optimal solution (K, u) to the following functional:

$$\mathcal{MS}(K, u) = \alpha \int_{\Omega \setminus K} |u - g|^2 \, \mathrm{dx} + \int_{\Omega \setminus K} |\nabla u|^2 \, \mathrm{dx} + \lambda \mathcal{H}^1(K \cap \Omega) \qquad (1)$$

where $\alpha, \lambda > 0$ and $\mathcal{H}^1$ denotes the 1-dimensional Hausdorff measure. We recognize in the first term the L_2 approximation to the input image, the second term requires the smoothness of u, while the last term penalizes the length of discontinuities K.

The MS functional is difficult to solve in this form, so many relaxations have been proposed to overcome this issue. We take an interest in the Ambrosio-Tortorelli relaxation [1], defined as:

$$\mathrm{AT}_\varepsilon(u,v) = \int_\Omega \alpha|u-g|^2 + v^2|\nabla u|^2 + \lambda\varepsilon|\nabla v|^2 + \frac{\lambda}{4\varepsilon}|1-v|^2 \; \mathrm{dx}, \qquad (2)$$

for functions $u,v \in W^{1,2}(\Omega)$ with $0 \le v \le 1$.

In (2), function u is a smooth approximation of the input image g. Function v is a smooth approximation of the set of discontinuities, and takes value close to 0 in this set, while being close to 1 outside discontinuities. A remarkable property of this functional is that it Γ-converges to (a relaxation of) the MS functional as ε tends to 0 [1]. The intuition is that a large ε induces a solution with a fuzzy set of discontinuities, which is then progressively narrowed to the crisp 1-dimensional set of discontinuites as ε goes to 0.

However the minimization of (2) with standard discretization schemes such as finite differences is not possible. Indeed, to achieve convergence, parameters ε, the grid-step h and the ratio $\frac{\varepsilon}{h}$ must all tend to zero [4]. So in practice we set $\varepsilon \approx 5h$ but the resulting set of discontinuities is thick and fuzzy (sometime more than 6 pixels wide), and the restoration is very poor in these regions. To overcome this issue, Bourdin and Chambolle [4] proposed a finite element method with adaptive domain refinement around discontinuities. It will be shown later that this method is still not satisfactory, despite the added complexity. These difficulties explains why the AT model is not a popular approach in image processing, and why TV, ROF, or graph cuts methods have been heavily used instead.

For more details about other similar variational models for image processing and more background about related works, we refer the reader to [11].

3   Discrete Calculus Formulations of AT Functional

In [11], a different formulation of the AT functional was proposed, which retains its main characteristics (piecewise smoothness, penalization of the length of the discontinuities), while being able to capture thin discontinuities. This reformulation uses the setting of discrete exterior calculus (DEC), as described in the context of computer graphics in [7] and image analysis in [13]. The advantage of this setting is that one can control easily where the variables are defined, and where they are coupled. In particular, the function v does not become identically one even when ε tends to zero.

Discrete exterior calculus. The idea is to decompose the image domain Ω into a cell complex K. Here, the faces of K are simply the pixels of the image, the edges of K are the sides shared by two pixels, while the vertices of K are the those shared by four pixels. For technical reasons, the dual complex $\bar{K}$ of K is also needed and is defined in the usual way: a vertex of K is thus associated one-to-one to a face of $\bar{K}$, etc. A *discrete k-dimensional form* is just a map that associates a scalar to a k-dimensional cell.[1] If the number of k-dimensional cells

---

[1] Although discrete forms can be defined without reference to the continuous setting, one can see them as the integration of k-dimensional differential form over a k-cell, resulting in a scalar per k-cell.

of K is denoted by n_k, then a discrete k-form is simply represented by a column vector of size $n_k \times 1$.

We then define the usual linear operators between k-forms (see Fig. 1). We denote by $\mathbf{d}_k$ and $\bar{\mathbf{d}}_k$ the standard discrete exterior primal and dual derivative operators. The derivative operator $\mathbf{d}_0$ is the oriented vertex-edge incidence matrix of K, and has size $n_1 \times n_0$. Since the complex K is the regular grid with edge size 1, the dual derivative $\bar{\mathbf{d}}_1$ is the transpose of $\mathbf{d}_0$. Similarly, the primal derivative $\mathbf{d}_1$ is the oriented edge-face incidence matrix of K, of size $n_2 \times n_1$, and the dual derivative $\bar{\mathbf{d}}_0$ is its transpose.

The Hodge star is an operator that maps a differential form onto its complementary differential form. Discrete Hodge star operators $\star$ sends k-forms of the primal complex K onto $n - k$-forms of the dual complex $\bar{K}$ (see again Fig. 1). In our setting, these operators reduce to identity operations except for a change of sign in some cases, and they also change the meaning of vectors. For instance, if f is a 0-form on the vertices of K, $\star f$ is a dual 2-form defined on the faces of $\bar{K}$. Clearly, it is also a vector of size $n_0 \times 1$ since there are n_0 faces in $\bar{K}$.

We define $\mathbf{M}_{01}$ the matrix which transforms a 0-form into a 1-form by averaging the values on the two edge extremities, i.e. $\mathbf{M}_{01} = \frac{1}{2}|\mathbf{d}_0|$. Moreover, we use the edge laplacian defined in [13] by $\bar{\star}\bar{\mathbf{d}}_0\star\mathbf{d}_1 + \mathbf{d}_0\bar{\star}\bar{\mathbf{d}}_1\star$.

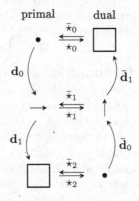

Fig. 1. Primal and dual complex and common Discrete Exterior Calculus (DEC) operators.

Discrete formulations of AT. We first set u and g to live on the faces and v to live on the vertices and edges. Pixels are faces, so functions u and g are 2-forms since they represent the gray levels of each pixel. On the contrary, v is an estimation of the set of discontinuities of u, and should be of null Hausdorff-1 measure when $\varepsilon \to 0$. Thus we set v in-between cells of non null measure, so in this case on vertices as a 0-form, and on edges by averaging with $\mathbf{M}_{01}$. We call this formulation $\mathrm{AT}_\varepsilon^{2,0}$. Looking at (2), the DEC reformulation is straightforward, except for the second term, where v is a 0-form and ∇u a 1-form. Hence we use matrix $\mathbf{M}_{01}$ to transport the 0-form v onto edges by simple averaging:

$$\text{AT}_\varepsilon^{2,0}(u,v) = \alpha\langle u - g, u - g\rangle_2 + \langle \mathbf{M}_{01}v \odot \bar{\star}\mathbf{d}_0\star u, \mathbf{M}_{01}v \odot \bar{\star}\mathbf{d}_0\star u\rangle_1$$

$$+ \lambda\varepsilon\langle \mathbf{d}_0 v, \mathbf{d}_0 v\rangle_1 + \frac{\lambda}{4\varepsilon}\langle 1 - v, 1 - v\rangle_0. \tag{3}$$

where $\odot$ denotes the point-wise multiplication.

A second possibility is to define u and g on the vertices and v on the edges. We denote this formulation $\text{AT}_\varepsilon^{0,1}$. Contrary to the previous formulation, the gray levels are seen as point mass on the center of pixels, so that functions u and g are both 0-forms. An alternative interpretation is to say that pixel values are dual 2-forms, while v is a dual 1-form in between u. It follows:

$$\text{AT}_\varepsilon^{0,1}(u,v) = \alpha\langle u - g, u - g\rangle_0 + \langle v \odot \mathbf{d}_0 u, v \odot \mathbf{d}_0 u\rangle_1$$

$$+ \lambda\varepsilon\langle(\mathbf{d}_1 + \bar{\star}\mathbf{d}_1\star)v, (\mathbf{d}_1 + \bar{\star}\mathbf{d}_1\star)v\rangle_1 + \frac{\lambda}{4\varepsilon}\langle 1 - v, 1 - v\rangle_1. \tag{4}$$

We further extend (3) and (4) to the vectorial case by associating to each component of the input image n forms $\{g_1, \ldots, g_n\}$, and the corresponding forms $\{u_1, \ldots, u_n\}$, and summing over the coordinates. In this paper, we will use $n = 1$ for gray-level images and $n = 3$ for RGB color images.

Optimization. The functionals $\text{AT}_\varepsilon^{2,0}$ and $\text{AT}_\varepsilon^{0,1}$ are both sums of quadratic terms, independently, but not simultaneously, convex in u and v. They must have null derivative at optimum. We thus propose to alternatively solve for u, then v. The derivatives can be given explicitly as linear systems. To simplify notations, let $\mathbf{A} := \mathbf{d}_0$, $\mathbf{B} := \mathbf{d}_1$, $\mathbf{A}' := \bar{\star}\mathbf{d}_1\star$ and $\mathbf{B}' := \bar{\star}\mathbf{d}_0\star$. It is worth to note $\mathbf{A}'$ and $\mathbf{B}'$ are the respective transpose of $\mathbf{A}$ of $\mathbf{B}$, except on the boundary of the image. We get at optimum:

$$\begin{cases} \left[\alpha\mathbf{Id} - \mathbf{B}'^\mathsf{T}\text{diag}\left(\mathbf{M}_{01}v\right)^2\mathbf{B}'\right]u = \alpha g, \\ \left[\frac{\lambda}{4\varepsilon}\mathbf{Id} + \lambda\varepsilon\mathbf{A}^\mathsf{T}\mathbf{A} + \mathbf{M}_{01}^\mathsf{T}\text{diag}\left(\mathbf{B}'u\right)^2\mathbf{M}_{01}\right]v = \frac{\lambda}{4\varepsilon}\mathbf{1}. \end{cases} \tag{5}$$

for the derivative of $\text{AT}_\varepsilon^{2,0}$, and

$$\begin{cases} \left[\alpha\mathbf{Id} - \mathbf{A}^\mathsf{T}\text{diag}\left(v\right)^2\mathbf{A}\right]u = \alpha g, \\ \left[\frac{\lambda}{4\varepsilon}\mathbf{Id} + \lambda\varepsilon(\mathbf{A}'^\mathsf{T}\mathbf{A}' + \mathbf{B}^\mathsf{T}\mathbf{B}) + \text{diag}\left(\mathbf{A}u\right)^2\right]v = \frac{\lambda}{4\varepsilon}\mathbf{1}. \end{cases} \tag{6}$$

for the derivative of $\text{AT}_\varepsilon^{0,1}$. Since all matrices are symmetric, definite and positive, we use a Cholesky factorization to solve alternatively the two equations of (5) (resp. (6)). Because of the $\mathbf{Id}$ additive term, the left-hand side is full rank, yielding a unique minimum at each iteration. It is a known result in convex analysis linked to block coordinate descent algorithms [3, Prop. 2.7.1], that these iterations must converge to a stationary point of $\text{AT}_\varepsilon^{2,0}$ (resp. $\text{AT}_\varepsilon^{0,1}$). In the optimization process, we start with a large enough ε_1, in order to capture the discontinuities, and after convergence for a given ε, we decrease it by dividing it by ε_r, until $\varepsilon = \varepsilon_2$. We denote this process by $\varepsilon = \varepsilon_1 \searrow \varepsilon_2$. The main loop stops when v reaches stability. Figure 2 illustrates that our AT model are able to capture discontinuities as a 1-dimensional set, since v is defined on 0- and 1-dimensional cells.

OPTIMIZE-AT($(g_1, ..., g_n)$: 2-forms (resp. 0-forms), $(\alpha, \lambda, \varepsilon_1, \varepsilon_2, \varepsilon_r)$: reals);
Var $(u_1, ..., u_n)$: 2-forms (resp. 0-forms), (v, v'): 0-forms (resp. 1-forms), ε: real ;
begin

    foreach $i \in \{1, ..., n\}$ **do** $u_i \leftarrow g_i$;

    $v \leftarrow 1, \varepsilon \leftarrow \varepsilon_1$;

    while $\varepsilon \geq \varepsilon_2$ **do**

1   **repeat**

           $v' \leftarrow v$;

           Solve 1st line of (5) (resp. (6)) for all u_i;

           Solve 2nd line of (5) (resp. (6)) for v;

        until $\|v - v'\|$ *is small*;

        $\varepsilon \leftarrow \varepsilon/\varepsilon_r$;

    end

    return $((u_1, ..., u_n), v)$;

end

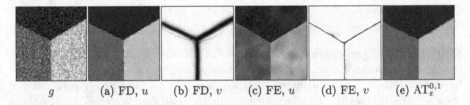

    g (a) FD, u (b) FD, v (c) FE, u (d) FE, v (e) $\mathrm{AT}_\varepsilon^{0,1}$

Fig. 2. Minimization of AT with finite differences (FD), finite elements (FE) from [4] and our approach $\mathrm{AT}_\varepsilon^{2,0}$ on a triple point image with PSNR = 20.3 dB.

Limit cases. As is the case with many image restoration methods, our approach assumes stationary noise and blur. Some spatially variant noise occurs in nature, for instance Poisson noise [21]. As is illustrated on Fig. 3, when the noise is spatially variant, suboptimal results are achieved. This is due to the parameters α and λ being constant for the entire image. For future work, we plan to let α and λ depend on x and thus choose locally the optimal pair (α, λ), and to adapt

Fig. 3. In this figure we have added a spatially-variant noise to the Mandrill image. In this case it is not possible to find an optimal (α, λ) pair that denoises and segments the image appropriately with our current model.

AT to use data fidelity terms that are appropriate for some non-stationary noise models [14].

4   Comparisons with Other Relaxations of MS and AT Functionals

A frequent criticism about MS and AT functionals is that they are non convex. Current optimization techniques thus do not extract the global optimum,

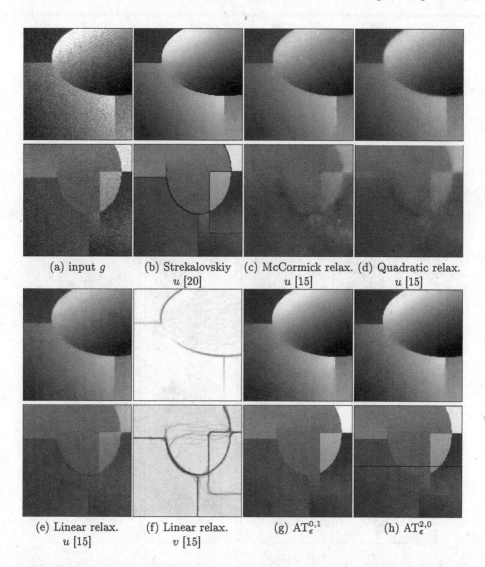

(a) input g (b) Strekalovskiy   (c) McCormick relax.   (d) Quadratic relax.
                          u [20] u [15] u [15]

(e) Linear relax.   (f) Linear relax.   (g) $AT_\varepsilon^{0,1}$ (h) $AT_\varepsilon^{2,0}$
    u [15] v [15]

Fig. 4. Comparison of the minimization of convex relaxations of AT (extracted from [15]), MS [20] and our approach on images extracted from [15]. In all cases, parameters were fixed to get best possible SNR.

and results are subject to initialization. This is for instance why TV models have gained so much popularity, despite known problems (most notably staircasing instead of smoothing). Other people have followed a different path and proposed convex approximations of MS or AT. Strekalovskiy and Cremers have proposed a truncated quadratic potential to approach directly the MS model [20], which leads them to a fast algorithm for segmentation and cartooning. Kee an Kim proposed in [15] three convex relaxations of AT: a quadratic relaxation, a linear relaxation, and the last one based on a factorization theorem

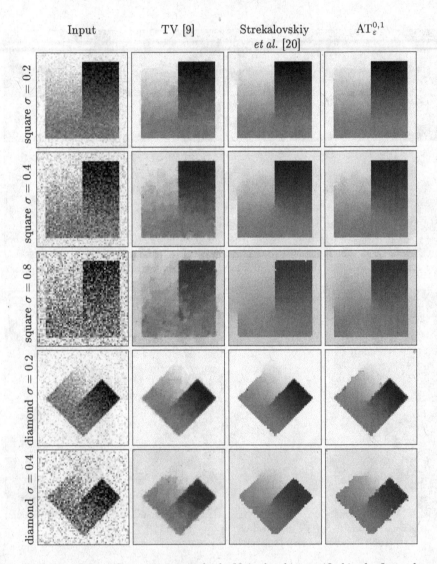

Fig. 5. Comparison with competing methods. Noise level is specified in the first column.

due to McCormick [16]. They used a gradient descend algorithm to compute the minimizers, and observed that the best results are obtained with the linear relaxation. We compare in Fig. 4 the results of Kee and Kim, the results of Strekalovskiy and Cremers, and our approach on the images used in [15].

We can see that the McCormick relaxation (Fig. 4(c)) retains many artifacts while the quadratic relaxation (Fig. 4(d)) leads to blurry reconstructions. The results obtained with the linear relaxation (Fig. 4(e)) are piecewise smooth, but we observe a poor reconstruction of angles in the vectorial case. Furthermore we see on Fig. 4(f) that they obtain diffuse and sometimes false contours.

The convex relaxation of Strekalovskiy and Cremers leads to piecewise smooth results (Fig. 4(b)), with sharp discontinuities, similar to our approaches (Fig. 4(g)–(h)).

In Fig. 5, we compare the results of TV model implemented in [9], the results of Strekalovskiy et $al.$ [20], and our approach on synthetic images. For all methods, we set the parameters that maximize the PSNR (see Table 1). We observe the characteristic staircasing effect with the TV method. Strekalovskiy et $al.$ and our method are robust to noise and yield piecewise smooth results.

Table 1. Best PSNRs results are in bold.

	TV [9]	Strek et $al.$ [20]	$AT_{\varepsilon}^{2,0}$	$AT_{\varepsilon}^{0,1}$
square $\sigma = 0.2$	29.1528	30.3717	30.7517	**30.8439**
square $\sigma = 0.4$	23.7067	24.7827	24.8512	**25.2425**
square $\sigma = 0.8$	17.6858	17.3795	17.1204	**18.3949**
diamond $\sigma = 0.2$	27.3675	26.6616	**27.7706**	27.2441
diamond $\sigma = 0.4$	**21.8341**	21.1176	21.7719	21.6394

5   Influence of Parameters and Scale Spaces

The Γ-convergence parameter ε controls the thickness of the contours. Large values of ε convexify the AT functional and help to detect the discontinuities. Then, as ε goes to 0, the contours become thinner and thinner (see Fig. 6).

On the other hand, for a large enough and fixed λ, the minimization of AT is equivalent to a diffusion with a small perturbation dependent on α. Hence parameter α can be chosen for an initial blur of the input data: the smaller α is, the stronger the initial blur is (see Fig. 7).

Finally, for fixed α (chosen so as to remove noise), the parameter λ controls the length of discontinuities. Hence, for a large enough λ, the set of discontinuities is empty because the minimization of AT is equivalent to a diffusion. As the parameter λ decreases, more and more discontinuities are detected and delineated, as we can see in Fig. 8. Note that results of $AT_{\varepsilon}^{0,1}$ and $AT_{\varepsilon}^{2,0}$ are almost identical for this image.

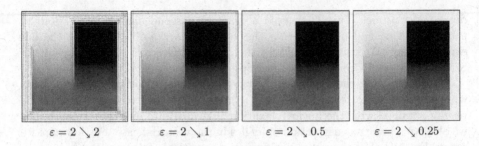

$$\varepsilon = 2 \searrow 2 \qquad \varepsilon = 2 \searrow 1 \qquad \varepsilon = 2 \searrow 0.5 \qquad \varepsilon = 2 \searrow 0.25$$

Fig. 6. ε scale space, for fixed $\lambda = 0.006$ and $\alpha = 0.1$.

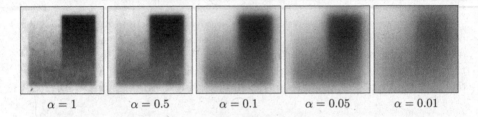

$$\alpha = 1 \qquad \alpha = 0.5 \qquad \alpha = 0.1 \qquad \alpha = 0.05 \qquad \alpha = 0.01$$

Fig. 7. α scale space, for fixed $\lambda = 1.0$ and $\varepsilon = 2 \searrow 0.25$.

$$\lambda = 0.2 \qquad \lambda = 0.1 \qquad \lambda = 0.05 \qquad \lambda = 0.025 \qquad \lambda = 0.0125$$

Fig. 8. λ scale space of $\mathrm{AT}_\varepsilon^{2,0}$, for fixed $\alpha = 0.48$ and $\varepsilon = 2 \searrow 0.25$.

6 Potential of the Model in Image Inpainting

It is easy to adapt the AT models for image inpainting. It suffices to have a parameter α that varies across the image. More precisely, it is set to 0 wherever the user selected a damaged zone while it is kept to its normal value elsewhere. Furthermore, forms u are initialized with random values at these places.

We have checked if our discrete AT models can be interesting for image inpainting. As illustrated on Fig. 9, it appears that model $\mathrm{AT}_\varepsilon^{0,1}$ introduces too many artefacts on artificial examples. Indeed, it optimizes the $L1$-length of discontinuities, which is not a natural inpainting for a human eye. The problem is that the $L1$-length has a very flat minimum, which is composed of all the discrete paths in some rectangle joining two constraints. Model $\mathrm{AT}_\varepsilon^{0,1}$ picks anyone of these paths: this is governed by the order of cells in the linear systems.

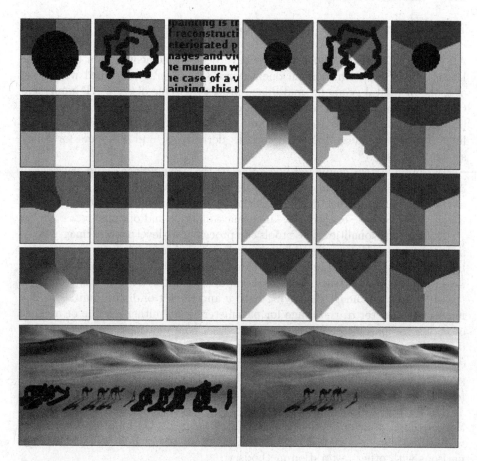

Fig. 9. Using discrete AT functionals for image inpaiting. Top row: input images. Second row: results of $\mathrm{AT}_\varepsilon^{0,1}$ with $\varepsilon = 4 \searrow 0.25$. Third row: results of $\mathrm{AT}_\varepsilon^{2,0}$ with $\varepsilon = 4 \searrow 0.25$. Fourth row: results of $\mathrm{AT}_\varepsilon^{2,0}$ with $\varepsilon = 1 \searrow 0.25$. Fifth row: inpainting of real picture with $\mathrm{AT}_\varepsilon^{0,1}$ and $\varepsilon = 4 \searrow 0.25$.

However, model $\mathrm{AT}_\varepsilon^{2,0}$ seems much more interesting. It is able to detect the two triple points that optimize a four region contact as well as the 120° angle for a three region contact. The reason is that this model averages the $L1$-length of discontinuities especially when ε is large. Hence, the diffused $L1$-length is closer to the natural $L2$-length and the model chooses a better $L1$-path for large ε. As ε decreases, discontinuities stay at the correct location while getting crispier. This explains why triple points are correctly detected by $\mathrm{AT}_\varepsilon^{2,0}$, if we start from a large enough ε, which be must proportional to the width of the damaged zone. In Fig. 9, setting $\varepsilon = 4 \searrow 0.25$ was good for all examples.

Of course, variational methods for image inpainting should be combined with some non-local/texture filtering to compete with state-of-the-art approaches, but we may conclude that $\mathrm{AT}_\varepsilon^{2,0}$ is a candidate for such a hybrid inpainting method.

7 Implementation in the DGtal Library

All presented material and programs have been implemented as a tool in the DGtal library [22], which is an open-source C++ library, bundled with a set of tools for digital geometry and image processing. Our discrete AT implementation relies heavily on the Discrete Exterior Calculus package. This package provides data-structures and algorithms for manipulating discrete forms on cellular complexes, linear operators such as derivatives, and wrappers for linear system solvers.

We provide two command-line tools in the `imageProcessing` package of `DGtalTools` (http://dgtal.org/doc/tools/nightly/imageProcessing), one called `at-u0-v1` that implements $AT_\varepsilon^{0,1}$, the other called `at-u2-v0` that implements $AT_\varepsilon^{2,0}$. They provide exactly the same functionalities and options.

Among functionalities, these tools can process grey-level or color images given in PBM format. You may either restore the whole image or perform inpainting by giving a mask image specifying damaged zone. SNR computation is provided if you provide ground truth. Both tools export the restored image u as well as an (possibly zoomed) image displaying both u and the set of discontinuities v. You may set parameter α, the range for parameter ε, and either a value or a range of values for parameter λ. In the latter case, computations are performed in descending λ order, delineating progressively more and more discontinuities. All options are described in pages associated to these tools. Note also that several generic classes have been created to facilitate the development of further image tools that use a discrete exterior calculus formulation.

For further works, we plan to develop an on-line demo of these image restoration methods, which uses the IPOL (Image Processing On-Line) platform. This will facilitate even more the reproducibility of our research as well as fair comparisons with other restoration methods.

References

1. Ambrosio, L., Tortorelli, V.M.: Approximation of functional depending on jumps by elliptic functional via t-convergence. Commun. Pure Appl. Math. **43**(8), 999–1036 (1990)
2. Bar, L., Chan, T.F., Chung, G., Jung, M., Kiryati, N., Mohieddine, R., Sochen, N., Vese, L.A.: Mumford and Shah Model and its Applications to Image Segmentation and Image Restoration, pp. 1095–1157. Springer, New York (2011)
3. Bertsekas, D.P.: Nonlinear Programming. Athena scientific, 2nd edn. (1999)
4. Bourdin, B., Chambolle, A.: Implementation of an adaptive finite-element approximation of the mumford-shah functional. Numer. Math. **85**(4), 609–646 (2000)
5. Chambolle, A.: An algorithm for total variation minimization and applications. J. Math. Imaging Vis. **20**(1–2), 89–97 (2004)
6. Chan,T.F., Vese, L.A.: Active contours without edges. IEEE Trans. Image Process.**10**(2), 266–277 (2001)
7. Desbrun, M., Hirani, A.N., Leok, M., Marsden, J.E.: Discrete exterior calculus. arXiv preprint arXiv:math/0508341 (2005)

8. Duan, J., Wenqi, L., Pan, Z., Bai, L.: New second order mumford-shah model based on γ-convergence approximation for image processing. Infrared Phys. Technol. **76**, 641–647 (2016)

9. Duran, J., Coll, B., Sbert, C.: Chambolle's projection algorithm for total variation denoising. Image Process. Line **311–331**, 2013 (2013)

10. Esedoglu, S., Shen, J.: Digital inpainting based on the mumford-shah-euler image model. Eur. J. Appl. Math. **13**(04), 353–370 (2002)

11. Foare, M., Lachaud, J.-O., Talbot, H.: Image restoration and segmentation using the ambrosio-tortorelli functional and discrete calculus. In: Proceedings of the IAPR International Conference on Pattern Recognition (ICPR2016), Cancun, Mexico (2016)

12. Grady, L., Alvino, C.V.: The piecewise smooth mumford-shah functional on an arbitrary graph. IEEE Trans. Image Process. **18**(11), 2547–2561 (2009)

13. Grady, L.J., Polimeni, J.: Discrete Calculus: Applied Analysis on Graphs for Computational Science. Springer, London (2010)

14. Jezierska, A., Chouzenoux, E., Pesquet, J.-C., Talbot, H., et al.: A convex approach for image restoration with exact poisson-gaussian likelihood (2013)

15. Kee, Y., Kim, Y.: A convex relaxation of the ambrosio-tortorelli elliptic functionals for the mumford-shah functional. In: Proceedings of the IEEE Conference on Computer Vision and Pattern Recognition, pp. 4074–4081 (2014)

16. McCormick, G.P.: Computability of global solutions to factorable nonconvex programs: Part i - convex underestimating problems. Math. Program. **10**(1), 147–175 (1976)

17. Mumford, D., Shah, J.: Optimal approximations by piecewise smooth functions and associated variational problems. Commun. Pure Appl. Math. **42**(5), 577–685 (1989)

18. Nikolova, M., Esedoglu, S., Chan, T.F.: Algorithms for finding global minimizers of image segmentation and denoising models. SIAM J. Appl. Math **66**(5), 1632–1648 (2006)

19. Rudin, L.I., Osher, S., Fatemi, E.: Nonlinear total variation based noise removal algorithms. Phys. D Nonlinear Phenom. **60**(1), 259–268 (1992)

20. Strekalovskiy, E., Cremers, D.: Real-time minimization of the piecewise smooth mumford-shah functional. In: Fleet, D., Pajdla, T., Schiele, B., Tuytelaars, T. (eds.) ECCV 2014. LNCS, vol. 8690, pp. 127–141. Springer, Cham (2014). doi:10.1007/978-3-319-10605-2_9

21. Talbot, H., Phelippeau, H., Akil, M., Bara, S.: Efficient poisson denoising for photography. In: Proceedings of IEEE ICIP 2009, Cairo, Egypt, pp. 3881–3883 (2009)

22. DGtal: Digital Geometry tools and algorithms library. http://dgtal.org

23. Vese, L.A., Le Guyader, C.: Variational Methods in Image Processing. CRC Press, Boca Raton (2015)

RSSL: Semi-supervised Learning in R

Jesse H. Krijthe[1,2]([✉])

[1] Pattern Recognition Laboratory, Delft University of Technology,
Delft, The Netherlands
jkrijthe@gmail.com
[2] Department of Molecular Epidemiology, Leiden University Medical Center,
Leiden, The Netherlands

Abstract. In this paper, we introduce a package for semi-supervised learning research in the R programming language called RSSL. We cover the purpose of the package, the methods it includes and comment on their use and implementation. We then show, using several code examples, how the package can be used to replicate well-known results from the semi-supervised learning literature.

Keywords: Semi-supervised learning · Reproducibility · Pattern recognition · R

1 Introduction

Semi-supervised learning is concerned with using unlabeled examples, that is, examples for which we know the values for the input features but not the corresponding outcome, to improve the performance of supervised learning methods that only use labeled examples to train a model. An important motivation for investigations into these types of algorithms is that in some applications, gathering labels is relatively expensive or time-consuming, compared to the cost of obtaining an unlabeled example. Consider, for instance, building a web-page classifier. Downloading millions of unlabeled web-pages is easy. Reading them to assign a label is time-consuming. Effectively using unlabeled examples to improve supervised classifiers can therefore greatly reduce the cost of building a decently performing prediction model, or make it feasible in cases where labeling many examples is not a viable option.

While the R programming language [22] offers a rich set of implementations of a plethora of supervised learning methods, brought together by machine learning packages such as `caret` and `mlr` there are fewer implementations of methods that can deal with the semi-supervised learning setting. This both impedes the spread of the use of these types of algorithms by practitioners, and makes it harder for researchers to study these approaches or compare new methods to existing ones. The goal of the RSSL package is to make a step towards filling this hiatus, with a focus on providing methods that exemplify common behaviours of semi-supervised learning methods.

B. Kerautret et al. (Eds.): RRPR 2016, LNCS 10214, pp. 104–115, 2017.
DOI: 10.1007/978-3-319-56414-2_8

Until recently, no package providing multiple semi-supervised learning methods was available in R[1]. In other languages, semi-supervised learning libraries that bring together several different methods are not available either, although there are general purpose machine learning libraries, such as scikit-learn in Python [21] that offer implementations of some semi-supervised algorithms. A broader set of implementations is available for Matlab, since the original implementations provided by the authors of many of the approaches covered by our package are provided for Matlab. The goal of our package is to bring some of these implementations together in the R environment by providing common interfaces to these methods, either implementing these methods in R, translating code to R or providing interfaces to C++ libraries.

The goal of this work is to give an overview of the package and make some comments how it is implemented and how it can be used. We will then provide several examples on how the package can be used to replicate various well-known results from the semi-supervised learning literature.

2   Overview of the Package

2.1   Classifiers

The package focuses on semi-supervised classification. We give an overview of the classifiers that are available in Table 1. We consider it important to compare the performance of semi-supervised learners to their supervised counterparts. We therefore include several supervised implementations and sets of semi-supervised methods corresponding to each supervised method. Most of the methods are new implementations in R based on the description of the methods in the original research papers. For others, we either provide a (close to) direct translation of the original code into R code or an R interface to the original C++ code. For the latter we make use of the Rcpp package [6]. In some cases (WellSVM and S4VM) it was necessary to also include a customized version of LIBSVM [2] on which these implementations depend.

A common wrapper method for semi-supervised learning, self-learning, is available for all supervised learners, since it merely requires a supervised classifier and some unlabeled objects. Other types of semi-supervised methods that are available for multiple supervised classifiers are the moment (or intrinsically) constrained methods of [16,17], the implicitly constrained methods of [10,12,13] and the Laplacian regularization of [1].

All the classifier functions require as input either matrices with feature values (one for the labeled data and one for the unlabeled data) and a `factor` object containing the labels, or a `formula` object defining the names input and target variables and a corresponding `data.frame` object containing the whole dataset. In the examples, we will mostly use the latter style, since it fits better with the use of the pipe operator that is becoming popular in R programming.

---

[1] Recently, the SSL package was introduced whose implementations are mostly complementary to those offered in our package: https://CRAN.R-project.org/package=SSL.

Each classifier function returns an object of a specific subclass of the `Classifier` class containing the trained classifier. There are several methods that we can call on these objects. The `predict` method predicts the labels of new data. `decisionvalues` returns the value of the decision function for new objects. If available, the `loss` method returns the classifier specific loss (the surrogate loss used to train the classifier) incurred by the classifier on a set of examples. If the method assigns responsibilities –probabilities of belonging to a particular class– to the unlabeled examples, `responsibilities` returns the responsibility values assigned to the unlabeled examples. For linear classifiers, we often provide the `line_coefficients` method that provides the coefficients to plot a 2-dimensional decision boundary, which may be useful for plotting the classifier in simple 2D examples.

2.2   Utility Functions

In addition to the implementations of the classifiers themselves, the package includes a number of functions that simplify setting up experiments and studying these classifiers. There are three main categories of functions: functions to generate simulated datasets, functions to evaluate classifiers and run experiments and functions for plotting trained classifiers.

Generated Datasets. A number of functions, of the form `generate*`, create datasets sampled from archetypical simulated problems. An overview of simulated datasets is given in Fig. 1. You will notice that these datasets mostly show examples where the structure of the density of the feature values is either very informative or not informative at all for the estimation of the conditional distribution of the labels given the feature value. A major theme in semi-supervised learning research is how to leverage this connection between the distribution of the features and the conditional distribution of the labels, and what happens if this connection is non-existent. These simulated datasets offer some simple but interesting test cases for semi-supervised methods.

Classifier Evaluation. To evaluate the performance of different methods, the package contains three types of functions that implement standard procedures for setting up such experiments. The first is by splitting a fully labeled dataset into a labeled set, an unlabeled set and a test set. For data in the form of a matrix, the `split_dataset_ssl` can be used. For data in the form of a data frame, the easiest way is to use `magrittr`'s pipe operator, splitting the data using the `split_random` command, using `add_missinglabels_mar` to randomly remove labels, and `missing_labels` or `true_labels` to recover these labels when we want to evaluate the performance on the unlabeled objects. The second type of experiment is to apply cross-validation in a semi-supervised setting using `CrossValidationSSL`. Distinct from the normal cross-validation setting, the data in the training folds get randomly assigned to the labeled or unlabeled set. The third type of experiment enabled by the package is to generate learning

Table 1. Overview of classifiers available in RSSL

Classifier	R	Interface	Port	Reference
(Kernel) least squares classifier	✓			[8]
Implicitly constrained	✓			[13]
Implicitly constrained projection	✓			[12]
Laplacian regularized	✓			[1]
Updated second moment	✓			[23]
Self-learning	✓			[20]
Optimistic/"Expectation Maximization"	✓			[11]
Linear discriminant analysis	✓			[25]
Expectation maximization	✓			[5]
Implicitly constrained	✓			[10]
Maximum contrastive pessimistic			✓	[18]
Moment constrained	✓			[17]
Self-learning	✓			[20]
Nearest mean classifier	✓			[25]
Expectation maximization	✓			[5]
Moment constrained	✓			[16]
Self-learning	✓			[20]
Support vector machine	✓			
SVMlin		✓		[24]
WellSVM			✓	[14]
S4VM			✓	[15]
Transductive SVM (convex concave procedure)	✓			[3,9]
Laplacian SVM	✓			[1]
Self-learning	✓			[20]
Logistic regression	✓			
Entropy regularized logistic regression	✓			[7]
Self-learning	✓			[20]
Harmonic energy minimization	✓			[27]

curves using the LearningCurveSSL function. These are performance curves for increasing numbers of unlabeled examples or an increasing fraction of labeled examples. For both the learning curves and cross-validation, multiple datasets can be given as input and the performance measures can be user defined, or one could use one of the supplied measure_* functions. Also in both cases, the experiments can optionally be run in parallel on multiple cores to speed up computation.

Plotting. Three ways to plot classifiers in simple 2D examples are provided. The most general method relies on the ggplot2 package [26] to plot

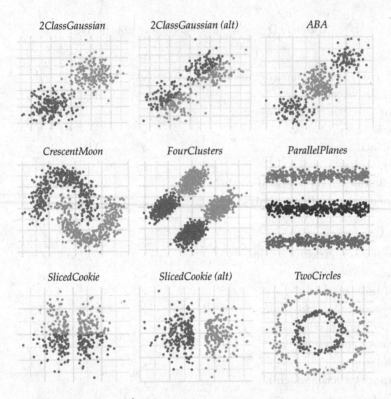

Fig. 1. Simulated Datasets. Each can be generated using a function of the form generate*, where * should be replaced by the name of the dataset. (alt) indicates non-default parameters were used when calling the function

the data and is provided in the form of the stat_classifier that can add classification boundaries to ggplot2 plots. geom_linearclassifier works in a similar way, but only works for a number of linear classifiers that have an associated line_coefficients method. Lastly, for these classifiers line_coefficients can be used directly to get the parameters that define the linear decision boundary, for use in a custom plotting function. In the examples, we will illustrate the use of stat_classifier and geom_linearclassifier.

3   Installation

The package is available from the Comprehensive R Archive Network (CRAN). As such, the easiest way to install the package is to run the following command using a recent version of R:

```
install.packages("RSSL")
```

The latest development version of the package can be installed using:

```
# If devtools is not installed run: install.packages("devtools")
devtools::install_github("jkrijthe/RSSL")
```

4   Examples

In this section, we will provide several examples of how the RSSL package can be used to illustrate or replicate results from the semi-supervised learning literature. Due to space constraints, we provide parts of the code for the examples in the text below. The complete code for all examples can be found in the source version of this document, which can be found on the author's website[2].

4.1   A Failure of Self-learning

While semi-supervised learning may seem to be obviously helpful, the fact that semi-supervised methods can actually lead to worse performance than their supervised counterparts has been both widely observed and described [4]. We will generate an example where unlabeled data is helpful (using the 2ClassGaussian problem from Fig. 1) and one where unlabeled data actually leads to an increase in the classification error (2ClassGaussian (alt) in Fig. 1), for the least squares classifier and self-learning as the semi-supervised learner. This can be done using the following code:

```
library(RSSL)
set.seed(1)

# Set the datasets and corresponding formula objects
datasets <- list("2 Gaussian Expected"=
                    generate2ClassGaussian(n=2000,d=2,expected=TRUE),
                 "2 Gaussian Non-Expected"=
                    generate2ClassGaussian(n=2000,d=2,expected=FALSE))
formulae <- list("2 Gaussian Expected"=formula(Class~.),
                 "2 Gaussian Non-Expected"=formula(Class~.))

# Define the classifiers to be used
classifiers <- list("Supervised" =
                       function(X,y,X_u,y_u) { LeastSquaresClassifier(X,y)},
                    "Self-learning" =
                       function(X,y,X_u,y_u) { SelfLearning(X,y,X_u,
                                          method = LeastSquaresClassifier)})

# Define the performance measures to be used and run experiment
measures <- list("Error" = measure_error, "Loss" = measure_losstest)
results_lc <- LearningCurveSSL(formulae,datasets,
                  classifiers=classifiers,
                  measures=measures,verbose=FALSE,
                  repeats=100,n_l=10,sizes = 2^(1:10))
```

---

[2] www.jessekrijthe.com.

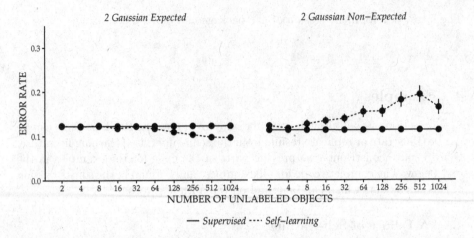

Fig. 2. Example where self-learning leads to better performance as we add more unlabeled data (left) and increasingly worse performance as unlabeled data is added (right). The classifier used is the least squares classifier. The datasets are similar to the ones shown in Fig. 1.

When we plot these results (using the `plot` method and optionally changing the display settings of the plot), we get the figure shown in Fig. 2. What this shows is that, clearly, semi-supervised methods can be outperformed by their supervised counterpart for some datasets, for some choice of semi-supervised learner. Given that one may have little labeled training data to accurately detect that this is happening, in some settings we may want to consider methods that inherently attempt to avoid this deterioration in performance. We will return to this in a later example.

4.2   Graph Based Semi-supervised Learning

Many methods in semi-supervised learning attempt to use the assumption that labels change smoothly over dense regions in the feature space. An early attempt to encode this assumption is offered by [27] who propose to minimize an energy function for the labels of the unlabeled objects that penalizes large deviations between labels assigned to objects that are close, for some measure of closeness. This so-called harmonic energy formulation can also be interpreted as a propagation of the labels from the labeled objects to the unlabeled objects, through a graph that encodes a measure of closeness. We recreate [27]'s Fig. 2, which can be found in Fig. 3. Due to space constraints, we will defer the code to the online version of this document, since it is similar to the code for the next example.

4.3   Manifold Regularization

Belkin et al. [1] build on the ideas of [27] by formulating the smoothness of the labeling function over the data manifold as a regularization term. In RSSL this Laplacian regularization term is included in both an SVM formulation and a regularized least squares formulation. For the Laplacian SVM formulation, Fig. 2 from [1] provides an example of its performance on a simulated dataset. We can replicate this result using the following code. The results are shown in Fig. 4.

```
library(RSSL)
library(dplyr)
library(ggplot2)
plot_style <- theme_classic() # Set the style of the plot

set.seed(2)
df_unlabeled <- generateCrescentMoon(n=100,sigma = 0.3) %>%
  add_missinglabels_mar(Class~.,prob=1)
df_labeled <- generateCrescentMoon(n=1,sigma = 0.3)
df <- rbind(df_unlabeled,df_labeled)

c_svm <- SVM(Class~.,df_labeled,scale=FALSE,
         kernel = kernlab::rbfdot(0.05),
         C=2500)

c_lapsvm1 <- LaplacianSVM(Class~.,df,scale=FALSE,
               kernel=kernlab::rbfdot(0.05),
               lambda = 0.0001,gamma=10)

c_lapsvm2 <- LaplacianSVM(Class~.,df,scale=FALSE,
               kernel=kernlab::rbfdot(0.05),
               lambda = 0.0001,gamma=10000)

# Plot the results
# Change the arguments of stat_classifier to plot the Laplacian SVM
ggplot(df_unlabeled, aes(x=X1,y=X2)) +
  geom_point() +
  geom_point(aes(color=Class,shape=Class),data=df_labeled,size=5) +
  stat_classifier(classifiers=list("SVM"=c_svm),color="black") +
  ggtitle("SVM")+
  plot_style
```

4.4 Low Density Separation

A number of semi-supervised approaches attempt to leverage the assumption that the classification boundary may reside in a region of low-density. The Semi-supervised SVM or Transductive SVM [9] is one such approach. In [28, Chap. 6], an example is given for the potential problems this low-density assumption may cause when it is not valid by considering two artificial datasets. Here we replicate these results for a different classifier that makes use of the low-density assumption: entropy regularized logistic regression [7]. The results are shown in Fig. 5. The code to generate these results can be found in the source version of this document.

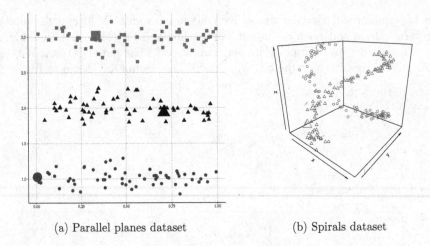

(a) Parallel planes dataset   (b) Spirals dataset

Fig. 3. Replication of Fig. 2 from [27] demonstrating harmonic energy minimization. The larger points indicate the labeled objects. The color indicates the predicted class.

4.5 Improvement Guarantees

We now return to the example of deterioration in performance from Fig. 2. The goal of our work in [11,12,18] is to construct methods that are guaranteed to outperform the supervised alternative. The guarantee that is given in these works is that the semi-supervised learner outperforms the supervised learner on the full, labeled and unlabeled, training set in terms of the surrogate loss (cf. [19]). The following code trains semi-supervised classifiers in these cases and returns the mean loss on the whole training set, the output is shown below the code example. It shows that indeed, these methods do not deteriorate performance in terms of the surrogate loss, while the self-learning method does show this deterioration in performance.

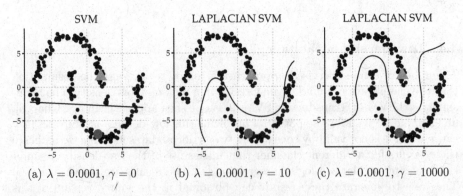

(a) $\lambda = 0.0001, \gamma = 0$ (b) $\lambda = 0.0001, \gamma = 10$ (c) $\lambda = 0.0001, \gamma = 10000$

Fig. 4. Replication of Fig. 2 from [1]. Laplacian SVM for various values of the influence of the unlabeled data.

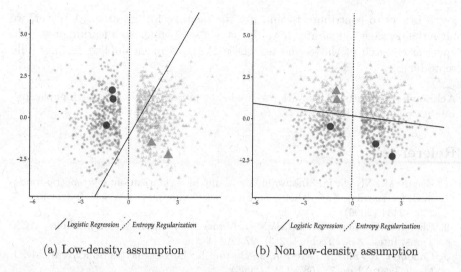

/ Logistic Regression ,·' Entropy Regularization   / Logistic Regression ,·' Entropy Regularization

(a) Low-density assumption   (b) Non low-density assumption

Fig. 5. Demonstration of potential problems when the low density assumption does not hold, similar to Fig. 6.5 in [28].

```
library(RSSL)
set.seed(1)

# Generate Example
df <- generate2ClassGaussian(n=1000, d=2, expected=FALSE)
df_semi <- add_missinglabels_mar(df, Class~., prob=0.995)

# Train and evaluate classifiers
mean(loss(LeastSquaresClassifier(Class~.,df_semi),df))
mean(loss(SelfLearning(Class~.,df_semi,method=LeastSquaresClassifier),df))
mean(loss(ICLeastSquaresClassifier(Class~.,df_semi),df))
mean(loss(ICLeastSquaresClassifier(Class~.,df_semi,
                 projection="semisupervised"),df))

## [1] 0.1763921
## [1] 0.4813863
## [1] 0.1185772
## [1] 0.1236701
```

5   Conclusion

We presented RSSL, a package containing implementations and interfaces to implementations of semi-supervised classifiers, and utility methods to carry out experiments using these methods. We demonstrated how the package can be used to replicate several results from the semi-supervised learning literature. More usage examples can be found in the package documentation. We hope the package inspires practitioners to consider semi-supervised learning in their work and we invite others to contribute to and use the package for research. Moreover, we hope the package contributes towards making semi-supervised learning research, and the research of those who use these methods in an applied setting, fully reproducible.

Acknowledgements. This work was funded by project P23 of the Dutch public/private research network COMMIT.

References

1. Belkin, M., Niyogi, P., Sindhwani, V.: Manifold regularization: a geometric framework for learning from labeled and unlabeled examples. J. Mach. Learn. Res. **7**, 2399–2434 (2006)
2. Chang, C.C., Lin, C.J.: LIBSVM: a library for support vector machines. ACM Trans. Intell. Syst. Technol. **2**(3), 27 (2011)
3. Collobert, R., Sinz, F., Weston, J., Bottou, L.: Large scale transductive SVMs. J. Mach. Learn. Res. **7**, 1687–1712 (2006)
4. Cozman, F.G., Cohen, I., Cirelo, M.C.: Semi-supervised learning of mixture models. In: Proceedings of the 20th International Conference on Machine Learning, pp. 99–106 (2003)
5. Dempster, A., Laird, N., Rubin, D.: Maximum likelihood from incomplete data via the EM algorithm. J. R. Stat. Soc. Ser. B **39**(1), 1–38 (1977)
6. Eddelbuettel, D., Francois, R.: Rcpp: seamless R and C++ Integration. J. Stat. Softw. **40**(1), 1–18 (2011)
7. Grandvalet, Y., Bengio, Y.: Semi-supervised learning by entropy minimization. In: Saul, L.K., Weiss, Y., Bottou, L. (eds.) Advances in Neural Information Processing Systems, vol. 17, pp. 529–536. MIT Press, Cambridge (2005)
8. Hastie, T., Tibshirani, R., Friedman, J.H.: The Elements of Statistical Learning, 2nd edn. Springer, New York (2009)
9. Joachims, T.: Transductive inference for text classification using support vector machines. In: Proceedings of the 16th International Conference on Machine Learning, pp. 200–209. Morgan Kaufmann Publishers, San Francisco (1999)
10. Krijthe, J.H., Loog, M.: Implicitly constrained semi-supervised linear discriminant analysis. In: Proceedings of the 22nd International Conference on Pattern Recognition, Stockholm, pp. 3762–3767 (2014)
11. Krijthe, J.H., Loog, M.: Optimistic semi-supervised least squares classification. In: Proceedings of the 23rd International Conference on Pattern Recognition (2016)
12. Krijthe, J.H., Loog, M.: Projected estimators for robust semi-supervised classification. Mach. Learn. (to appear, 2017). http://arxiv.org/abs/1602.07865
13. Krijthe, J.H., Loog, M.: Robust semi-supervised least squares classification by implicit constraints. Pattern Recogn. **63**, 115–126 (2017)
14. Li, Y., Tsang, I., Kwok, J., Zhou, Z.: Convex and scalable weakly labeled SVMs. J. Mach. Learn. Res. **14**, 2151–2188 (2013). http://arxiv.org/abs/1303.1271
15. Li, Y.F., Zhou, Z.H.: Towards making unlabeled data never hurt. IEEE Trans. Pattern Anal. Mach. Intell. **37**(1), 175–188 (2015)
16. Loog, M.: Constrained parameter estimation for semi-supervised learning: the case of the nearest mean classifier. In: Balcázar, J.L., Bonchi, F., Gionis, A., Sebag, M. (eds.) ECML PKDD 2010. LNCS (LNAI), vol. 6322, pp. 291–304. Springer, Heidelberg (2010). doi:10.1007/978-3-642-15883-4_19

17. Loog, M.: Semi-supervised linear discriminant analysis through moment-constraint parameter estimation. Pattern Recogn. Lett. **37**, 24–31 (2014)
18. Loog, M.: Contrastive pessimistic likelihood estimation for semi-supervised classification. IEEE Trans. Pattern Anal. Mach. Intell. **38**(3), 462–475 (2016)
19. Loog, M., Jensen, A.C.: Semi-supervised nearest mean classification through a constrained log-likelihood. IEEE Trans. Neural Netw. Learn. Syst. **26**(5), 995–1006 (2014)
20. McLachlan, G.J.: Iterative reclassification procedure for constructing an asymptotically optimal rule of allocation in discriminant analysis. J. Am. Stat. Assoc. **70**(350), 365–369 (1975)
21. Pedregosa, F., Varoquaux, G., Gramfort, A., Michel, V., Thirion, B., Grisel, O., Blondel, M., Prettenhofer, P., Weiss, R., Dubourg, V., Vanderplas, J., Passos, A., Cournapeau, D., Brucher, M., Perrot, M., Duchesnay, E.: Scikit-learn: machine learning in Python. J. Mach. Learn. Res. **12**, 2825–2830 (2011)
22. R Core Team: R: a language and environment for statistical computing. R Foundation for Statistical Computing, Vienna (2016). https://www.r-project.org/
23. Shaffer, J.P.: The Gauss-Markov theorem and random regressors. Am. Stat. **45**(4), 269–273 (1991)
24. Sindhwani, V., Keerthi, S.S.: Large scale semi-supervised linear SVMs. In: Proceedings of the 29th Annual International ACM SIGIR Conference on Research and Development in Information Retrieval, pp. 477–484. ACM (2006)
25. Webb, A.: Statistical Pattern Recognition, 2nd edn. John Wiley, New York (2002)
26. Wickham, H.: ggplot2: Elegant Graphics for Data Analysis. Springer, New York (2009). http://ggplot2.org
27. Zhu, X., Ghahramani, Z., Lafferty, J.: Semi-supervised learning using Gaussian fields and harmonic functions. In: Proceedings of the 20th International Conference on Machine Learning, pp. 912–919 (2003)
28. Zhu, X., Goldberg, A.B.: Introduction to Semi-supervised Learning. Morgan & Claypool, San Rafael (2009)

On the Implementation of Centerline Extraction Based on Confidence Vote in Accumulation Map

Bertrand Kerautret[1,2(✉)], Adrien Krähenbühl[4], Isabelle Debled-Rennesson[1,2], and Jacques-Olivier Lachaud[3]

[1] Université de Lorraine, LORIA, UMR 7503, 54506 Vandoeuvre-lès-Nancy, France
{bertrand.kerautret,isabelle.debled-rennesson}@loria.fr
[2] CNRS, LORIA, UMR 7503, 54506 Vandoeuvre-lès-Nancy, France
[3] LAMA (UMR CNRS 5127), Université Savoie Mont Blanc, 73376 Chambéry, France
jacques-olivier.lachaud@univ-savoie.fr
[4] LaBRI (UMR CNRS 5800), 351, Cours de la Libération, 33405 Talence Cedex, France
adrien.krahenbuhl@labri.fr

Abstract. This paper focuses on the implementation details of a recent method which extracts the centerline of 3D shapes using solely partial mesh scans of these shapes. This method [9] extracts the shape centerline by constructing an accumulation map from input points and normal vectors and by filtering it with a confidence vote. This paper presents in details all the algorithms of the method and describes the implementation and development choices. Some experiments test the robustness to the parameter variability and show the current limitations allowing to consider further improvements.

1 Introduction

Extracting the centerline of a shape is a classical problem in geometry processing and in image analysis. It can be seen as a special case of skeleton extraction for shapes with local approximate cylindrical symmetry. This problem has been addressed many times in the literature, one can refer to Tagliasacchi *et al.* [18] and Saha *et al.* [15] for recent surveys. As mentioned in the first survey, the wide deployment of such methods in many relevant applications is still missing [18]. In order to make easier the concrete deployment of academic centerline extraction methods in industrial applications, we present in details a recent method specialized for the extraction of centerlines of approximately tubular shapes with possibly branching [9] and we provide its complete implementation. This method presents several advantages: it can process partial mesh scans, it is robust to perturbations and relatively independent to parameters, it is not difficult to reproduce and implement. For instance, the replication of the

J.-O. Lachaud—This work was partially supported by the ANR grants DigitalSnow ANR-11-BS02-009.

B. Kerautret et al. (Eds.): RRPR 2016, LNCS 10214, pp. 116–130, 2017.
DOI: 10.1007/978-3-319-56414-2_9

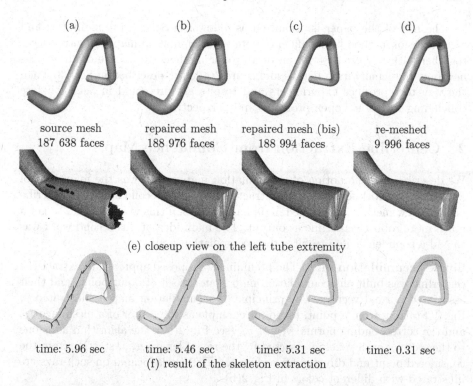

(a) (b) (c) (d)

| source mesh | repaired mesh | repaired mesh (bis) | re-meshed |
| 187 638 faces | 188 976 faces | 188 994 faces | 9 996 faces |

(e) closeup view on the left tube extremity

time: 5.96 sec   time: 5.46 sec   time: 5.31 sec   time: 0.31 sec
(f) result of the skeleton extraction

Fig. 1. Measure of the sensibility of the skeleton extraction method of [17] on data with different qualities: (a) raw data extracted directly from the scanner, (b) repaired mesh with hole closure, (c) mesh (b) + face intersection removal, (d) new re-meshing by keeping 5000 points.

method (in the meaning of Goodman's definition [8]) was demonstrated with its integration in an industrial framework by a company manufacturing tubular shapes for aircraft cabins.

The originality of this new method compared to existing works was already presented in the latter reference [9], and is not the main topic of this paper. Nevertheless we examine the sensibility with respect to input data quality of a recent method [17] publicly available in the $CGAL$ library [1]. Figure 1 displays the different results obtained by running this method respectively on raw mesh scans (column (a)), on mesh repaired by hole closure (column (b)), on mesh (b) repaired by face intersection (column (c)), and finally after a complete re-meshing and keeping a reduced number of faces (column (d)). Such repairing processes were obtained using the *geogram* library [3,4], which proposes a complete set of re-meshing tools based on different methods [11,12,19]. It appears that the quality of output centerlines depends directly of the mesh quality. In particular, for the source mesh (column (a) of Fig. 1), the resulting skeleton appears really noisy. Its quality is then significantly improved with mesh repaired and re-meshed (columns (b) to (d)). We will see in the following that the proposed method is far less sensitive to the quality of the input data, and even does not use their topology.

The rest of the paper is organized as follows: in Sect. 2, the main idea and algorithms of method [9] (confidence vote in accumulation map) are introduced, together with a short description of a former method [10] at the origin of this new one. Implementation details and source code are described in Sect. 3. Then the way to reproduce experiments and results are presented in Sect. 4 before concluding with some open problems and perspectives.

2   Centerline Extraction from Confidence Map

We describe first the notion of accumulation map, which was the main idea of a preliminary work for centerline extraction [10]. In a second stage, we describe how the new method introduced in [9] has built upon this work in order to get a much more robust centerline as output. The main idea of this second work was to add a confidence vote to filter the accumulation map.

Single accumulation map. The preliminary proposed approach to extract the centerline was built an accumulation map from the set of input points and their associated normal vectors. The principle of accumulation map is illustrated in Fig. 2. Starting from a point, taken for example as the center of a mesh face f_k, and the corresponding normal vector $\overrightarrow{n_k}$ (see Fig. 2(a)), the algorithm adds one to the score of each voxel intersected by the ray of length d_{acc}, starting from the considered point and directed toward vector $\overrightarrow{n_k}$. Voxels located on such rays are illustrated with different colors in Fig. 2(b).

From the resulting accumulation map (see Fig. 2(c)), the centerline points are tracked by moving from the peaks of this map in the direction orthogonal to intersecting rays. This approach is robust enough to handle a simple shape without branching. The algorithm was successfully exploited and reproduced in a concrete application dealing with the detection of wood trunk defects [13]. However such an application is not adapted to deal with a branched centerline.

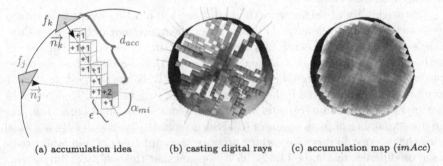

(a) accumulation idea   (b) casting digital rays   (c) accumulation map ($imAcc$)

Fig. 2. Main steps of the preliminary approach [10]. The image (a) shows how digital rays are casted from input data to define the accumulation map. The voxels intersected by the same ray are displayed in the same color on image (b). The resulting accumulation map, stored as an image, is illustrated in image (c), where the red (resp. blue) color corresponds to a high (resp. low) accumulation. (Color figure online)

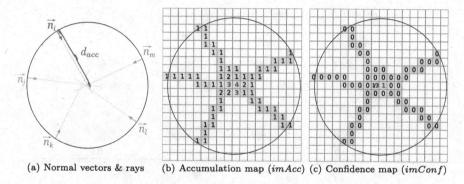

(a) Normal vectors & rays   (b) Accumulation map (*imAcc*) (c) Confidence map (*imConf*)

Fig. 3. Construction of the confidence map from the accumulation map. (Color figure online)

Therefore a new notion of confidence in the accumulation value was proposed to extend the centerline detection method to branched tubular objects.

Notion of confidence in accumulation. The centerline extraction was significantly improved by adding a confidence value in the vote that represent the accumulation scores [9]. The main idea is to define a confidence map (*imConf*), which is deduced from the accumulation map (*imAcc*) with a maximality principle. More precisely, let v be a voxel and let v_{acc} be the number of rays traversing it, then v_{max} is defined as the number of rays passing trough v and for which v_{acc} is a strict maximum value along the whole ray. Figure 3(b) illustrates this maximality principle where red values are maximal accumulation values for at least one ray. Then, from these v_{max} values, the confidence value v_{conf} is simply defined as the ratio between values v_{max} and v_{acc}:

$$v_{conf} = \frac{v_{max}}{v_{acc}}$$

As illustrated in Fig. 3, the confidence scores appear to be more concentrated near the center of the circular shape than the accumulation map scores. Such quality was already analyzed in a previous work by computing the number of connected components resulting of different confidence/accumulation thresholds (see Fig. 5 in [9]). These analysis were obtained on a single class of shapes. The analysis Fig. 4 complete it on meshes with various quality levels. The better behavior of the confidence map with respect to the sole accumulation map is also well visible: even if we consider partial data, voxels located near the center of the shape are well identified in the confidence map even for very different thresholds, while this is not the case for the accumulation map. The measures can be reproduced from the `compAccFromMesh` program (see Sect. 3) and for instance the experiments presented in Fig. 4(a) are obtained with the command lines in Code 1.1 (and by using the minimum threshold parameter (`-m 25`)).

120   B. Kerautret et al.

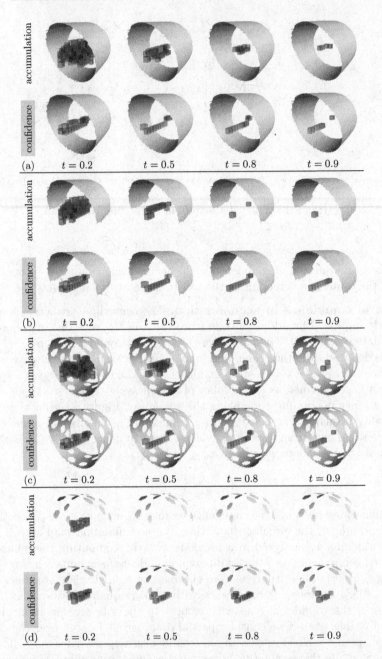

Fig. 4. Experimental comparisons of sensitivity to thresholding between the accumulation map and the confidence map. Thresholds were set between 0 (min accumulation/confidence value) and 1 (max accumulation/confidence value) on all meshes. Note that the parameter t for the accumulation was rescaled according the the maximal value of accumulation. The same maximal radius parameters $R = 7$ was used in all experiments.

Code 1.1. Command lines to compute and display the confidence map, used to generate the experiments presented in the second line in Fig. 4(a). Replace `confidence.longvol` by `accumulation.longvol` to obtain the accumulation map computed at the first line.

```
$ ./bin/compAccFromMesh -i ../SamplesIllustration/sectionATube1.off -r 7
$ longvol2vol -i confidence.longvol -o confidence.vol
$ 3dImageViewer -i confidence.vol -m 25 -M 255 -t 120 \
                --displayMesh ../SamplesIllustration/sectionATube1.off \
                --colorMesh 127 127 127 100
```

All detailed algorithms are given in the appendix: the global process (Algorithm 1) computes the accumulation map with (Algorithm 2) before using it as an input parameter in the algorithm computing the confidence map (Algorithm 3).

Centerline extraction from confidence map.
Since the confidence map locates centerline points in a more accurate and stable way, the former centerline extraction algorithm from [10] can be redefined to handle branchings. In particular, as illustrated in side Fig. 5, a simple threshold on the confidence map gives a set of voxels that is almost a connected path. A geodesic-based graph extraction was proposed in [9] to track it and is detailed in Algorithm 4. This algorithm consists in first applying a dilation on the thresholded confidence map before tracking center points according to a the geodesic distance map of $imConf$, computed from an initial point P_{init}. The geodesic map is divided in a set regions corresponding to connected components at a specific geodesic distance from P_{init}, then a representative point of each region is selected and the graph is reconstructed by linking the representative points of connected regions.

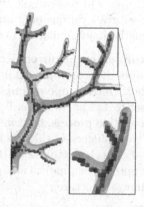

Fig. 5. Points resulting from a thresholding on confidence map.

Following this overview of the proposed method, the next section details the implementation of the different algorithms and describes the potential influence of the different parameters.

3   Implementation Description

The source code of the proposed implementation is available on Github:

https://github.com/kerautret/CDCVAM

The proposed implementation is written in C++ and is based on the *DGtal* library [2]. The algorithms computing accumulation and confidence maps can easily be implemented in another language. The only part of *DGtal* specifically exploited concerns the geodesic graph extraction method, which uses DGtal implementation of the Fast Marching Method [16]. This algorithm is used in Algorithm 4 both to compute the dilation and the geodesic images. Of course other strategies to reconstruct the graph can be defined like for instance the use of a metric graph algorithm [7]. Moreover, the implementation only deals with meshes as input but the first step consists to extract the point list and the normal vector field. It is really easy to create another wrappers allowing to deal with other entries without changing the core functions.

Sources organization. The main algorithms are implemented in the *src* directory, and organized into classes: the classes `NormalAccumulator` and `Geodesic-GraphComputer` implement respectively Algorithms 2 and 4. This directory also contains helper classes and functions with different purposes: adaptation of input data to accumulation map and confidence map algorithms (`Accumu-latorHelper`), optimization of the center line position (`CenterLineHelper`) as described in [10]. The main programs used for experiments are located in the *bin* directory (like the program of Code 1.1). Other programs which generate the figures and plots of [9] are also given in this directory. Finally the *tests* directory gives various programs to display and control the main key features of our method: accumulation map, confidence map, geodesic graph extraction.

Implementation choices. For the accumulation map algorithm, we chose to store the scores in a 3D image with bounds corresponding to the mesh bounding box. In the proposed implementation the choice of the grid size is automatically set to 1. The mesh can be scaled in order to have enough precision in the accumulation process, by using for instance the mean distance between input points. The influence of the grid size parameter is experimented in the next section.

The choice to use a 3D image is a first handy solution. For large shapes, this approach can induce a large memory cost. It should then be adapted to another image structure.

Handling other types of data. In the previous work [9] the experiments were exclusively defined on partial mesh scans. However since the proposed method takes as input only a set of points with normal vectors, it can process other types of data like set of points, digital objects and height maps. To process these other types of data one has only to estimate the normal vector at each point and then import these data in the main program `GeodesicGraphComputer`.

It is also useful to provide tools for processing shapes presenting long rectangular faces like in the image on the side. Such meshes are typically built by geometric modeling software when modeling tubular shapes. In this case, the centerline graph extraction  algorithm outputs a disconnected set of voxels. We thus adapt this algorithm by exploiting clusters of confident voxels and by using the main local direction estimated from the voting vectors (note that accumulation and confidence map algorithms remain the same). This case can however be adapted by exploiting clusters of confident voxels and by using the main local direction estimated from the voting vectors. The floating figure on the side illustrates the result that we obtain when using Code 1.1 with this particular type of mesh. All the voxels identifying a common tubular section are well detected and can be exploited for the reconstruction.

Optimizations not described in the algorithms. The proposed implementation of Algorithm 4 contains some optimizations which are not described in this paper for sake of clarity. In particular connected components are obtained with an union-find algorithm during the FMM extension. More details are given in the source files *GeodesicGraphComputer(.h/.cpp)*.

4   Reproducing the Results and Influence of Parameters

The reproduction of the results is straightforward from the programs provided in the *bin* directory of the *GitHub* repository. Results can be inspected with the visualisation tools coming from the *DGtal* companion repositories (*DGtalTools* [5] and *DGtalTools-Contrib* [6]). All command line tools provide a full description of their options. For instance, Code 1.2 shows a typical usage for centerline extraction, which builds the result displayed in Fig. 6.

Fig. 6.   Result obtained with Code 1.2.

Code 1.2. Command lines to extract and display the centerline of a given shape.

```
$ ./bin/centerLineGeodesicGraph -i ../Samples/tube3.off -R 6   -g 6
$ graphViewer -v resultVertex.sdp -e resultEdges.sdp \
                -m ../Samples/tube3.off --meshColor 250 100 100 25 -b 2
```

In order to integrate the proposed method in other frameworks you can use the code snippet given in Code 1.3. It shows how to compute the centerline of an arbitrary mesh stored as an OFF file. The computation itself is done in two main stages: (i) computation of the accumulation and confidence maps, (ii) threshold on the confidence map followed by graph reconstruction. Note that by importing normal vectors, you can adapt these code sample to process voxels or point clouds. For instance the tool *compAccFromSDP* extracts the centerline of a point cloud and uses the PCL library [14] to estimate normal vectors.

Code 1.3. Compute the centerline of a mesh given as the OFF file "example.off".

```
// Preliminary: read input off file:
DGtal::Mesh<P3d> aMesh; aMesh <<"example.off";

// Step i): compute the accumulation and confidence (with dacc=7)
NormalAccumulator acc(7);
acc.initFromMesh(aMesh);
acc.computeAccumulation();
acc.computeConfidence();
Image3Dd imConf = acc.getConfidenceImage();

// Step ii): apply the centerline extraction from confidence map.
GeodesicGraphComputer::TSet aConfidenceSet(imConf.domain());
// ii. a)  Thresholding the confidence map:
for (auto const &p: imConf.domain())
    if(imConf(p)>= 0.5)
        aConfidenceSet.insert(p);
P3d p0 = acc.getMaxAccumulationPoint();
// ii. b) Computing the graph:
GeodesicGraphComputer gg(4, aConfidenceSet, 3,  acc.getDomain(), p0);
gg.computeGraphFromGeodesic();
```

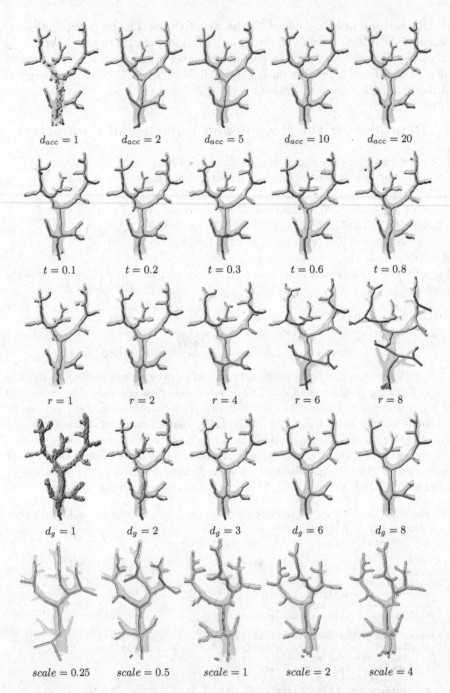

$d_{acc} = 1$ $d_{acc} = 2$ $d_{acc} = 5$ $d_{acc} = 10$ $d_{acc} = 20$

$t = 0.1$ $t = 0.2$ $t = 0.3$ $t = 0.6$ $t = 0.8$

$r = 1$ $r = 2$ $r = 4$ $r = 6$ $r = 8$

$d_g = 1$ $d_g = 2$ $d_g = 3$ $d_g = 6$ $d_g = 8$

$scale = 0.25$ $scale = 0.5$ $scale = 1$ $scale = 2$ $scale = 4$

Fig. 7. Influence of parameters when extracting the centerline of *playmobil* tree. For all experiments (expect for the scale) the other parameters were set to their default values ($d_g = 3$, $r = 2$, $t = 0.5$, $d_{acc} = 6$). For the scale parameter experiment, default parameters were scaled accordingly.

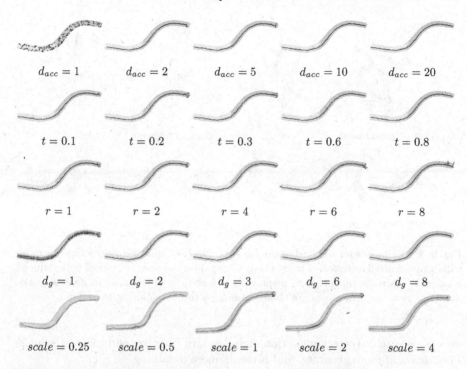

$d_{acc} = 1$ $d_{acc} = 2$ $d_{acc} = 5$ $d_{acc} = 10$ $d_{acc} = 20$

$t = 0.1$ $t = 0.2$ $t = 0.3$ $t = 0.6$ $t = 0.8$

$r = 1$ $r = 2$ $r = 4$ $r = 6$ $r = 8$

$d_g = 1$ $d_g = 2$ $d_g = 3$ $d_g = 6$ $d_g = 8$

$scale = 0.25$ $scale = 0.5$ $scale = 1$ $scale = 2$ $scale = 4$

Fig. 8. Influence of parameters when extracting the centerline of a tube shape. For all experiments (expect for the scale) the other parameters were set to their default values ($d_g = 3$, $r = 2$, $t = 0.5$, $d_{acc} = 6$). For the scale parameter experiment, default parameters were scaled accordingly.

Influence of Parameters. The proposed method is tuned by several parameters which can be set according to properties of the shape under study. The first stage of the algorithm has two parameters: the maximal distance of accumulation (d_{acc}) and the threshold on the confidence score (t). As illustrated in Figs. 7 and 8, the method is not very sensitive to these two parameters and they can be chosen arbitrarily in a wide range of values. Significant changes are only visible in the output if we choose a too small distance of accumulation ($d_{acc} = 1$) or a too high threshold on confidence map ($t = 0.8$). The latter disconnects some branches of the *playmobil* tree. A rule of the thumb is to choose for parameter d_{acc} a value greater than the maximal possible radius, and to set $t = 0.5$.

In the same way the parameters of the second stage of the algorithm, which are the dilatation radius (d_r) and the geodesic step distance (d_g) have not a significant influence (if we omit extremal values). Finally, we have measured the effect of a scale change in the input mesh (equivalent to change the grid resolution during the accumulation process, i.e. to reduce the input point density). As expected, increasing the scale makes the computation time longer (with the

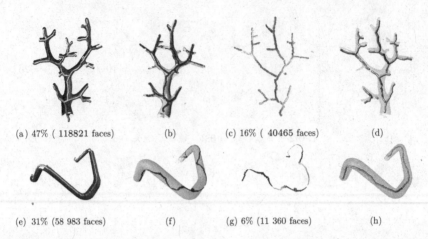

(a) 47% (118821 faces)   (b)   (c) 16% (40465 faces)   (d)

(e) 31% (58 983 faces)   (f)   (g) 6% (11 360 faces)   (h)

Fig. 9. Experiments on reduced scans by applying the centerline extraction on mesh with a very limited selection of faces. Images (a,e) show the result obtained with reduced scan parts (in red). Images (b,f) display the selected faces (isolated in images (c,g)), and the extracted centerlines are shown in images (d,h). (Color figure online)

increase of size of the accumulation digital space) but the resulting centerline is smoother and more accurate, and presents more details.

Robustness to missing parts in mesh scans. To conclude this section, the sensitivity to partial data in meshes was tested. Even if experiments of partial scans of real objects were given in the previous publication, we measure here extreme cases for the method with a major removal of information: first on a partial scan obtained by filtering the normal direction (see Fig. 9(a to d)), and second on a thin portion of the original mesh to measure the limitations of the method (see Fig. 9(e to h)). In both cases, the confidence map is remarkably stable, and the algorithm is able to approach the centerline located inside the original shape, with a slight loss in accuracy in the second experiment. Note that the optimization process was not included here but it could potentially significantly increase the quality of the result.

5   Conclusion and Discussions

We have presented in full details a method for centerline extraction from meshes. Algorithms, code organization, tools and dependencies were described, and the complete source code is available online. Reproducibility was demonstrated with complementary experiments, and a particular attention was devoted to the sensibity of the method to parameter tuning. The method was presented here only on triangulated mesh data type, but the method can easily be tailored to other data types (like point clouds or digitized objects) from the provided source codes. The extension of the confidence map method to process volumetric grayscale images is a future challenging task and would have many applications in the medical imaging domain, with for instance the extraction of 3d vascular vessels or bronchial trees.

A   Appendix

In this section we present in details the different algorithms that were mentioned in the method description. These algorithms were implemented almost as is in our C++ code. They are already proposed in another manner in the paper [9].

Algorithm 1. Global process that computes the normal vector accumulation image $imAcc$ and the corresponding confidence image $imConf$ from an input set of points and the corresponding normal filed.

---

procedure GLOBALPROCESS

Input

  List<Point3D> sp ▷ List of surface points

  List<Vector3D> nv ▷ Normal vectors of sp

  Int d_{acc} ▷ Accumulation distance

  Double r ▷ Morphological dilatation radius

  Double d_{geo} ▷ Geodesic step distance

  Double t_{conf} ▷ Threshold on imConf, in $[0, 1]$

Output

  Graph $graph$ ▷ Resulting centerline

Begin

  Image3D<Int> $imAcc = $ COMPUTEACC(sp, nv, d)   ▷ Accumulation image

  Image3D<Double> $imConf = $ COMPUTECONF($sp, nv, imAcc, d_{acc}$)

                  ▷ Confidence image

  Image3D<Double> $imConf_T = $ THRESHOLD($imConf, t_{conf}$)

  $graph = $ COMPUTEGRAPH($imAcc, imConf_T, r, d_{geo}$)

  return $graph$

End

Algorithm 2. Compute the accumulation image $imAcc$ from a normal vector field nv with an accumulation distance d.

```
procedure COMPUTEACC
Input
    List<Point3D> sp                                    ▷ Surface points
    List<Vector3D> nv                                   ▷ Normal vectors
    Int d_acc                                           ▷ Accumulation distance
Output
    Image3D<Int> imAcc                                  ▷ Accumulation image
Begin
    for  i : 0 → nv.size()−1 do
        Vector 3D norm = nv[i]
        Point3D orig = sp[i]
        Point3D pos = orig
        while  orig.distanceTo(pos) < d_acc do
            imAcc(pos)++
            pos.translate(norm)
    return imAcc
End
```

Algorithm 3. Compute the confidence map $imConf$ for each accumulation value of $imAcc$ from each normal vector of nv contributing to this accumulation value.

```
1: procedure COMPUTECONF
2: Input
3:     List<Point3D> sp                                ▷ Surface points
4:     List<Vector3D> nv                               ▷ Normal vectors
5:     Image3D<Int> imAcc                              ▷ Accumulation map
6:     Int d_acc                                       ▷ Accumulation distance
7: Output
8:     Image3D<Double> imConf                          ▷ Confidence map
9: Begin
10:    for  i : 0 → nv.size() - 1 do
11:        Vector3D norm = nv[i]
12:        Point3D orig, pos, maxPos = sp[i]
13:        Int maxAcc = 0
14:        while  orig.distanceTo(pos) < d_acc  do
15:            if  imAcc(pos) > maxAcc then
16:                maxAcc = imAcc(pos)
17:                maxPos = pos
18:            pos.translate(norm)
19:        imConf(maxPos)++
20:    for all  pos ∈ imConf.domain()  do
21:        imConf(pos) = imConf(pos) ÷ imAcc(pos)
22:    return imConf
23: End
```

Algorithm 4. Compute the geodesic graph from an accumulation map $imAcc$ and a thresholded confidence map $imConf_T$.

---

procedure COMPUTEGRAPH
Input
    Image3D<Int> $imAcc$ ▷ Accumulation map
    Image3D<Double> $imConf_T$ ▷ Thresholded confidence map
    Double r ▷ Dilatation radius
    Double d_{geo} ▷ Geodesic step distance
Output
    Graph $graph$ ▷ Resulting graph
Begin
    Image3D<Bool> $imConf_B$ = binarize($imConf_T$,0)
    Image3D<Bool> $imConf_D$ = dilate($imConf_B$,r)
    Point3D P_{init} = maximumCoordinates($imAcc$)
    Image3D<Double> $imGeo$ = geodesicDistanceTransform($imConf_D$,P_{init})
    Map<Int,Vector<Point3D>> $regions$ ▷ Geodesic regions
    for all $pos \in imGeo$.domain() **do**
        $regions[floor(imGeo(pos)/d_{geo})]$.push(pos)
    Map<Int,List<Vector<Point3D>>> $regionCCs$ ▷ Connected components
    for all $key, region \in regions$ **do**
        List<Vector<Point3D>> CCs = splitIntoCCs($region$)
        $regionCCs[key]$.push(CCs)
    for all $key, CCList \in regionCCs$ **do**   ▷ Graph building
        for all $CC \in CCList$ **do**
            Point3D $bary$ = barycenter(CC)
            $graph$.addVertex($bary$)
            for all $childCC \in regionCC[key+1]$ **do** ▷ key+1 repr. the next region
                if areConnected(CC,$childCC$) **then**
                    $graph$.addEdge($bary$, barycenter($childCC$))
    return $graph$
End

References

1. CGal: release 4.8. http://www.cgal.org
2. DGtal: digital Geometry tools and algorithms library. http://dgtal.org
3. Geogram: release 1.0.0. http://alice.loria.fr/software/geogram/doc/html/index.html
4. Geogram vorpaview: online demonstration. http://webloria.loria.fr/levy/GEOGRAM/vorpaview.html
5. Dgtaltools: companion repository of DGtal library (2016). https://github.com/DGtal-team/DGtalTools
6. Dgtaltools-contrib: companion repository of DGtal library (2016). https://github.com/DGtal-team/DGtalTools-contrib
7. Aanjaneya, M., Chazal, F., Chen, D., Glisse, M., Guibas, L., Morozov, D.: Metric graph reconstruction fron noisy data. Int. J. Comput. Geom. Appl. **22**(04), 305–325 (2012). http://www.worldscientific.com/doi/abs/10.1142/S0218195912600072

8. Goodman, S.N., Fanelli, D., Ioannidis, J.P.: What does research reproducibility mean? Sci. Transl. Med. **8**(341), 341ps12 (2016). http://stm.sciencemag.org/content/8/341/341ps12

9. Kerautret, B., Krahenbül, A., Debled Rennesson, I., Lachaud, J.O.: Centerline detection on partial mesh scans by confidence vote in accumulation map. In: The proceedings of ICPR 2016 (2016, to appear)

10. Kerautret, B., Krähenbühl, A., Debled-Rennesson, I., Lachaud, J.-O.: 3D geometric analysis of tubular objects based on surface normal accumulation. In: Murino, V., Puppo, E. (eds.) ICIAP 2015. LNCS, vol. 9279, pp. 319–331. Springer, Cham (2015). doi:10.1007/978-3-319-23231-7_29

11. Liu, Y., Wang, W., Lévy, B., Sun, F., Yan, D.M., Lu, L., Yang, C.: On centroidal voronoi tessellation - energy smoothness and fast computation. ACM Trans. Graph. **28**(4), 32 (2009). Article No. 101, Presented at SIGGRAPH 2010

12. Lévy, B., Bonneel, N.: Variational anisotropic surface meshing with voronoi parallel linear enumeration. In: Jiao, X., Weill, J.C. (eds.) Proceedings of the 21st International Meshing Roundtable, pp. 349–366. Springer, Heidelberg (2012)

13. Nguyen, V.T., Kerautret, B., Debled Rennesson, I., Colin, F., Piboule, A., Constant, T.: Segmentation of defects on log surface from terrestrial Lidar data. In: soumis à ICPR 2016 (2016)

14. Rusu, R.B., Cousins, S.: 3D is here: point cloud library (PCL). In: IEEE International Conference on Robotics and Automation (ICRA), Shanghai, China, 9–13 May 2011

15. Saha, P.K., Borgefors, G., di Baja, G.S.: A survey on skeletonization algorithms and their applications. Pattern Recogn. Lett. **76**, 3–12 (2016)

16. Sethian, J.A.: Fast marching methods. SIAM Rev. **41**(2), 199–235 (1999). http://epubs.siam.org/doi/abs/10.1137/S0036144598347059

17. Tagliasacchi, A., Alhashim, I., Olson, M., Zhang, H.: Mean curvature skeletons. Comp. Graph. Forum **31**(5), 1735–1744 (2012). http://dx.doi.org/10.1111/j.1467-8659.2012.03178.x

18. Tagliasacchi, A., Delamé, T., Spagnuolo, M., Amenta, N., Telea, A.: 3D skeletons: a state-of-the-art report. Comput. Graph. Forum **35**(2), 573–597 (2016)

19. Yan, D., Lévy, B., Liu, Y., Sun, F., Wang, W.: Isotropic remeshing with fast and exact computation of restricted voronoi diagram. In: ACM/EG Symposium on Geometry Processing/Computer Graphics Forum (2009)

An Algorithm to Decompose
Noisy Digital Contours

Phuc Ngo[1,2]([⊠]), Hayat Nasser[1,2], Isabelle Debled-Rennesson[1,2],
and Bertrand Kerautret[1,2]

[1] Université de Lorraine, LORIA, UMR 7503, 54506 Vandoeuvre-lès-Nancy, France
[2] CNRS, LORIA, UMR 7503, 54506 Vandoeuvre-lès-Nancy, France
{hoai-diem-phuc.ngo,hayat.nasser,
isabelle.debled-rennesson,bertrand.kerautret}@loria.fr

Abstract. From the previous digital contour decomposition algorithm, this paper focuses on the implementation and on the reproduction of the method linking to an online demonstration. This paper also gives improvement of the previous method with details on the intern parameter choice and shows how to use the C++ source code in other context.

Keywords: Digital contours representation · Image vectorisation · Discrete geometry

1 Introduction

The representation of a digital contour is a key point for the quality of image vectorisation algorithms. Such algorithms are mainly exploited in commercial or open source softwares such as *Adobe Illustrator* or *Inskape* when importing a bipmap image and converting it into a vectorized format like *postscrip* or *svg*. The quality of the resulting vectorisation depends on the contour geometry which is mostly related to the choice of geometric primitive types (segments, arcs or others). It also depends on the presence of noise which can degrade the quality of the resulting image in terms of primitive number or from visual quality point of view. Furthermore, the potential noise presence and the setting of user parameter can as well influence the result quality.

In this work, we focus on the contour representation based on two types of primitive which are arcs and segments by taking into account locally the potential noise presence in digital contours. A special attention is given on the implementation and reproduction of the proposed algorithm which was presented in previous work [12] with some new improvements.

In the following section we recall the main decomposition algorithm with its prerequisite notions before describing how to reproduce results (Sect. 3). The experiments and details are given in Sect. 4.

© Springer International Publishing AG 2017
B. Kerautret et al. (Eds.): RRPR 2016, LNCS 10214, pp. 131–149, 2017.
DOI: 10.1007/978-3-319-56414-2_10

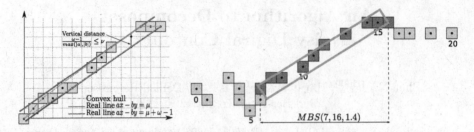

Fig. 1. Example of (left) blurred segment (greys points) and (right) maximal blurred segment (green points). (Color figure online)

2   Decomposition Algorithm [12,14]

2.1   Prerequisite

Maximal Blurred Segment. The notion of blurred segment is introduced in [3] as an extension of arithmetical discrete line [18] with a width parameter ν for noisy or disconnected digital contours. This notion is defined as follows.

Definition 1. *A sequence of points S_f is a blurred segment of width ν iff*

- $\forall (x,y) \in S_f$, $\mu \le ax - by < \mu + \omega$ where $a, b, \mu, \omega \in \mathbb{Z}$ and $gcd(a,b) = 1$, and
- *the vertical (or horizontal) distance $d = \frac{\omega - 1}{\max(|a|,|b|)}$ equals to the vertical (or horizontal) thickness of the convex hull of S_f, and*
- $d \le \nu$.

Given a discrete curve C, let $C_{i,j}$ be the sequence of points indexed from i to j in C. We denote the predicate "$C_{i,j}$ is a blurred segment of width ν" as $BS(i,j,\nu)$. Then, C_{ij} is said to be *maximal* if it can not be extended (i.e. no point added) on the left nor on the right, and noted by $MBS(i,j,\nu)$. Illustration of blurred segment and maximal blurred segment are given in Fig. 1.

The sequence of the maximal blurred segments of width ν along a curve is called *width ν tangential cover* (see Fig. 2(a)). This structure is used in numerous discrete geometric estimators such as length, tangent, curvature estimators ... (see [10] for a state of the art). In [14], an extension of width ν tangential cover, namely *adaptive tangential cover (ATC)*, is proposed to handle with noisy curves. In particular, ATC is composed of MSB of different width values deduced from the noise estimation of *meaningful thickness* [9] in which two parameters are set: (1) sampling step size –namely, **samplingStep**– and (2) maximal thickness –namely, **maxScale**– for which the shape is analysed for the meaningful thickness (see [9] for more details). Examples of ATC are given in Figs. 2(b) and 3. Still in [14], an algorithm is proposed to compute the ATC of discrete noisy curves.

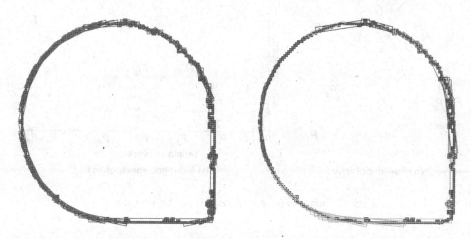

Fig. 2. Examples of (left) width ν tangential cover with $\nu = 2$ and (right) adaptive tangential cover (ATC) with different widths transmitted from meaningful thickness detection.

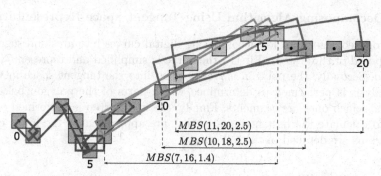

Fig. 3. Example of adaptive tangential cover (ATC) with three width values $\nu = 1, 1.4$ and 2.5 (in blue, green and red respectively). Considering the last three MBS of the ATC, in yellow are points in the common zone, and in orange are its two endpoints. (Color figure online)

Tangent Space Representation. This notion is presented in [1,11] as a tool for shape characterization and comparing polygonal shapes.

Definition 2. *Let* $P = \{P_i\}_{i=0}^m$ *be a polygon,* l_i *length of segment* P_iP_{i+1} *and* $\alpha_i = \angle(\overrightarrow{P_{i-1}P_i}, \overrightarrow{P_iP_{i+1}})$ *such that* $\alpha_i > 0$ *if* P_{i+1} *is on the right side of* $\overrightarrow{P_{i-1}P_i}$ *and* $\alpha_i < 0$ *otherwise. A tangent space representation* $T(P)$ *of* P *is a step function which is constituted of segments* $T_{i2}T_{(i+1)1}$ *and* $T_{(i+1)1}T_{(i+1)2}$ *for* $0 \le i < m$ *with*

- $T_{02} = (0, 0)$,
- $T_{i1} = (T_{(i-1)2}.x + l_{i-1}, T_{(i-1)2}.y)$ *for* $1 \le i \le m$,
- $T_{i2} = (T_{i1}.x, T_{i1}.y + \alpha_i)$, $1 \le i \le (m - 1)$.

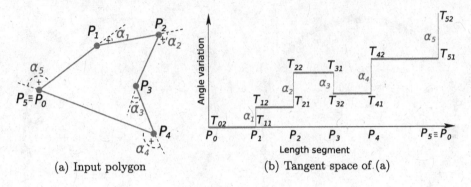

(a) Input polygon   (b) Tangent space of (a)

Fig. 4. Tangent space representation of a polygon.

Roughly speaking, the tangent space of a polygon is the representation of exterior angles versus segment lengths of the polygon as illustrated in Fig. 4.

2.2   Decomposing Algorithm Using Tangent Space Representation

The proposed algorithm for decomposing digital curves into arcs and segments is composed of three steps. Firstly, the curve is simplified and represented by a polygon. Secondly, the polygon is transformed into the tangent space in which the analysis is performed to determined which parts of the polygon belong to arcs and which ones are segments. Finally, the fitting step is performed on arc parts to calculate the best fitting arcs that are approximated the input curve. These steps are detailed in the following.

Polygonal Simplification. This step consists in finding the characteristic points, namely *dominant points*, to form a polygon approximating/representing the given discrete curve. This step, called *polygonal simplification*, allows to use only the characteristic points, instead of all points of the curve, for the decomposition into arcs and segments using the tangent space.

Issued from the dominant point detection method proposed in [13,17], an algorithm is presented in [14] to determine the characteristic points of noisy curves using ATC notion. The idea is that the candidates of dominant point are localized in common zone of successive MBS of the ATC of the given curve, and such common zone can be easily found by checking the starting and ending indices of MBS (see Fig. 3). Then, dominant point in each common zone is the point having the smallest curvature which is estimated as the angle between the point and the left and right endpoints of the left and right MBS constituting in the common zone, as illustrated in Fig. 5.

Due to the nature of ATC, common zones detected are mostly over-much and stay very near. As a consequence, the obtained dominant points in common zones are sometimes redundant which is presumably undesirable for polygonal simplification and in particular for curve decomposition algorithm. Therefore,

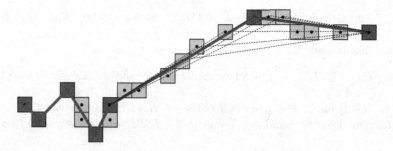

Fig. 5. Dominant points are detected as point having the smallest angle measure w.r.t. the two end points. Dominant points of the curve are depicted in red, and the common zone in Fig. 3 is depicted yellow. (Color figure online)

Algorithm 1. Dominant point detection

Input: $C = (C_i)_{0 \leq i \leq n-1}$ discrete curve of n points
Output: D set of dominant points
1   $ATC(C) = \{MBS(B_j, E_j, .)\}_{j=0}^{m-1}$ adaptive tangential cover of C
    /* Detection of dominant points in common zones   */
2   $q = 0; p = 1; D = \emptyset$
3   **while** $p < m$ **do**
4      $D = D \cup \{min_{i \in [\![B_{p-1}, E_q]\!]} Angle(C_{B_q}, C_i, C_{E_{p-1}})\}$
5      $q = p - 1$

    /* Optimization process to get significant dominant points   */
6   $F = FOM_2(D)$
7   **repeat**
8      $\widehat{F} = F$
9      $D = D \setminus \{min_{p \in D} Weight(p)\}$
10     $F = FOM_2(D)$
    until $F < \widehat{F}$;

---

we propose an optimization process to eliminate certain dominant points to achieve a high compression of the approximated polygon while preserving the principle angular deviation of the input curve. More precisely, each detected dominant point is associated to a weight describing its importance w.r.t. the approximating polygon of the curve. This weight is computed as the ratio of ISSE[1] and angle with the two dominant point neighbours; $ISSE/angle$ [13]. Then, the optimization process removes one by one the dominant points of small

---

[1] Integral sum of square errors is calculated by $ISSE = \sum_{i=1}^{n} d_i^2$, where d_i is distance from i-th curve point to approximating polygon. The smaller ISSE, the better description of the shape by the approximating polygon.

weight until reaching the maximum FOM_2[2] criterion [19,20]. The algorithm is given in Algorithm 1.

The following auxiliary functions are used in Algorithm 1:

- $Angle(C_{B_q}, C_i, C_{E_{p-1}})$ (Line 3) calculates the angle between three points C_{B_q}, C_i and $C_{E_{p-1}}$
- $FOM_2(D)$ (Line 5, 9) calculates $FOM_2 = CR^2/ISSE$ of the set D
- $Weight(p)$ (Line 8) calculates the $weight = ISSE/angle$ associated to p

Tangent Space Analysis. In [15,16], the following result is obtained for the tangent space representation of a set of sequential chords are proposed.

Proposition 1. *Let* $P = \{P_i\}_{i=0}^m$ *be a polygon,* $l_i = | \overrightarrow{P_iP_{i+1}} |$, $\alpha_i = \angle(\overrightarrow{P_{i-1}P_i}, \overrightarrow{P_iP_{i+1}})$ *such that* $\alpha_i \leqslant \alpha \leqslant \frac{\pi}{4}$ *for* $0 \leq i < n$. *Let* $T(P)$ *be the tangent space representation of* P *and* $T(P)$ *constitutes of segments* $T_{i2}T_{(i+1)1}, T_{(i+1)1}T_{(i+1)2}$ *for* $0 \leq i < m$, $M = \{M_i\}_{i=0}^{m-1}$ *the midpoint set of* $\{T_{i2}T_{(i+1)1}\}_{i=0}^{m-1}$. *P is a polygon whose vertices are on a real arc only if the set* M *belongs to a small width strip bounded by two real parallel lines, namely quasi collinear points (see Fig. 6).*

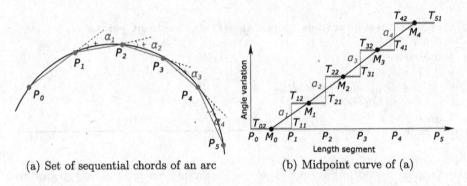

(a) Set of sequential chords of an arc   (b) Midpoint curve of (a)

Fig. 6. Tangent space and the curve of midpoints of a set of sequential chords. If the midpoints is *quasi collinear*, then the initial points belong to a circular arc [15,16].

Therefore, the arc detection of P becomes the problem of verifying the quasi collinearity of midpoints M in tangent space representation of P. In particular, this can be handled with the algorithm of recognition of MBS of width ν with midpoint curve in the tangent space.

---

[2] Figure of merit 2 is calculated by $FOM_2 = \frac{CR^2}{ISSE}$, where CR is the compression ratio between number of curve points and number of detected dominant points. FOM_2 compromises between the low approximation error and the benefit of high data reduction.

It should be mentioned for quasi collinear midpoints in the tangent space that the more points are recognized in MBS of width ν –namely, **thickness**– the more *surely* arc is estimated. Therefore, to enhance the arc detection using the tangent space, we define a threshold for the number of elements in a set of quasi collinear midpoints –namely, **nbPointCircle**. Then, the set of quasi collinear midpoints is associated to an arc if its cardinality is greater than or equal to the threshold. Moreover, any two points are always collinear, then nbPointCircle ≥ 3.

Still in [15,16], it is observed for non linear midpoints that

- a midpoint is an *isolated point* if it has the difference of ordinate values between it and *one of the two* neighboring midpoints is higher than a threshold α – namely, **alphaMax**– and it corresponds to a junction of two primitives,
- a midpoint is a *full isolated point* if it is isolated with *all two neighbors* and it corresponds to a segment primitive (see Fig. 7).

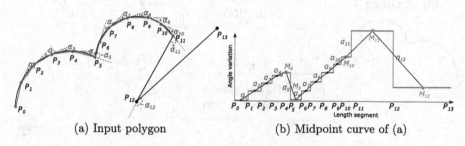

(a) Input polygon   (b) Midpoint curve of (a)

Fig. 7. Classification of midpoints in tangent space. Pink (resp. green) points are isolated points (resp. full isolated points) and correspond to junctions of two primitives (resp. segments), while black points are points of arcs. (Color figure online)

Fitting of Arcs. Proposition 1 allows to determine the sequence of points belonging to an arc. A fitting process is performed to find the most appropriate arc in least square sense. It should be mentioned that for the continuity of the decomposition in between the primitives, we consider the junctions as dominant points. More precisely, let M_i to M_j be quasi-collinear midpoints in the tangent space representation. Let C_{b_i} and C_{e_i} (resp. C_{b_j} and C_{e_j}) be starting and ending dominant points that correspond to the midpoint M_i (resp. M_j). Then, junction points are C_{b_i} and C_{e_j} which are also ending points of the arc. In order to determine an arc for points from C_{b_i} to C_{e_j}, we need at least three points. Due to a high angular deviation near the endpoints of an arc, the fitting arc is performed using least square distance with one point in the central one-third portion of C_{b_i} and C_{e_j}. Such the best fitting arc associated to C_{b_i} and C_{e_j} can be denoted by $Arc(O, R, \beta_b, \beta_e)$, where O is the arc center, and R is the radius with angles go from β_b to β_e (i.e from C_{b_i} to C_{e_j}) which is calculated as follows

$$Arc(O, R, \beta_b, \beta_e) = \min_{k \in [\frac{C_{b_i} + 2C_{e_j}}{3}, \frac{2C_{b_i} + C_{e_j}}{3}]} d^2(C_k, \mathcal{C}_{(C_{b_i}, C_k, C_{e_j})}(O, R)) \quad (1)$$

where $\mathcal{C}_{(C_{b_i},C_k,C_{e_j})}(O,R)$ is the circle passing through three points C_{b_i}, C_k, C_{e_j} and has the center O with radius R, and $d^2(C_k, \mathcal{C}_{(C_{b_i},C_k,C_{e_j})}(O,R))$ is the square distance of the point C_k to the circle $\mathcal{C}_{(C_{b_i},C_k,C_{e_j})}(O,R)$.

Furthermore, in some cases the approximation of a curve part by an arc may not be the optimal solution in particular when the part is quasi flat. Therefore, we propose a threshold of error approximation –namely **isseTol**– of the curve part using an arc and segments. More precisely, the curve part is an arc approximation if the ISSE by the arc is isseTol times smaller than this by segments.

Proposed Algorithm. Algorithm 2 puts all steps together for decomposing a noisy discrete curve into arcs and segments. The algorithm scheme is given in Fig. 8.

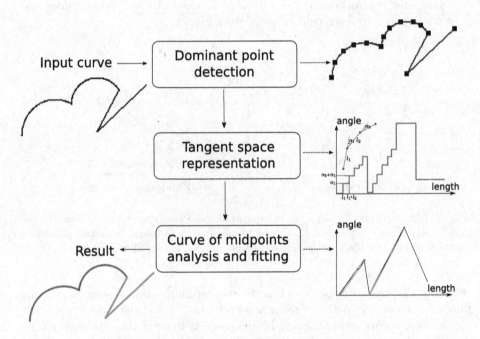

Fig. 8. Flowchart of the proposed algorithm.

Complexity Analysis. In Algorithm 2, Line 1 to detect the dominant points of C using Algorithm 1 is performed in $O(n \log n)$ [14] where n is the number of points of C. Lines 2–3 to transform the dominant points detected into the tangent space and to compute the midpoint curve is in $O(m)$ with $m \ll n$ is the number of dominant points. The loop iterates over the midpoints to find the corresponding segments and arcs (Lines 4–23) is performed in $O(nm)$. More precisely, Lines 6 for verifying admissible angle in the tangent space is done in $O(1)$. Then, Lines 10 for the recognition of MBS of the midpoint curve can be done in $O(m)$ [4]. For finding a segment associated to a part of the curve, Lines 7, 20, 22 are executed in $O(1)$ since the segment is determined by the extremities $C_{b_i}C_{e_i}$. For finding a best-fitting arc associated to $pArc$ of the curve, Lines 14–18

Algorithm 2. Curve Decomposition into Arcs and Segments

Input: $C = (C_i)_{0 \leq i \leq n-1}$ a discrete curve of n points

        thickness width of MBS for collinear test in the tangent space

        alphaMax threshold of admissible angle in the tangent space

        nbCirclePoint threshold of midpoint number belonging to an arc

        isseTol threshold of approximation by an arc or segments

Output: $ARCs$ and $SEGs$ sets of arcs and segments of C

1   $ARCs \leftarrow \emptyset, SEGs \leftarrow \emptyset, pARCs \leftarrow \emptyset, MBS_\nu \leftarrow \emptyset$

2   Detect the dominant point D of C (see Algorithm 1)

3   Transform D into the tangent space $T(D)$ (see Definition 2)

4   Construct the midpoint curve $\{M_i\}_{i=0}^{m-1}$ of $T(D)$ (see Proposition 1)

5   **for** $i \leftarrow 1$ *to* $m - 2$ **do**

6      $C_{b_i}C_{e_i}$ is the part of C corresponding to M_i

7   **if** $(| M_i.y - M_{i-1}.y | > alphaMax) \& (| M_i.y - M_{i+1}.y | > alphaMax)$ **then**

8          $SEGs \leftarrow SEGs \cup \{C_{b_i}C_{e_i}\}$

9          $MBS_\nu \leftarrow \emptyset$

       else

11   **if** $MBS_\nu \cup \{M_i\}$ *is a MBS of thickness* **then**

12             $MBS_\nu \leftarrow MBS_\nu \cup \{M_i\}$

13             $pARC \leftarrow pARC \cup \{C_{b_i}C_{e_i}\}$

         else

15   **if** $| MBS_\nu | \geq nbCirclePoint$ **then**

16                 $C_{b_i}C_{e_j}$ is the part of C corresponding to $pArc$

17                 $Arc(O, R, \beta_b, \beta_e)$ is the best fitting arc for $C_{b_i}C_{e_j}$ (see Eq. 1)

18   **if** $ISSE(C_{b_i}, C_{e_j}, Arc(O, R, \beta_b, \beta_e)) <$

                      $isseTol \sum_{C_{b_i}C_{e_i} | C_{b_i}C_{e_i} \in pARC} ISSE(C_{b_i}, C_{e_i}, \overline{C_{b_i}C_{e_i}})$ **then**

19                    $ARCs \leftarrow ARCs \cup \{Arc(O_i, R_i, \beta_b, \beta_e)\}$

                else

21                    $SEGs \leftarrow SEGs \cup \{C_{b_i}C_{e_i} \mid C_{b_i}C_{e_i} \in pARC\}$

            else

23                 $SEGs \leftarrow SEGs \cup \{C_{b_i}C_{e_i} \mid C_{b_i}C_{e_i} \in pARC\}$

24                 $pARC \leftarrow \emptyset$

---

are executed in $O(| pArc |)$ to compute the fitting error, and $| pArc | = n/3$ in the worst case. Finally, the complexity of the algorithm is $O(n \log n + nm)$.

3   Source Code

3.1   Download and Installation

The algorithm is implemented in C++ using the open source libraries DGtal[3] (Digital Geometry Tools and Algorithms) and ImaGene[4]. It is available at

---

[3] http://dgtal.org.

[4] https://gforge.liris.cnrs.fr/projects/imagene.

the github repository: https://github.com/ngophuc/CurveDecomposition. The installation is done through classical cmake procedure[5] (version $\geq$ 2.8) (see *INSTALLATION.txt* file).

3.2 Description and Usage

In the package of source code, there are:

- **decompositionAlgorithm.h,cpp** contain the proposed algorithm
- **functions.h,cpp** contain the auxiliary functions used in the algorithm

The proposed method (contained in **decompositionAlgorithm.h,cpp** files) is defined from the following functions:

- **adaptiveTangentCoverDecomposition** for computing of ATC of a curve
- **dominantPointDetection** for detecting dominant points (see Algorithm 1)
- **dominantPointSimplification** for reducing the detected dominant points to obtain an optimal representation of the shape (see Algorithm 1)
- **tangentSpaceTransform** for transforming the dominant point into tangent space representation
- **arcSegmentDecomposition** contains the implementation of Algorithm 2
- **drawDecomposition** for drawing the decomposed arcs and segments

The executable file is generated in the **build** directory and named **testContourDecom**.

Input: A sdp file contains the several contours as lists of points:

```
x0 y0 x1 y1 ... xn yn # Points of contour 1
xn+1 yn+1 xn+2 yn+2 ... xm ym # Points of contour 2
```

Such lists of contour points are obtained after a contour extraction from image. Note that there is a new line for the last contour.

Command line from the CODESOURCES/build for running the decomposition algorithm on **contour.sdp** file with *samplingStep* = 1.0, *maxScale* = 10, *alphaMax* = 0.78, *thickness* = 0.2, *nbPointCircle* = 3 and *isseTol* = 4.0 is

```
./testContourDecom -i contour.sdp -d IMAGENEDIRECTORY
--samplingStep 1.0 --maxScale 10 -a 0.78 -t 0.2 -n 3 -s 4.0
```

More details about the options are given in the command line helper.

Output: Several files are generated as output (in svg or eps format)

OutPts.svg	File of input points
ATC.svg	Result of ATC computation
DPnew.svg	Result of dominant point simplification
OnlyArcSeg.svg	Arc and segment decomposition result

---

[5] http://www.cmake.org.

4   Experimental Results

We now present some experiments using Algorithm 2 to decompose discrete curves into arcs and segments. Firstly, we show the decomposition results with noisy data. Secondly, the effects of the results to different sets of input parameters. Finally, some borderline cases are given.

In all experimental results, the arcs and segments are respectively colored in red and green. The contour points are extracted from images using the tool named *img2freeman* from DGtalTools[6] of DGtal library. It should be mentioned that the input of the algorithm is constituted of several sequences of points, thus different extraction methods can be used such as classical Canny contour detection [2] or smooth contour detection [5].

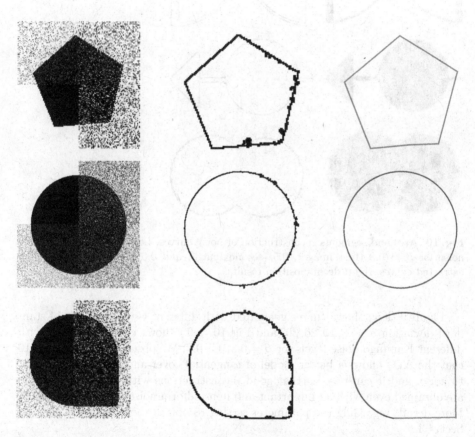

Fig. 9. Arcs and segments reconstruction of noisy curves. Left: input with Gaussian noise, middle: extracted curves, right: decomposition results.

---

[6] http://dgtal.org/tools.

4.1   Experiments on Various Noisy Shapes

We present in this section the decomposition results obtained with various noisy shapes. More precisely, noise is added uniformly in the input images in order to test the robustness of the proposed algorithm towards noise. Two noise models are considered: Gaussian noise and a statistical noise model similar to the Kanungo noise [6], in which the probability P_d of changing the pixel located at a distance d from the shape boundary is defined as $P_d = \beta^d$ with $0 < \beta < 1$.

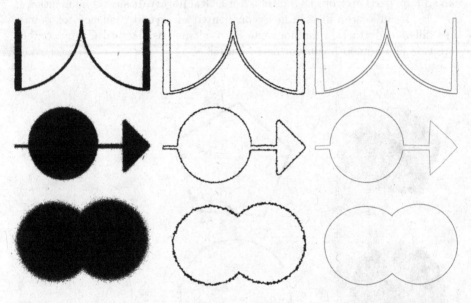

Fig. 10. Arcs and segments reconstruction of noisy curves. Left: input with Kanungo noise for $\beta = 0.3$ (first image), 0.5 (second image) and 0.5 (third image), middle: extracted curves, right: decomposition results.

Figure 9 (left) shows curves generated with different Gaussian noise of standard deviation $\sigma = 0, 10, 20, 30$, and Fig. 10 (left) shows curves obtained with different Kanungo noise levels for $\beta = 0.3, 0.5, 0.7$. We observe in Figs. 9 and 10 that the ATC allows a better model of tangential cover and thus more relevant to noise, and it can be seen that good reconstructions with arcs and segments are obtained even with an important and non-uniform noise on digital contours. More details regarding the parameter setting to obtain these results is given in Sect. 4.3.

4.2 Experiments on Real Images

Experiments are carried out as well on technical and real images. The results in Figs. 11 and 12 are obtained using the default parameters; *i.e.,*

- sampling step of meaningful thickness detection is *samplingStep* = 1
- maximal thickness of meaningful thickness detection is *maxScale* = 15
- admissible angle in the tangent space is $\alpha = \frac{\pi}{4} = 0.785$
- width for the quasi collinear test of MBS is $\nu = 0.2$
- minimum number of midpoints associated to an arc *nbCirclePoint* = 3
- ISSE tolerance between arc and segments approximation *isseTol* = 4

We observe a good reconstruction of the shapes by arcs and segments. It should be mentioned that the results of the decomposition algorithm depend a lot on the extracted curves from images. With the input images in Figs. 11 and 12 (left) a good threshold needs to be chosen to get such results for the decomposition.

Fig. 11. Arcs and segments reconstruction on real images using default parameter setting. Left: input images, middle: extracted curves, right: decomposition results.

Fig. 12. Arcs and segments reconstruction on technical images using default parameter setting. Left: input images, middle: extracted curves, right: decomposition results.

4.3 Effects of Parameter Changes

The decomposition of digital contours into arcs and segments depends on the result of dominant point detected which is changed regarding the values of *maxScale* and particularly *samplingStep*. More precisely, the bigger value of *maxScale*, a smoother dominant point detection is obtained. For examples, *samplingStep* = 0.2 or 0.5, we obtain a number of dominant points much greater than *samplingStep* = 1 or 2 (see Figs. 13 and 14). The other parameters such as *alphaMax*, *thickness*, *isseTol* and *nbPointCircle* control the arc approximation of the input curve. Figure 15 presents some borderline examples of the proposed algorithm in which a non-expected result is obtained for the decomposition of curves into arcs and segments using default parameter values. From Figs. 13 and 15, it can be clearly seen the sensibility of the decomposition w.r.t. to the parameter setting.

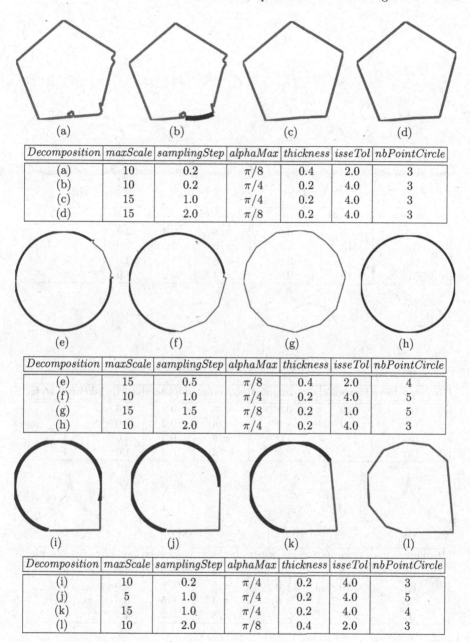

Decomposition	maxScale	samplingStep	alphaMax	thickness	isseTol	nbPointCircle
(a)	10	0.2	$\pi/8$	0.4	2.0	3
(b)	10	0.2	$\pi/4$	0.2	4.0	3
(c)	15	1.0	$\pi/4$	0.2	4.0	3
(d)	15	2.0	$\pi/8$	0.2	4.0	3

Decomposition	maxScale	samplingStep	alphaMax	thickness	isseTol	nbPointCircle
(e)	15	0.5	$\pi/8$	0.4	2.0	4
(f)	10	1.0	$\pi/4$	0.2	4.0	5
(g)	15	1.5	$\pi/8$	0.2	1.0	5
(h)	10	2.0	$\pi/4$	0.2	4.0	3

Decomposition	maxScale	samplingStep	alphaMax	thickness	isseTol	nbPointCircle
(i)	10	0.2	$\pi/4$	0.2	4.0	3
(j)	5	1.0	$\pi/4$	0.2	4.0	5
(k)	15	1.0	$\pi/4$	0.2	4.0	4
(l)	10	2.0	$\pi/8$	0.4	2.0	3

Fig. 13. Experiments on the sensibility to parameters of Fig. 9.

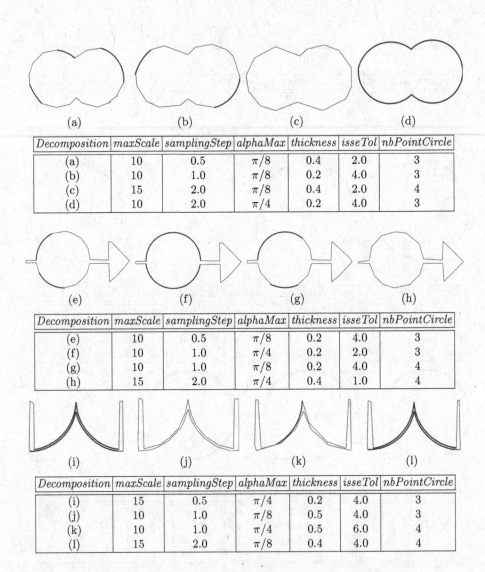

Decomposition	maxScale	samplingStep	alphaMax	thickness	isseTol	nbPointCircle
(a)	10	0.5	$\pi/8$	0.4	2.0	3
(b)	10	1.0	$\pi/8$	0.2	4.0	3
(c)	15	2.0	$\pi/8$	0.4	2.0	4
(d)	10	2.0	$\pi/4$	0.2	4.0	3

Decomposition	maxScale	samplingStep	alphaMax	thickness	isseTol	nbPointCircle
(e)	10	0.5	$\pi/8$	0.2	4.0	3
(f)	10	1.0	$\pi/4$	0.2	2.0	3
(g)	10	1.0	$\pi/8$	0.2	4.0	4
(h)	15	2.0	$\pi/4$	0.4	1.0	4

Decomposition	maxScale	samplingStep	alphaMax	thickness	isseTol	nbPointCircle
(i)	15	0.5	$\pi/4$	0.2	4.0	3
(j)	10	1.0	$\pi/8$	0.5	4.0	3
(k)	10	1.0	$\pi/4$	0.5	6.0	4
(l)	15	2.0	$\pi/8$	0.4	4.0	4

Fig. 14. Experiments on the sensibility to parameters of Fig. 10.

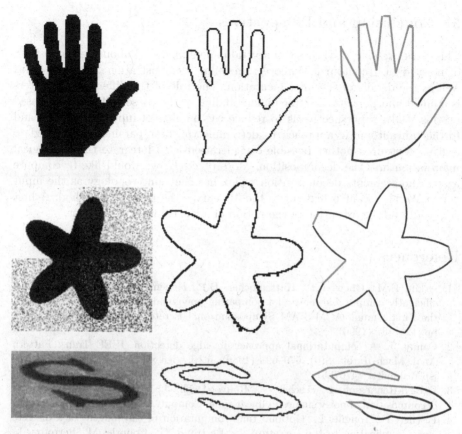

Fig. 15. Borderline cases of decomposition using default parameter setting. Left: input images, middle: extracted curves, right: decomposition results.

4.4   Image Credits

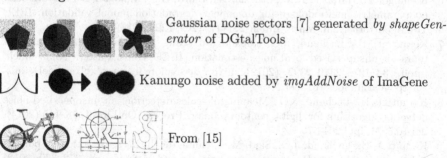

Gaussian noise sectors [7] generated *by shapeGenerator* of DGtalTools

Kanungo noise added by *imgAddNoise* of ImaGene

From [15]

 From [8]

All other images by the authors.

5   Conclusion and Perspectives

This work presents a synthesis of several papers [9,12–17] about decomposition of noisy digital contours. Moreover, an online demonstration[7] is proposed as well as the details of the implementation. The role of the different parameters is studied and permits a better understanding of the presented method. Based on this study, a perspective is to reduce the number of input parameters and further an automatic approach to determine the best parameters adapted to a given contour. Another possible consideration is to integrate the topological information into the decomposition. More precisely, we would like to compute a arcs-and-segments decomposition which has the same topology as the input curve. We also want to extend to the 3D curves the proposed method. A first step could be the extension of the notion of adaptive tangential cover.

References

1. Arkin, E.M., Chew, L.P., Huttenlocher, D.P., Kedem, K., Mitchell, J.S.B.: An efficiently computable metric for comparing polygonal shapes. In: Proceedings of the First Annual ACM-SIAM Symposium on Discrete Algorithms, SODA 1990, pp. 129–137 (1990)
2. Canny, J.: A computational approach to edge detection. IEEE Trans. Pattern Anal. Mach. Intell. 8(6), 679–698 (1986). http://ieeexplore.ieee.org/xpls/abs_all.jsp?arnumber=4767851
3. Debled-Rennesson, I., Feschet, F., Rouyer-Degli, J.: Optimal blurred segments decomposition of noisy shapes in linear time. Comput. Graph. 30(1), 30–36 (2006)
4. Feschet, F., Tougne, L.: Optimal time computation of the tangent of a discrete curve: application to the curvature. In: Bertrand, G., Couprie, M., Perroton, L. (eds.) DGCI 1999. LNCS, vol. 1568, pp. 31–40. Springer, Heidelberg (1999). doi:10.1007/3-540-49126-0_3
5. von Gioi, R.G., Randall, G.: Unsupervised smooth contour detection. Image Processing on Line (2016). http://www.ipol.im/pub/pre/175/
6. Kanungo, T., Haralick, R.M., Stuezle, W., Baird, H.S., Madigan, D.: A statistical, nonparametric methodology for document degradation model validation. IEEE Trans. Pattern Anal. Mach. Intell. 22(11), 1209–1223 (2000)
7. Kerautret, B., Lachaud, J.O.: Meaningful scales detection along digital contours for unsupervised local noise estimation. IEEE Trans. Pattern Anal. Mach. Intell. 34(12), 2379–2392 (2012). http://ieeexplore.ieee.org/xpl/articleDetails.jsp?tp=&arnumber=6138862
8. Kerautret, B., Lachaud, J.O.: Meaningful scales detection: an unsupervised noise detection algorithm for digital contours. Image Process. On Line 4, 98–115 (2014). doi:10.5201/ipol.2014.75
9. Kerautret, B., Lachaud, J.O., Said, M.: Meaningful thickness detection on polygonal curve. In: Pattern Recognition Applications and Methods, pp. 372–379 (2012)
10. Lachaud, J.-O.: Digital shape analysis with maximal segments. In: Köthe, U., Montanvert, A., Soille, P. (eds.) WADGMM 2010. LNCS, vol. 7346, pp. 14–27. Springer, Heidelberg (2012). doi:10.1007/978-3-642-32313-3_2

---

[7] http://ipol-geometry.loria.fr/~phuc/ipol_demo/RRPR_demo.

11. Latecki, L.J., Lakämper, R.: Shape similarity measure based on correspondence of visual parts. IEEE Trans. Pattern Anal. Mach. Intell. **22**(10), 1185–1190 (2000)
12. Ngo, P., Nasser, H., Debled Rennesson, I.: A discrete approach for decomposing noisy digital contours into arcs and segments. In: Workshop on Discrete Geometry and Mathematical Morphology for Computer Vision, Tapei, Taiwan (2016)
13. Ngo, P., Nasser, H., Debled-Rennesson, I.: Efficient dominant point detection based on discrete curve structure. In: Barneva, R.P., Bhattacharya, B.B., Brimkov, V.E. (eds.) IWCIA 2015. LNCS, vol. 9448, pp. 143–156. Springer, Cham (2015). doi:10. 1007/978-3-319-26145-4_11
14. Ngo, P., Nasser, H., Debled-Rennesson, I., Kerautret, B.: Adaptive tangential cover for noisy digital contours. In: Normand, N., Guédon, J., Autrusseau, F. (eds.) DGCI 2016. LNCS, vol. 9647, pp. 439–451. Springer, Cham (2016). doi:10.1007/ 978-3-319-32360-2_34
15. Nguyen, T.P., Debled-Rennesson, I.: Arc segmentation in linear time. In: Real, P., Diaz-Pernil, D., Molina-Abril, H., Berciano, A., Kropatsch, W. (eds.) CAIP 2011. LNCS, vol. 6854, pp. 84–92. Springer, Heidelberg (2011). doi:10.1007/ 978-3-642-23672-3_11
16. Nguyen, T.P., Debled-Rennesson, I.: Decomposition of a curve into arcs and line segments based on dominant point detection. In: Heyden, A., Kahl, F. (eds.) SCIA 2011. LNCS, vol. 6688, pp. 794–805. Springer, Heidelberg (2011). doi:10.1007/ 978-3-642-21227-7_74
17. Nguyen, T.P., Debled-Rennesson, I.: A discrete geometry approach for dominant point detection. Pattern Recogn. **44**(1), 32–44 (2011)
18. Reveillès, J.P.: Géométrie discrète, calculs en nombre entiers et algorithmique, thèse d'état. Université Louis Pasteur, Strasbourg (1991)
19. Rosin, P.L.: Techniques for assessing polygonal approximations of curves. IEEE Trans. Pattern Anal. Mach. Intell. **19**(6), 659–666 (1997)
20. Sarkar, D.: A simple algorithm for detection of significant vertices for polygonal approximation of chain-coded curves. Pattern Recogn. Lett. **14**(12), 959–964 (1993)

Algorithms and Implementation for Segmenting Tree Log Surface Defects

Van-Tho Nguyen[1], Bertrand Kerautret[2(✉)], Isabelle Debled-Rennesson[2],
Francis Colin[1], Alexandre Piboule[3], and Thiéry Constant[1]

[1] LERFOB, AgroParisTech, INRA, 54000 Nancy, France
[2] LORIA, UMR CNRS 7503, Université de Lorraine,
54506 Vandœuvre-lés-Nancy, France
bertrand.kerautret@loria.fr
[3] ONF, RDI, 5 Rue Girardet, 54000 Nancy, France

Abstract. This paper focuses on the algorithms and implementation details of a published segmentation method defined to identify the defects of tree log surface. Such a method overcomes the difficulty of the high variability of the tree log surface and allows to segment the defects from the tree bark. All the algorithms used in this method are described in link to their source code which guarantees a full reproducible method associated to an online demonstration.

1 Overview of the Segmentation of Defects on Log Surface

In the computer imagery domain, the tubular objects are present in various applications of which segmentation and analysis are of most importance like in medicine (with the blood vessel segmentation [9,12]), biology (with the wood knot detections [11]) or industry [4,7]. In this work, we focus on the problem of wood quality estimation in relation to the presence of internal wood knots (Fig. 1). Since the latters have a structural link with defects on the surface of the trunk, the non destructive Terrestrial Laser Scanning (TLS) can be used to obtain an estimation of the wood quality. As described in previous work [14], different approaches were proposed following this strategy with for instance the fitting of primitive such as cylinder [10,17,18] or circle [19,20]. However, the existing approaches are not fully satisfactory in regards to the specificity of some species [20,21] or for the automation of the method [10,17,18]. Another limitation is the implementation details which are often missing and limit the reproduction of the methods.

A generic method to segment automatically defects on tree log surface that is robust to various tree species is still missing. In [14], we presented a novel approach to segment defects on tree logs from TLS data that is robust to different tested tree species in regard to bark roughness, longitudinal flexuosity or cross-sectional ovality. However, being limited on the number of pages, we were not able to provide enough details about algorithms, implementations and also how

© Springer International Publishing AG 2017
B. Kerautret et al. (Eds.): RRPR 2016, LNCS 10214, pp. 150–166, 2017.
DOI: 10.1007/978-3-319-56414-2_11

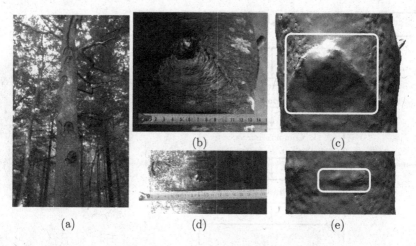

Fig. 1. (a) Defects on a standing tree in forest. (b,c) A Chinese mustache and its corresponding mesh. (d,e) A small defect in ellipse shape and its corresponding mesh.

to reproduce the best results. As a complement of [14], this paper aims to provide the implementation details of the main algorithms and to discuss the choice of parameter values and the reader can also access to the source code and other resources to reproduce the published results.

Our approach to segment tree log surface defects consists of four main steps (see Fig. 2(a)). In the first step, we compute the centerline of the tree log by the accumulation of surface normal vectors. In the second step, based on this centerline, we can compute the distance to the centerline and then convert the point cloud from the cartesian coordinate system to cylindrical coordinate system. The third step concerns the computation of the reference distance to the centerline using a patch of neighbouring points. Finally, in the fourth step we compute the difference between the reference and the real distances to the centerline before applying an automatic threshold to binarize the point cloud according to the statistical distribution of the values.

The following section describes the details and implementations of our algorithms. The Sect. 3 describes the steps to reproduce the results. We discuss how to choose the best values of the most important parameters and show some limitations of our method in the Sect. 4.

2   Algorithms and Implementations

In this section, we describe in detail our algorithms and its implementations. The program is written in $C++$ using libraries DGtal [1] for the normal accumulation and the visualization, PCL [16] for the kd-tree, GNU Scientific Library (GSL) [6] for the smoothing and interpolation of the centerline by cubic Spline. Figure 3 shows main classes and methods that will be described in detail in this section.

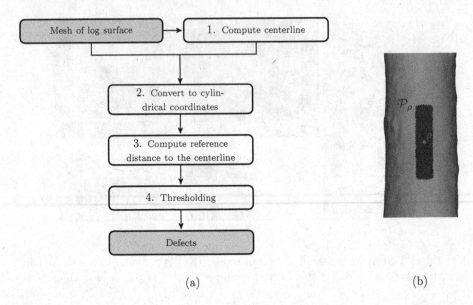

(a)   (b)

Fig. 2. (a) Overview of the algorithm. (b) Illustration of a patch $\mathcal{P}_\rho$ in blue which is used to estimate the reference distance to the centerline for the orange point. (Color figure online)

By convenience, our source files have the same name as class names. For example the class `Centerline` is implemented in the file *Centerline.h* and *Centerline.cpp*.

2.1   Compute Centerline

In the proposed method, the centerline plays an important role because the key variable is its distance to the input points. Thus, the centerline must be precisely assessed. Our method to compute the centerline is based on the surface normal accumulation proposed in [7] with modifications optimized to tree log data. The implementation of this method is simple (Fig. 4(a)) and consists of four steps: (i) accumulation of surface normal vector, (ii) tracking of the centerline, (iii) optimization by elastic forces (see Algorithm 1) and (iv) BSpline interpolation.

(i) Accumulation of surface normal vectors. This step consists in computation of a volumetric image of which voxel value stores score of the accumulation (Fig. 4(b)) which is computed as follows. Starting from a mesh face f_i with its normal vector $\overrightarrow{n_i}$ and applying a normal oriented directional scan along a distance d_{acc} (oriented toward the object interior). During this scan, we increase by one all voxels of the digitized space which are crossed by the 3D line defined from the face center and from the direction $\overrightarrow{n_i}$ (see Fig. 4(a,b)) and Algorithm 1 of [7] for more details).

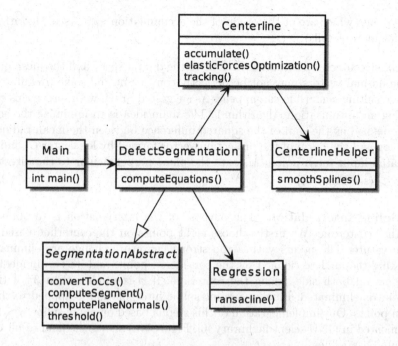

Fig. 3. Diagram class of our implementation.

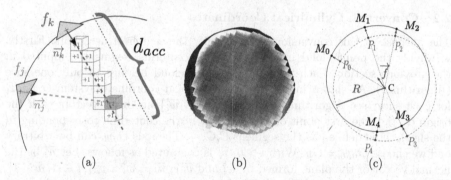

(a)   (b)   (c)

Fig. 4. Illustrations of the main ideas of the centerline method based on surface normal accumulation: (a) scan from mesh faces along a distance d_{acc}, (b) resulting accumulation score. (c) illustrates the step of elastic force optimization.

(ii) Tracking the centerline. Based on the result of previous algorithm, the centerline curve is obtained by a simple tracking process by looking at the local maxima accumulation points C_i of 2D patch image resulting from the projection in the $\vec{d}_k$ direction (see following figure). This direction $\vec{d}_k$ is computed from

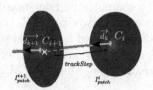

all the points which are at the origin of the accumulation value (see Algorithm 2 of [7] for more details).

(iii) Elastic force optimization. Due to the digital space and the mesh quality, the normal vectors may not be perfectly convergent and some irregularities on the resulting centerline can appear. As suggested in [7], we improve this step by using an optimization Algorithm 1. The main idea is to minimize the error $E_s(C)$ defined as the sum of the squared difference between the mean radius $\bar{R}$ of the log and the norm of the projection vector formed by log center C_i and its associated input mesh points M_i onto the plane perpendicular to the direction vector $\overrightarrow{d_i}$ (see Fig. 4(c)).

(iv) Spline Interpolation. The purpose of the interpolation is to obtain a smoother centerline. We firstly choose eight points on the centerline based on the curvature. The points with a too strong curvature change are eliminated by testing the angle ϕ defined by the considered point, and its two immediate neighbors on both sides along the centerline. If ϕ is smaller than $3\pi/4$ then the point is eliminated. Finally, a cubic spline interpolation is applied to these chosen points. Our implementation of this step is based on cubic spline which is implemented in GNU scientific library [6]. Figure 5(a) shows the final result of a computed centerline.

2.2   Convert to Cylindrical Coordinates

The purpose of this conversion is to simplify the search of neighbors. Firstly, we divide the point cloud into slices by the centerline segment computed in the previous section. Each point in the point cloud belongs to only one slice (Algorithm 2). As shown in [14], we define a local coordinate system $O_i x_i y_i z_i$ for each slice (see Algorithm 4) where $\{\overrightarrow{u_i}, \overrightarrow{v_i}, \overrightarrow{w_i}\}$ are basis vectors with the origin O_i (i.e. the first point on the segment of the centerline corresponding to the slice). $\overrightarrow{w_i}$ is defined as the segment $C_i C_{i+1}$. The axis $O_0 y_0$ can be arbitrary and we choose $O_0 y_0 = Oy$. With $i > 0$, $\overrightarrow{v_i}$ is computed as follows. Let $\overrightarrow{n_i}$ be the normal vector of the plane formed by $\overrightarrow{w_i}$ and $\overrightarrow{v_{i-1}}$: $\overrightarrow{n_i} = \overrightarrow{w_i} \times \overrightarrow{v_{i-1}}; i \in [1, m-1]$. $\overrightarrow{v_i}$ is the cross product of $\overrightarrow{w_i}$ and $\overrightarrow{n_i}$. And finally, $\overrightarrow{u_i}$ is computed by the cross product of $\overrightarrow{v_i}$ and $\overrightarrow{w_i}$. Figure 5(b) shows the computation of coordinate system for a point from its Cartesian coordinates.

2.3   Compute Reference Distance to the Centerline

To compute the reference distance to the centerline of the point ρ, we need to query a narrow patch $\mathcal{P}_\rho$ containing the neighbors of ρ (see Fig. 2(b)). The patch size is defined by two parameters φ and τ with $\varphi = l/\bar{r}$ where τ (resp. l) is the length (resp. arc length) of the patch and $\bar{r}$ is the mean of the distance to the centerline of all points. More formally the patch $\mathcal{P}_\rho$ can be defined as:

$$\mathcal{P}_\rho = \{\rho_j \mid |\theta_{\rho_j} - \theta_\rho| \leq \frac{\varphi}{2}, |z_{\rho_j} - z_\rho| \leq \frac{\tau}{2}\} \tag{1}$$

Algorithm 1. elasticForcesOptimisation: Optimize the centerline by elastic forces

```
   Data: rawCenterline // Raw centerline, output of Algorithm 2 of [7]
   Data: mesh // Input mesh to recover faces associated to centerline points
   Output : optimizedCenterline
   Variable: epsilon //Error
1  //store associated faces in the 2D patches
2  mapFaces = emptyMap()
3  sumradii=0
4  foreach point in rawCenterline do
5      faces = get2DpatchImage(point, mesh)
6      mapFaces[point] = faces
7      foreach face in faces do
8          centerPoint = face.center()
9          vectorNormal = face.getVectorNormal()
10         vectorRadial = centerPoint - point
11         sumradii = vectorRadial.norm()

12 meanRadii = sumradii / mesh.nbFaces()
13 DeltaError = infinity
14 previousTotalError
15 first=true
16 while DeltaError > epsilon do
17     totalError = 0.0
18     for i = 0 to rawCenterline.size() - 1 do
19         point = optimizedCenterline[i]
20         faces = mapFaces[point]
21       , sumForce = {0,0,0}
22         count=0
23         foreach face in faces do
24             centerPoint = face.center()
25             vectorNormal = face.getVectorNormal()
26             radialVector = centerPoint - point
27             alpha = anglebetween(vectorNormal, radialVector)
28             if alpha ¿ π/6 then
29                 continue
30             forceMagnitude = radialVector.norm() - meanRadii
31             force = radialVector.normalized()*forceMagnitude
32             totalError += forceMagnitude*forceMagnitude
33             sumForce += force
34             count++
35         //project of sumForces to normal vector
36         direction = dirImage[rawCenterline[i]].normalized()
37         sumForcesDir = direction.dot(sumForces)/vectDir.norm()/vectDir.norm()*vectDir;
38         radialForces = sumForces - sumForcesDir;
39         if count > 0 then
40             optimizedCenterline[i] += radialForces/count
41     if first then
42         DeltaError = totalError first = false
43     else
44         DeltaError = abs(totalError - previousTotalError)
45     previousTotalError = totalError - previousTotalError
46 return optimizedCenterline
47 .
```

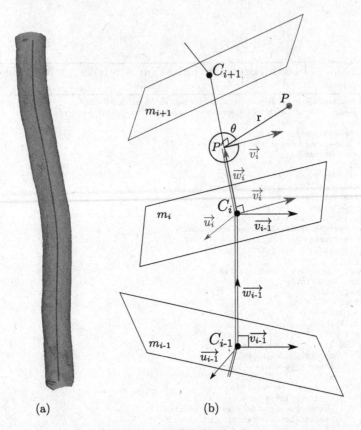

(a)   (b)

Fig. 5. (a) Centerline of a Beech log. (b) Computation of the coordinate system $\rho(r, \theta, z)$ from the point P with z is the red line. (Color figure online)

Algorithm 2. computePlanes: Compute normal vector of planes that divide the log into slices

Data: Centerline $\mathcal{C} = \{C_0, C_1, \ldots, C_m\}$
Result: List of normal vector m

1 m = emptySet()

2 $m[0] = \dfrac{\overrightarrow{C_0 C_1}}{\left\| \overrightarrow{C_0 C_1} \right\|}$

3 **for** $i = 1$ **to** $m - 1$ **do**

4      $m[i] = \dfrac{\overrightarrow{C_{i-1} C_i} + \overrightarrow{C_i C_{i+1}}}{\left\| \overrightarrow{C_{i-1} C_i} + \overrightarrow{C_i C_{i+1}} \right\|}$

5 **end**

6 **return** m

Because the number of points may be large, we use a kd-tree to speedup the query. We use the kd-tree implemented in the *Flann* library [3,13] which is included in the *PCL* library [16]. This library provides a range base query, so

---

Algorithm 3. getSegmentId: Compute the corresponding segment of a point

---

Data: Point P
Data: Centerline $\mathcal{C} = \{C_0, C_1, \ldots, C_m\}$
Result: segmentId
1   $lastSign \leftarrow 1$
2   **for** $i = 1$ *to* m **do**
3      $sign = \overrightarrow{C_i P}.ns[i]$;
4   **if** $sign * lastSign \, \text{¡}= 0$ **then**
5 | **return** i - 1;
6   **end**
7   lastSign = sign;
8   **end**
9   **return** m -1

Algorithm 4. convertToCcs: Convert the point cloud to cylindrical coordinate system

---

Data: Point cloud $\mathcal{P}_d = \{P_0, P_1, \ldots, P_n\}$
Data: Centerline $\mathcal{C} = \{C_0, C_1, \ldots, C_m\}$
Data: Local coordinate systems $\mathcal{L} = \{O_0 x_0 y_0 z_0, O_1 x_1 y_1 z_1, \ldots, O_{m-1} x_{m-1} y_{m-1} z_{m-1}\}$
Result: Point cloud in cylindrical coordinate system
1   **for** $i = 1$ *to* n **do**
2      $s = getSegmentId(P_i)$ //Algorithm 2
3      $\vec{d} = \dfrac{\overrightarrow{C_s C_{s+1}}}{\left\| \overrightarrow{C_s C_{s+1}} \right\|}$ //projection of P_i onto segment s of the centerline
4      $P' = \vec{d}.\overrightarrow{C_s P_i}$;
5      $r_i = \left\| \overrightarrow{P' P_i} \right\|$
6   **if** $s \, \text{¿} \, 0$ **then**
7 | $z_i = \sum\limits_{j=1}^{s} \left\| \overrightarrow{C_{j-1} C_j} \right\| + \overrightarrow{C_j P_i}.\vec{d}$
8   **else**
9 | $z_i = \overrightarrow{C_j P_i}.\vec{d}$
10   **end**
11      $\theta = \dfrac{\arccos \overrightarrow{P' P}.\vec{v_s}}{\left\| \overrightarrow{P' P} \right\|}$
12   //correction of angle
13      $\vec{t} = \vec{v_s} \times \vec{d}$
14   **if** $\vec{t}.\overrightarrow{P' P} < 0$ **then**
15 | $\theta = 2\pi - \theta$;
16   **end**
17   **end**

---

that at the point ρ, we query all the neighbors located inside the sphere of center ρ and $radius = \dfrac{\tau}{2}$:

$$Q_\rho = \{\rho_j \mid |z_{\rho_j} - z_\rho| \le \frac{\tau}{2}\} \tag{2}$$

The return must be refined to get the patch:

$$\mathcal{P}_\rho = \{\rho_j \in Q \mid |\theta_{\rho_j} - \theta_\rho| \le \frac{\varphi}{2}\} \tag{3}$$

Note that the query of patch can be improved by using a kd-tree for the θ and z coordinates in the cylindrical coordinate system with a regard of the circular problem of θ.

To compute the reference distance to the centerline (denoted $\hat{r}$) of the point i, we consider the profile of r by z and then compute a RANSAC [5] based linear regression (i.e. $\hat{r} = az + b$, see Fig. 6).

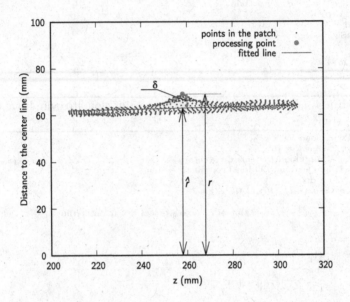

Fig. 6. Computation of the reference distance to the centerline for a given point.

2.4   Thresholding

After computing the reference distance to the centerline of points in the point cloud, we use the unimodal thresholding method proposed by Rosin in [15] to binarize the point cloud. Firstly, at each point ρ, we compute the difference between the distance to the centerline r and the reference distance to the centerline $\hat{r}$ for all points ($\delta_\rho = r_\rho - \hat{r}_\rho$).

Then, we compute the histogram of δ_ρ of all points in the cloud. The algorithm firstly finds the bin with maxima frequence (B_1) and then finds the first null bin (B_2) at the right size of the histogram. Finally, the algorithm loops over the bins situated between B_1 and B_2 and chooses the bin that maximizes the distance to the line $B_1 B_2$ (Fig. 7). The Algorithm 5 shows the details of the implementation.

Algorithm 5. threshold: Compute threshold by the Rosin method

Data: $\mathcal{D} = \{\delta_0, \delta_1, \ldots, \delta_n\}$
Data: $binSize$
Result: threshold T
1   nbBins = $\dfrac{max(\mathcal{D}) - min(\mathcal{D})}{binSize}$
2   histogram = array[nbBins]
3   **for** $i = 1$ *to* n **do**
4   binId = $\dfrac{\rho_i - min(\mathcal{D})}{binSize}$
5   histogram[binId]++
6   **end**
7   maxFrequence = max(histogram)
8   maxFrequenceIndex = indexOf(maxFrequence)
9   nullFrequenceIndex = nbBins -1
10 **for** $i = maxFrequenceIndex$ to $nbBins$ **do**
11   **if** *histogram[i] == 0* **then**
12   nullFrequenceIndex = i
13   break
14   **end**
15 **end**
16 bestDist = 0
17 bestDistIndex = maxFrequenceIndex
18 **for** $i = maxFrequenceIndex$ to $nullFrequenceIndex$ **do**
19     $AB = line(\{maxFrequenceIndex, maxFrequence\}, \{nullFrequenceIndex, 0\})$
20   **if** *distance(i, histogram[i], AB)* ¿ *bestDist* **then**
21   bestDist= distance(i, histogram[i], AB)
22   bestDistIndex = i
23   **end**
24 **end**
25 **return** $T = bestDistIndex * binSize + min(\mathcal{D})$

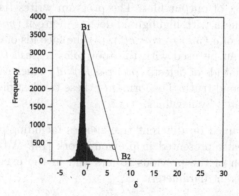

Fig. 7. Computation of the threshold T. Due to the different scales on the two axis, the two perpendicular lines are not shown correctly.

3 Reproducing the Results

The source code used to generate the present results is given at the following *GitHub* repository:

https://github.com/vanthonguyen/treelogdefectsegmentation

and an online demonstration is available at the following url:

http://ipol-geometry.loria.fr/~kerautre/ipol_demo/TDD_IPOLDemo/

The command to reproduce the results is:

```
segmentation -i mesh.off --voxelSize 5 --accRadius 100 --trackStep 20 \
--patchWidth 25 --patchHeight 100 --binWidth 5 --invertNormal true -o prefix
```

The program accepts the following parameters:

- voxelSize: the voxel size which is related to the resolution of the point cloud. In our experiments, the density of the point cloud is about 25 points per cm^2, we have chosen the voxel size as the squared root of the density which is 5.
- accRadius: the radius of the normal accumulation which should be greater than the real radius of the log.
- trackStep: the distance between two points in the tracking of the centerline.
- patchWidth, patchHeight: the width and height of the patch in the search of neighbors. The choice of the patch size must guarantee that the height is several time greater than the width and that the width is enough large to avoid an empty patch. In our experiments, we fixed the width equals to 25 mm and the height equals to 100 mm.
- binWidth: the width of histogram bins used to compute the threshold by the Rosin method.
- invertNormal: used when the direction of normal vectors is outside of the object.
- output: the prefix of output files. The program writes the output on some files: (1) output mesh with highlighted defects in green (*prefix-defect.off*), (2) the distance map of δ (*prefix-error.off*), (3) the face ids of defects (*prefix-def-faces.id*) which can be used with the tool *colorizeMesh* (included in source code), (4) the point ids of defects (*prefix-defect.id*) which can be used to compare with the ground truth. The format of these two last files are simply a list of integers separated by newlines.

The results obtained on different tree species including ground truth error measures were already presented in previous work [14]. We focus in this part on the reproduction of the previous results and in the experimental stability measure of the different parameters.

Reproducing results on various species. From the previous command line, the method can be applied directly to different species without the need to change the default parameters. The Fig. 8 presents some results generated from the example directory of the *GitHub* repository. All the results were generated with the same default parameters: voxelSize = 5 mm, accRadius is chosen by 1.5 time the maximum radius of the log (by default set to 200), the patchWidth = 25 mm, patchHeight = 100 mm. Note that the similar results are available on the demo site [2] with other examples.

Reproducing ground-truth comparisons. The Fig. 9 illustrates the comparisons of the previous results with the ground truth constructed by INRA experts

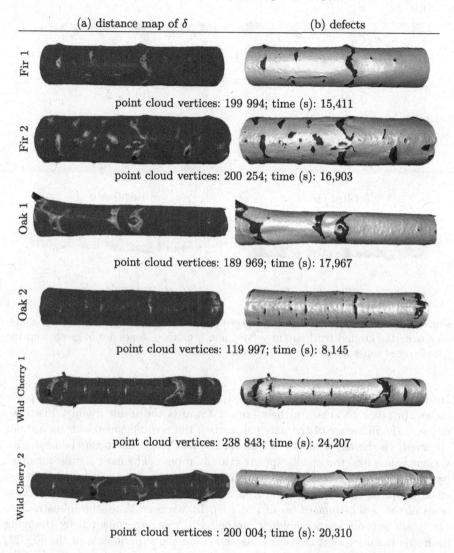

Fig. 8. Visualization of the distance map of δ (column (a)) and defects (column (b)) obtained on various species with the same default parameters (voxelSize = 5, accRadius = 200, trackStep = 20, patchWidth = 25, patchHeight = 100, binWidth = 0.01). The execution time were obtained on a *MacOS* 2,5 GHz *Intel Core i7*.

built from logs of different tree species and diameters, with a one meter length. Such comparisons can also be reproduced from the following command line:

```
colorizeMesh -i examples/WildCherry1.off -r examples/WildCherry1-grountruth.id
-t res_WildCherry-def-faces.id  -o compareWildCherry.off
```

To ensure reproducibility the ground-truth files are also given in the *GitHub* repository.

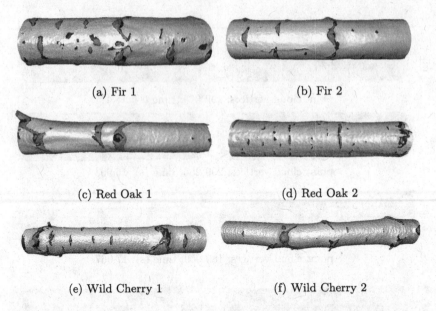

(a) Fir 1   (b) Fir 2

(c) Red Oak 1   (d) Red Oak 2

(e) Wild Cherry 1   (f) Wild Cherry 2

Fig. 9. Segmentation results of the proposed method for some logs: the detected zones, overlaying the ground truth are in yellow, non overlaying zones are in green, and the non-detected zones are in red. (Color figure online)

Influence of the parameters. We experimented the influence of some parameters in order to measure their impact towards the result quality. First, we measure the influence of the patch size when the recommended criteria are not observed. In the experiments of Fig. 10, the patch size has been changed with various values and the results appear visually robust. The most significant quality variations are visible only when using not recommended values (cases of too small (resp. big) size (images (f) resp. (d) of Fig. 10) or in case of bad orientations of the patch (images (e) of Fig. 10)). In a second time, the robustness of the Rosin automatic thresholding method [15] was experimented by changing its inside parameters (binWidth). As shown on the experiments of the Fig. 11, the change of this parameter is not very sensitive (see images (a–d)). Finally, the change of multiple default parameters also show small quality variations (see Fig. 11(e,f)).

4   Discussions

The previous results show that our method can precisely segment the defects and seems to be robust to different tree species or to geometrical variations. It must be preferred to the cylindrical-based method. The actual limitations appear when protruding branches are present on the log surface. To overcome this configuration, we envisage to use an additional method to segment branches before applying the proposed algorithms.

distance map of δ defects

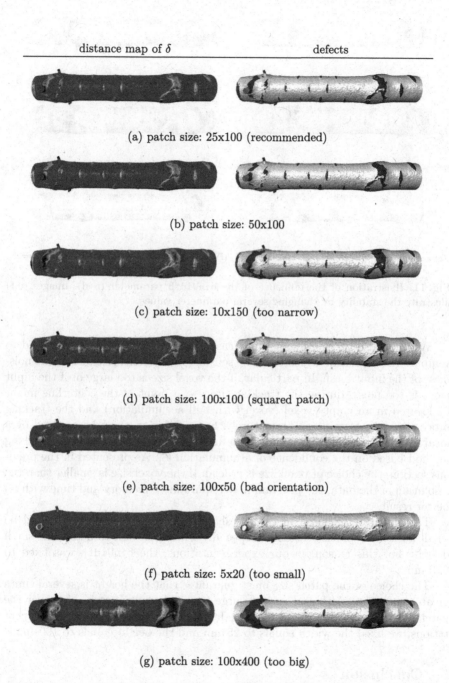

(a) patch size: 25x100 (recommended)

(b) patch size: 50x100

(c) patch size: 10x150 (too narrow)

(d) patch size: 100x100 (squared patch)

(e) patch size: 100x50 (bad orientation)

(f) patch size: 5x20 (too small)

(g) patch size: 100x400 (too big)

Fig. 10. Experimentation of the method stability towards the patch size parameters
(patchWidth, patchHeight).

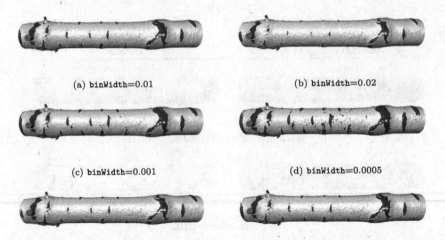

(a) binWidth=0.01   (b) binWidth=0.02

(c) binWidth=0.001   (d) binWidth=0.0005

(e) accRadius=300, voxelSize=3, trackStep=10   (f) accRadius=100, voxelSize=10, trackStep=25

Fig. 11. Illustration of the influence of the binWidth parameter (a–d). Images (e,f) illustrate the stability by changing several parameter values.

We have also observed some limit cases for the tracking algorithm used to compute the centerline which could be sensible to the voxel size and to the noisiness of the input mesh. In particular, if the voxel size is too large or if the input mesh is too noisy, during the tracking process, a point of the centerline might be located in an empty voxel (voxel with null accumulation) and the tracking process may be terminated prematurely. Even if this case can be resolved by a local search of non null accumulation, in future work we plane to use the tracking method based on the confidence of accumulation [8]. As presented in the previous section, the choice of voxelSize is crucial. If the voxel size is smaller than the resolution of the data, the program may require more memory and time with no better result.

The width of bin used in the thresholding method (binWidth) should be small for a more precise threshold especially when one want to detect the small defects. For this reason, in our experimentations, the binWidth was fixed to 0.01 mm.

The choice of the patch size must guarantee that the height is several times greater than the width and enough large to avoid empty patch. Moreover the patch height should be greater than the largest defect height. In our experimentations, we fixed the width equals to 25 mm and the height equals to 100 mm.

5   Conclusion

This paper has presented the implementation details of our novel algorithms to segment the defects on the surface of tree logs from Terrestrial Laser Scanning data. The proposed method consists in algorithms to precisely compute the centerline of tree logs and algorithms to compute the reference distance to the centerline and to threshold the point cloud. The experiments showed that the method could precisely segment defects with complex shape like the Chinese mustaches and small defects. The actual limit case are the logs with very prominent defects like a living branch for which the proposed method did not have a good performance. All the results presented in this paper are reproducible both from the source code or from the online demonstration.

Acknowledgment. This work was supported by the French National Research Agency through the Laboratory of Excellence ARBRE (ANR-12- LABXARBRE-01) and by the Lorraine French Region.

References

1. DGtal: Digital Geometry tools and algorithms library. http://dgtal.org
2. Online demonstration. http://ipol-geometry.loria.fr/~kerautre/ipol_demo/TrunkDefaultMeasure
3. Flann library, October 2016
4. Bauer, U., Polthier, K.: Generating parametric models of tubes from laser scans. Comput. Aided Des. **41**(10), 719–729 (2009)
5. Fischler, M.A., Bolles, R.C.: Random sample consensus: a paradigm for model fitting with applications to image analysis and automated cartography. Commun. ACM **24**(6), 381–395 (1981)
6. Gough, B.: GNU Scientific Library Reference Manual. Network Theory Ltd., London (2009)
7. Kerautret, B., Krähenbühl, A., Debled-Rennesson, I., Lachaud, J.-O.: 3D geometric analysis of tubular objects based on surface normal accumulation. In: Murino, V., Puppo, E. (eds.) ICIAP 2015. LNCS, vol. 9279, pp. 319–331. Springer, Cham (2015). doi:10.1007/978-3-319-23231-7_29
8. Kerautret, B., Krahenbl, A., Debled Rennesson, I., Lachaud, J.O.: Centerline detection on partial mesh scans by confidence vote in accumulation map. In: Proceedings of ICPR 2016 (2016). To appear
9. Kirbas, C., Quek, F.: A review of vessel extraction techniques and algorithms. CSUR **36**(2), 81–121 (2004)
10. Kretschmer, U., Kirchner, N., Morhart, C., Spiecker, H.: A new approach to assessing tree stem quality characteristics using terrestrial laser scans. Silva Fenn **47**, 14 (2013)
11. Krhenbhl, A., Kerautret, B., Debled-Rennesson, I., Mothe, F., Longuetaud, F.: Knot segmentation in 3D CT images of wet wood. Pattern Recogn. **47**(12), 3852–3869 (2014)
12. Lesage, D., Angelini, E.D., Bloch, I., Funka-Lea, G.: A review of 3D vessel lumen segmentation techniques: models, features and extraction schemes. Med. Image Anal. **13**(6), 819–845 (2009)
13. Muja, M., Lowe, D.G.: Scalable nearest neighbor algorithms for high dimensional data. IEEE Trans. Pattern Anal. Mach. Intell. **36**(11), 2227–2240 (2014)
14. Nguyen, V.T., Kerautret, B., Debled-Rennesson, I., Colin, F., Pipoule, A., Constant, T.: Segmentation of defects on log surface from terrestrial lidar data. In: Proceedings of ICPR 2016 (2016). To appear

15. Rosin, P.L.: Unimodal thresholding. Pattern Recogn. **34**(11), 2083–2096 (2001)
16. Rusu, R.B., Cousins, S.: 3D is here: point cloud library (PCL). In: IEEE International Conference on Robotics and Automation (ICRA), Shanghai, China, 9–13 May 2011
17. Schütt, C., Aschoff, T., Winterhalder, D., Thies, M., Kretschmer, U., Spiecker, H.: Approaches for recognition of wood quality of standing trees based on terrestrial laserscanner data. ISPRS **36**, 179–182 (2004)
18. Stängle, S.M., Brüchert, F., Kretschmer, U., Spiecker, H., Sauter, U.H.: Clear wood content in standing trees predicted from branch scar measurements with terrestrial lidar and verified with X-ray computed tomography 1. Can. J. For. Res. **44**(2), 145–153 (2013)
19. Thomas, L., Mili, L.: A robust GM-estimator for the automated detection of external defects on barked hardwood logs and stems. IEEE Trans. Signal Process. **55**(7), 3568–3576 (2007)
20. Thomas, L., Shaffer, C.A., Mili, L., Thomas, E.: Automated detection of severe surface defects on barked hardwood logs. For. Prod. J. **57**(4), 50 (2007)
21. Thomas, L., Thomas, R.E.: A graphical automated detection system to locate hardwood log surface defects using high-resolution three-dimensional laser scan data. In: 17th Central Hardwood Forest Conference. vol. 78, p. 92 (2010)

The Multiscale Line Segment Detector

Yohann Salaün[1,2], Renaud Marlet[1], and Pascal Monasse[1(✉)]

[1] LIGM, UMR 8049, École des Ponts, UPE, Champs-sur-Marne, France
{yohann.salaun,renaud.marlet,pascal.monasse}@enpc.fr
[2] CentraleSupélec, Châtenay-Malabry, France

Abstract. We propose a multiscale extension of a well-known line segment detector, LSD. We show that its multiscale nature makes it much less susceptible to over-segmentation and more robust to low contrast and less sensitive to noise, while keeping the parameter-less advantage of LSD and still being fast. We also present here a dense gradient filter that disregards regions in which lines are likely to be irrelevant. As it reduces line mismatches, this filter improves the robustness of the application to structure-from-motion. It also yields a faster detection.

1 Introduction

Among proposed line detectors, LSD [2] is one of the best and most popular methods. It accurately detects segments and does not use any threshold tuning, relying instead on the *a contrario* methodology. Though results are very good for small images (up to 1 Mpixel), it tends to give poorer results with high resolution images (5 Mpixels and more). As explained by Grompone von Gioi et al. [2], the detection is different after scaling or croping the picture. For high resolution images, detections are often over-segmented into small bits of segments and some lines are not even detected (see Fig. 1).

These poor results can be traced back to the greedy nature of LSD. Detected segments are in fact rectangular areas that contain a connected cluster of pixels with gradients that are similarly oriented. After they are identified, a score representing a number of false alarms (NFA) validates the detection as an actual segment or not. However, in high resolution cases, edges tend to be less strong which breaks the connectivity between pixel clusters and yields over-segmentation or lack of detection in low-contrast areas.

We propose a method that generalizes LSD to any kind of images, without being affected by their resolution. For this, we use a multiscale framework and information from coarser scales to better detect segments at finer scales. In our companion paper [3], we compare it to other state-of-the-art line detectors, namely LSD [2] and EDLines [1], as a building block of a structure from motion (SfM) pipeline [4] to obtain quantitative, objective results.

2 Notation

We use the same notations as the companion paper [3], recalled here. In the following, the k index will denote the scale associated with the feature.

B. Kerautret et al. (Eds.): RRPR 2016, LNCS 10214, pp. 167–178, 2017.
DOI: 10.1007/978-3-319-56414-2_12

Fig. 1. Lines detected with LSD [2] (left) or with MLSD [3] (right). The picture has a resolution of 15 Mpixels.

2.1 Upscaled Segment

Given a coarse segment s_i^{k-1} of direction $\theta(s_i^{k-1})$ detected with some angular tolerance πp_i^{k-1} ($0 \le p_i^{k-1} \le 1$ represents a probability), we define $\mathcal{A}_i^k$ as the rectangular area of s_i^{k-1} upscaled in I^k, and $\mathcal{P}_i^k$ as the subset of pixels in $\mathcal{A}_i^k$ that have the same direction as s_i^{k-1} up to πp_i^{k-1}:

$$\mathcal{P}_i^k = \left\{ q \in \mathcal{A}_i^k \text{ s.t. } |\theta(q) - \theta(s_i^{k-1})|_{(\text{mod } \pi)} < \pi p_i^{k-1} \right\}. \tag{1}$$

where $\theta(q)$ is the direction orthogonal to the gradient at pixel q. Note that we only consider a gradient direction if the gradient magnitude is above a given threshold $\rho = 2/\sin(45°/2)$ as in the original LSD because it is a good trade-off between good and fast detections.

2.2 Fusion Score

Given n segments $S = \{s_1, ..., s_n\}$, let $Seg(\cup_{i=1}^n s_i)$ be the best segment computed from the union of the clusters s_i, defined as the smallest rectangle that contains the rectangles associated to all segments s_i. The corresponding fusion score of the set of segments is defined as:

$$\mathcal{F}(s_1, ..., s_n) = \log \left(\frac{\text{NFA}_{\mathcal{M}}(s_1, ..., s_n, p)}{\text{NFA}_{\mathcal{M}}(Seg(\cup_{i=1}^n s_i), p)} \right). \tag{2}$$

The NFA is computed with Eq. (3) of the companion paper [3]:

$$\text{NFA}_{\mathcal{M}}(S, p) = \gamma N_L \binom{(NM)^{\frac{5}{2}}}{n} \prod_{i=1}^n (|s_i| + 1)\mathcal{B}(|s_i|, k_{s_i}, p) \tag{3}$$

in an $N \times M$ image, where γ is the number of tested values for the probability p, N_L the number of possible segments in the image, and k_s the number of pixels in the rectangle aligned with its direction, with tolerance πp. It uses the tail of the binomial law:

$$\mathcal{B}(|s|, k_s, p) = \sum_{j=k_s}^{|s|} \binom{|s|}{j} p^j (1-p)^{|s|-j}. \tag{4}$$

The fusion score defines a criterion for segment merging that does not rely on any parameter. If positive, the segments $s_1, ..., s_n$ should be merged into $\mathcal{S}eg(\cup_{i=1}^n s_i)$ otherwise they should be kept separate.

3 Dense-Gradient Filter

For SfM purpose, a too high density of segment detections in some area, such as a grid pattern, often leads to incorrect results for line matching. The density of similar lines also leads to less accurate calibration because it weighs too much similar information and thus tends to reduce or ignore information from lines located in other parts of the image. To address this issue, we designed a filter that disables detections in regions with too dense gradients. It also allows a faster detection as these regions often generate many tiny aligned segments that would need to be merged during our post-detection merging.

For this, we first detect regions with a local gradient density above a given threshold. The segment detection is then disabled in these areas. The process is fast because we apply it only at the coarsest scale using summed area tables.

With this filter, we may obtain a less exhaustive segment detection in these areas and at their borders. However, it leads to a better matching and a better calibration. It also decreases computation time for images with this type of regions.

4 Implementation

Our implementation is available on GitHub (https://github.com/ySalaun/MLSD).

4.1 Main Algorithm

Our algorithm consists in an iterative loop of three steps for each considered scale of the picture:

1. **Multiscale transition:** Upscale information from previous, coarser scale and use this information to compute segments at current, finer scale.
2. **Detection:** Detect segments using the standard LSD algorithm [2].
3. **Post-detection merging:** Merge neighboring segments at current scale.

Note that step 2 uses the exact same procedure as LSD and thus will not be described in this paper. The dense-gradient filter can optionally be used at the coarsest scale.

The number of considered scales is noted K. Though it can be chosen by the user, we compute it automatically depending on the size of the picture:

$$K = \min\{k \in \mathbb{N} \text{ s.t. } \max(w, h) \leq 2^k s_{max}\},$$

Input: Image I
Output: Set of segments S

for $k = 0$ to K **do**
　　Compute downscaled image I^k (I^K is the original image)

　　// 1. Initialize segment set at this scale from previous scale information, if any

　　if $k = 0$ **then**
　　　　$S^k \leftarrow \emptyset$
　　　　Optionally, disable detection in some regions with *dense-gradient filter*
　　else
　　　　$S^k \leftarrow \text{UPSCALE}(S^{k-1})$
　　end if

　　// 2. Add the segments detected with LSD [2]:
　　$S^k \leftarrow S^k \cup \text{LSD}(I^k)$

　　// 3. Merge aligned neighbors
　　$S^k \leftarrow \text{MERGE}(S^k)$
end for

return S^K

Fig. 2. Multiscale Line Segment Detector (MLSD).

where w (resp. h) is the width (resp. height) of the picture. We use a scale step of 2 and chose $s_{max} = 1000$ as we did not observe over-segmentation for images of size lower than 1000×1000 pixels and reducing too much the picture size can create artifacts.

The overall algorithm is described in Fig. 2. The successive steps are described below with a pseudo-code giving the main steps and additional details in the text.

4.2 Dense-Gradient Filter

The general idea of the dense-gradient filter is to discard from detection areas in which there is a high density of pixels with strong gradients.

Experimentally, we observed that it is difficult to set a density threshold for a proper filtering. If the density threshold is too low, it tends to discard pixels that may belong to interesting segments. If it is too high, it does not filter out enough pixels. For this reason, we perform the filtering in two steps. First, we identify which pixels are at the center of dense-gradient areas. Second, we disregard a region which is larger than the one that is used to evaluate the density of strong gradients.

This procedure is implemented in our code with the function *denseGradient-Filter* and described in Fig. 3. It consists in 3 steps:

Input: Image at coarsest scale I^0
Output: Mask $\tilde{I}^0$ of valid pixels
Compute summed area table of pixels with significant gradient magnitude for I^0
$\tilde{I}^0 \leftarrow$ valid
for all pixel $p \in I^0$ **do**
    Compute density τ of pixels with significant gradient near p
    if $\tau > \tau_{DENSE}$ **then**
        Invalidate pixel p in $\tilde{I}^0$
    end if
end for
Expand invalidated pixels in $\tilde{I}^0$ by dilation
return $\tilde{I}^0$

Fig. 3. Dense gradient filter.

1 **Summed area table:** We use a value of 1 for pixels with a gradient above ρ
   and 0 otherwise.
2 **Filtering:** For each pixel, we estimate the local density τ of pixels within a
   5×5 window. The filtered pixels are those with a density $\tau > \tau_{DENSE} = 0.75$.
3 **Expansion:** For each filtered pixels p, we also discard every pixel inside a
   21×21 window centered at p.

4.3 Multiscale Transition

We use a multiscale exploration that propagates detection information at coarse
scales to finer scales, which contributes in reducing over-segmentation.

This procedure is implemented in our code with the function *refineRawSeg-
ments*, described in Fig. 4 and some parts are illustrated in Fig. 5. It iterates over
each segment detected at the previous scale:

Input: Set of segments S^{k-1} detected at former scale
Output: Set of upscaled segments S^k

$S^k \leftarrow \emptyset$
for all $s_i \in S^{k-1}$ **do**
    1. Upscale s_i coordinates and select in this area the pixels whose gradient direc-
       tion is similar to the orthogonal direction to s_i (i.e., compute $\mathcal{P}_i^k$)
    2. Aggregate pixels inside $\mathcal{P}_i^k$ into 8-connected components
    3. Merge w.r.t. fusion score (2)
    4. Add to S^k the resulting segments, if meaningful enough
end for

return S^k

Fig. 4. Multiscale transition.

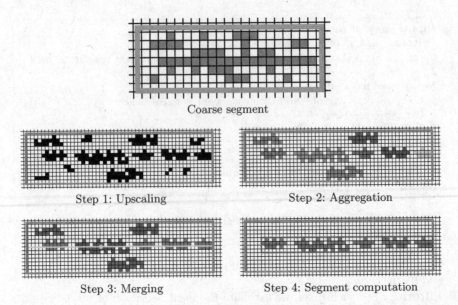

Coarse segment

Step 1: Upscaling   Step 2: Aggregation

Step 3: Merging   Step 4: Segment computation

Fig. 5. Illustration of the multiscale processing steps. The large orange rectangular box represent the upscaled region of the coarser segment. The blue rectangular box at step 4 represents the region of the detected segment at the finer scale. $\mathcal{P}_i^k$ is represented at step 1 with black pixels. After aggregation we only keep regions with at least 10 pixels. At step 3, we treat each cluster as an LSD segment with a barycenter, width and direction. We then consider the line that goes through its barycenter and with its direction (represented in yellow) to find merge candidates. (Color figure online)

1 **Upscaling:** The segment coordinates are upscaled and we compute the set $\mathcal{P}_i^k$ of pixels aligned with the segment direction (1).
2 **Aggregation:** Pixels inside $\mathcal{P}_i^k$ initialize clusters and are aggregated following an 8-neighborhood greedy method.
3 **Merging:** The clusters found at step 2 are merged according to the fusion score (2). As we cannot practically consider all the possible groups of clusters, we sort them by increasing NFA (i.e., decreasing meaningfulness) and queue them. Then, for each cluster c, we find the set of clusters that intersects with the line corresponding to c and try to merge the whole set. If merging is validated by the fusion score, we add the new segment inside the queue and dequeue the merged segments.
4 **Segment computation:** For each resulting cluster, if the NFA is low enough, we compute its corresponding segment and add it to the current set $\mathcal{S}^k$.

In the case where no pixel is selected at step 1 ($\mathcal{P}_i^k = \emptyset$) or no segment is added at step 4, we add the original segment into $\mathcal{S}^k$ with a scale information. It is kept as is, unrefined until all scales are explored. This allows detecting segments in low-contrast areas. Following LSD [2], we use a threshold $\epsilon = 1$ for NFA which corresponds to one false detection per image. LSD authors have shown that with values of TODO, the results do not change too much. In the code, this value is represented by the variable *logeps*.

4.4 Post-detection Merging

As new segments may be detected by LSD at the current scale, in addition to the segments originating from coarser scales, and as these segments may correspond to some form of over-segmentation, we apply another pass of segment merging, similar to the one used in multiscale transition but simplified to consider a reduced number of possible fusions.

This procedure is implemented in our code with the function *mergeSegments* and described in Fig. 6. It iterates on each segment previously detected. For this, as above, we first sort them by increasing NFA and push them to a queue. We then iterate the following steps until the queue is empty:

1 **Clustering:** For each segment s_i, we consider its central line as in multiscale transition (Sect. 4.3). For each of the two directions of the line, we examine the first cluster intersecting the line and such that its direction is similar to the direction of s_i up to tolerance πp_i.

2 **Merging:** The previously selected segments are merged if needed using the fusion score as a reference (2).

3 **Queuing:** If a merged segment was created, add the new segment to the queue and dequeue the merged segments.

Input: Set of segments $\mathcal{S}^k$ detected at current scale
Output: Set of merged segments $\tilde{\mathcal{S}}^k$
for all $s_i \in \mathcal{S}^k$ **do**
   1. Find aligned neighbors
   2. Possibly merge them into a single new segment w.r.t. fusion score (2)
   3. Add the new segment, if any, in $\mathcal{S}^k$
end for
return $\mathcal{S}^k$

Fig. 6. Post-detection merging.

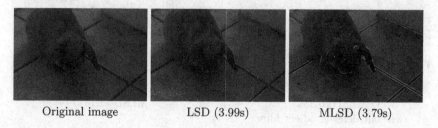

Original image   LSD (3.99s)   MLSD (3.79s)

Fig. 7. Lines detected with LSD [2] (middle) and with MLSD [3] (right) in a 15 Mpixels image (left).

5   Examples

In this section, we compare MLSD to LSD using images that specifically illustrate the limitations of LSD. Computation time are given for both methods.

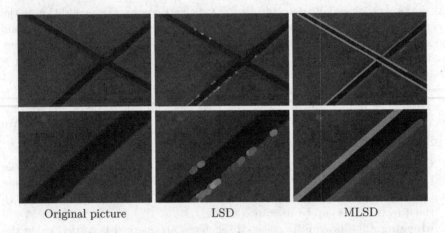

Original picture   LSD   MLSD

Fig. 8. Zoom of the bottom-right corner of pictures in Fig. 7.

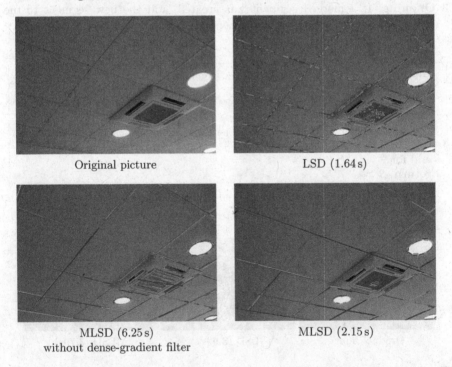

Original picture   LSD (1.64 s)

MLSD (6.25 s)   MLSD (2.15 s)
without dense-gradient filter

Fig. 9. Comparison between MLSD with and without dense-gradient filter.

5.1   Low-Contrast Images

We first consider an image with low contrast (Fig. 7). As can be seen when zooming the picture (see Fig. 8), the image is also noisy. As the gradient is also noisy around edges, the tile borders are hardly detected at all, whereas MLSD does detect them and does not create much over-segmentation.

5.2   Dense-Gradient Filter

Figure 9 illustrates the efficiency of the dense-gradient filter. The main difference between the two MLSD results occurs in the central part of the image where there is a grid pattern whereas the other parts are not affected. This type of pattern tends to slow the algorithm a lot (typically by a factor 3). Moreover, as argued above, the added segments are similar to each other and tend to deteriorate matching, and thus SfM results.

5.3   Effect on Scaling and Crop

Figures 10 and 11 illustrate the differences between LSD and MLSD for images with different resolutions. In Fig. 10, we decreased the size of the image (four times in both height and width) and in Fig. 11, we increased the size of the image (four times in both height and width).

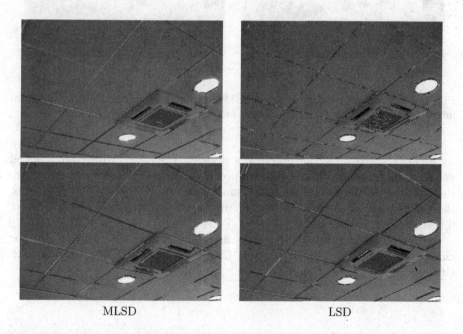

MLSD   LSD

Fig. 10. Comparison between LSD and MLSD on the same image with original resolution (above, 5 Mpixels) and four times reduced (below, 330 kpixels).

MLSD   LSD

Fig. 11. Comparison between LSD and MLSD on the same image with original resolution (above, 360 kpixels) and resolution four times larger (below, 5.8 Mpixels).

Figure 12 illustrates the differences between LSD and MLSD for cropped versions of the same image. We cropped the original picture into a 2 times smaller picture and then in a 4 times smaller picture. Whereas MLSD does not show significant changes from one picture to the other, LSD tends to detect differently segments.

Although in each case the results are different for both algorithms, the changes are limited for MLSD, whereas LSD gives sensibly different results with either a change of resolution or a crop.

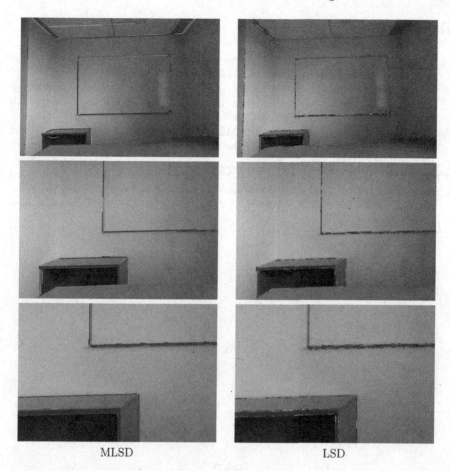

MLSD   LSD

Fig. 12. Comparison between LSD and MLSD on the same image (top, 18 Mpixels) but with cropped versions (no resolution changes) of respectively 5.6 Mpixels (middle) and 1.5 Mpixels (bottom).

6 Conclusion

We presented MLSD, a multiscale extension to the popular Line Segment Detector (LSD). MLSD is less prone to over-segmentation and is more robust to noise and low contrast. Being based on the a contrario theory, it retains the parameterless advantage of LSD, at a moderate additional computation cost. The source code accompanying this paper is not yet at as clean and readable as it could be. We plan to clean it and build an online demonstration with it on the IPOL website (http://www.ipol.im/).

References

1. Akinlar, C., Topal, C.: EDLines: a real-time line segment detector with a false detection control. Pattern Recogn. Lett. **32**(13), 1633–1642 (2011)
2. Grompone von Gioi, R., Jakubowicz, J., Morel, J.-M., Randall, G.: LSD: a line segment detector. Image Process On Line (IPOL 2012) **2**, 35–55 (2012). http://dx.doi.org/10.5201/ipol.2012.gjmr-lsd
3. Salaün, Y., Marlet, R., Monasse, P.: Multiscale line segment detector for robust and accurate SfM. In: Proceedings of the 23rd International Conference on Pattern Recognition (ICPR) (2016)
4. Salaün, Y., Marlet, R., Monasse, P.: Robust and accurate line- and/or point-based pose estimation without Manhattan assumptions. In: Leibe, B., Matas, J., Sebe, N., Welling, M. (eds.) ECCV 2016. LNCS, vol. 9911, pp. 801–818. Springer, Cham (2016). doi:10.1007/978-3-319-46478-7_49

Author Index

Printed in the United States
By Bookmasters